COMPUTABILITY

COMPUTABILITY

An introduction to recursive function theory

NIGEL CUTLAND

Department of Pure Mathematics, University of Hull

CAMBRIDGE UNIVERSITY PRESS

Published by the Press Syndicate of the University of Cambridge
The Pitt Building, Trumpington Street, Cambridge CB2 1RP
40 West 20th Street, New York, NY 10011-4211, USA
10 Stamford Road, Oakleigh, Melbourne 3166, Australia

First published 1980

Reprinted 1983, 1984, 1986, 1988, 1989, 1992, 1994

Printed in Great Britain by Athenæum Press Ltd, Gateshead, Tyne & Wear

Library of Congress Cataloguing in Publication Data

Cutland, Nigel.
Computability: an introduction to recursive function theory.

Bibliography: p.
Includes index.
1. Computable functions. 2. Recursion theory. I. Title.
QA9.59.C87 519.4 79-51823

ISBN 0 521 29465 7 paperback

Contents

Preface

The emergence of the concept of a *computable function* over fifty years ago marked the birth of a new branch of mathematics: its importance may be judged from the fact that it has had applications and implications in fields as diverse as computer science, philosophy and the foundations of mathematics, as well as in many other areas of mathematics itself. This book is designed to be an introduction to the basic ideas and results of computability theory (or recursion theory, as it is traditionally known among mathematicians).

The initial purpose of computability theory is to make precise the intuitive idea of a computable function; that is, a function whose values can be calculated in some kind of automatic or effective way. Thereby we can gain a clearer understanding of this intuitive idea; and only thereby can we begin to explore in a mathematical way the concept of computability as well as the many related ideas such as decidability and effective enumerability. A rich theory then arises, having both positive *and* negative aspects (here we are thinking of *non*-computability and *un*decidability results), which it is the aim of this book to introduce.

We could describe computability theory, from the viewpoint of computer science, as beginning with the question What can computers do *in principle* (without restrictions of space, time or money)? – and, by implication – What are their inherent theoretical limitations? Thus this book is *not* about real computers and their hardware, nor is it about programming languages and techniques. Nevertheless, our subject matter is part of the theoretical background to the real world of computers and their use, and should be of interest to the computing community.

For the basic definition of computability we have used the 'idealised computer' or register machine approach; we have found that this is readily grasped by students, most of whom are aware of the idea of a computer. (We do not, however, assume such an awareness (although it is helpful) and even less do we assume any practical experience with computers or calculators.) Our approach is mathematically equivalent to the many others that have been discovered, including Turing machines, the favourite of many. (We discuss these equivalences in chapter 3.)

This text grew out of a course given to undergraduates in mathematics and computer science at the University of Hull. The reader envisaged is a mathematics student with no prior knowledge of this subject, or a student of computer science who may wish to supplement his practical expertise with something of the theoretical background to his subject. We have aimed at the second or third year undergraduate level, although the earlier chapters covering the basic theory (chapters 1–7) should be within the grasp of good students in sixth forms, high schools and colleges (and their teachers). The only prerequisites are knowledge of the mathematical language of sets and functions (reviewed in the Prologue) and the ability to follow a line of mathematical reasoning.

The later chapters (8–12) are largely independent of each other. Thus a short introductory course could consist of chapters 1–7 supplemented by selection according to taste from chapters 8–12. It has been our aim in these later chapters to provide an introduction to some of the ramifications and applications of basic computability theory, and thereby provide a stepping stone towards more advanced study. To this end, the final chapter contains a brief survey of possible directions for further study, and some suggestions for further reading. (The two main texts that might be regarded as natural sequels to this one are M. L. Minsky, *Computation: Finite and Infinite Machines*, which would complement the present volume by its broad and comprehensive study of *computation* (as opposed to computability), and H. Rogers, *Theory of Recursive Functions and Effective Computability*, which provides a more advanced treatment of recursion theory in depth.)

Many people have helped towards the writing of this book. I would first thank John Cleave, who taught me recursive function theory in a graduate course at the University of Bristol in 1966, and introduced me to the register machine approach that I have used here. I have greatly appreciated the sustained interest and encouragement from Stan Wainer (who also made valuable suggestions for the material in chapters 10 and 12) and David Jordan: I thank them. I would also like to thank David Jordan and Dick Epstein for reading a draft of the manuscript and making many valuable comments and corrections. I am grateful to the Cambridge University Press for their interest and advice which has resulted in the emergence of the completed manuscript.

Finally, a big thank you to my wife Mary for her patience and encouragement during the many phases of writing and preparation of this book; her idealism and understanding have been a sustaining influence throughout.

Prologue
Prerequisites and notation

The only prerequisite to be able to read this book is familiarity with the basic notations of sets and functions, and the basic ideas of mathematical reasoning. Here we shall review these matters, and explain the notation and terminology that we shall use. This is mostly standard; so for the reader who prefers to move straight to chapter 1 and refer back to this prologue only as necessary, we point out that we shall use the word function to mean a *partial* function in general. We discuss this more fully below.

1. Sets

Generally we shall use capital letters $A, B, C, \ldots$ to denote sets. We write $x \in A$ to mean that x is a member of A, and we write $x \notin A$ to mean that x is not a member of A. The notation $\{x: \ldots x \ldots\}$ where $\ldots x \ldots$ is some statement involving x means the set of all objects x for which $\ldots x \ldots$ is true. Thus $\{x: x \text{ is an even natural number}\}$ is the set $\{0, 2, 4, 6, \ldots\}$.

If A, B are sets, we write $A \subseteq B$ to mean that A is contained in B (or A is a *subset* of B); we use the notation $A \subset B$ to mean that $A \subseteq B$ but $A \neq B$ (i.e. A is a *proper subset* of B). The *union* of the sets A, B is the set $\{x: x \in A \text{ or } x \in B \text{ (or both)}\}$, and is denoted by $A \cup B$; the *intersection* of A, B is the set $\{x: x \in A \text{ and } x \in B\}$ and is denoted by $A \cap B$. The *difference* (or relative complement) of the sets A, B is the set $\{x: x \in A \text{ and } x \notin B\}$ and is denoted by $A \setminus B$.

The empty set is denoted by $\varnothing$. We use the standard symbol $\mathbb{N}$ to denote the set of natural numbers $\{0, 1, 2, 3, \ldots\}$. If A is a set of natural numbers (i.e. $A \subseteq \mathbb{N}$) we write $\bar{A}$ to denote the complement of A relative to $\mathbb{N}$, i.e. $\mathbb{N} \setminus A$. We write $\mathbb{N}^+$ for the set of positive natural numbers $\{1, 2, 3, \ldots\}$, and as usual $\mathbb{Z}$ denotes the set of integers.

We write (x, y) to denote the *ordered pair* of elements x and y; thus $(x, y) \neq (y, x)$ in general. If A, B are sets, the *Cartesian product* of A and B is the set $\{(x, y): x \in A \text{ and } y \in B\}$, and is denoted by $A \times B$.

More generally, for elements $x_1, \ldots, x_n$ we write $(x_1, \ldots, x_n)$ to denote the *ordered n-tuple* of $x_1, \ldots, x_n$; an n-tuple is often represented by a single boldfaced symbol such as $\boldsymbol{x}$. If $A_1, \ldots, A_n$ are sets we write $A_1 \times \ldots \times A_n$ for the set of n-tuples $\{(x_1, \ldots, x_n): x_1 \in A_1 \text{ and } x_2 \in A_2 \ldots x_n \in A_n\}$. The product $A \times A \times \ldots \times A$ (n times) is abbreviated by A^n; A^1 means A.

2. Functions

We assume familiarity with the basic idea of a function, and the distinction between a function f and a particular value $f(x)$ at any given x where f is defined.[1] If f is a function, the *domain* of f is the set $\{x: f(x)$ is defined$\}$, and is denoted $\mathrm{Dom}(f)$; we say that $f(x)$ is *undefined* if $x \notin \mathrm{Dom}(f)$. The set $\{f(x): x \in \mathrm{Dom}(f)\}$ is called the *range* of f, and is denoted by $\mathrm{Ran}(f)$. If A and B are sets we say that f is a function *from A to B* if $\mathrm{Dom}(f) \subseteq A$ and $\mathrm{Ran}(f) \subseteq B$. We use the notation $f: A \to B$ to mean that f is a function from A to B with $\mathrm{Dom}(f) = A$.

A function f is said to be *injective* if whenever $x, y \in \mathrm{Dom}(f)$ and $x \neq y$, then $f(x) \neq f(y)$. If f is injective, then f^{-1} denotes the *inverse* of f, i.e. the unique function g such that $\mathrm{Dom}(g) = \mathrm{Ran}(f)$ and $g(f(x)) = x$ for $x \in \mathrm{Dom}(f)$. A function f from A to B is *surjective* if $\mathrm{Ran}(f) = B$.

If $f: A \to B$, we say that f is an *injection* (from A to B) if it is injective, and a *surjection* (from A to B) if it is surjective. It is a *bijection* if it is both an injection and a surjection.

Suppose that f is a function and X is a set. The *restriction* of f to X, denoted by $f|X$, is the function with domain $X \cap \mathrm{Dom}(f)$ whose value for $x \in X \cap \mathrm{Dom}(f)$ is $f(x)$. We write $f(X)$ for $\mathrm{Ran}(f|X)$. If Y is a set, then the *inverse image of Y under f* is the set $f^{-1}(Y) = \{x: f(x) \in Y\}$. (Note that this is defined even when f is not injective.)

If f, g are functions, we say that g *extends* f if $\mathrm{Dom}(f) \subseteq \mathrm{Dom}(g)$ and $f(x) = g(x)$ for all $x \in \mathrm{Dom}(f)$: in short, $f = g|\mathrm{Dom}(f)$. This is written $f \subseteq g$.

[1] Usually in mathematical texts a function f is defined to be a set of ordered pairs such that if $(x, y) \in f$ and $(x, z) \in f$, then $y = z$, and $f(x)$ is defined to be this y. We do not insist on this definition of a function, but our exposition is consistent with it.

The *composition* of two functions f, g is the function whose domain is the set $\{x: x \in \mathrm{Dom}(g) \text{ and } g(x) \in \mathrm{Dom}(f)\}$, and whose value is $f(g(x))$ when defined. This function is denoted $f \circ g$.

We denote by $f_\varnothing$ the function that is defined nowhere; i.e. $f_\varnothing$ has the property that $\mathrm{Dom}(f_\varnothing) = \mathrm{Ran}(f_\varnothing) = \varnothing$. Clearly $f_\varnothing = g|\varnothing$ for any function g.

Often in computability we shall encounter functions, or expressions involving functions, that are not always defined. In such situations the following notation is very useful. Suppose that $\alpha(\boldsymbol{x})$ and $\beta(\boldsymbol{x})$ are expressions involving the variables $\boldsymbol{x} = (x_1, \dots x_n)$. Then we write

$$\alpha(\boldsymbol{x}) \simeq \beta(\boldsymbol{x})$$

to mean that for any $\boldsymbol{x}$, the expressions $\alpha(\boldsymbol{x})$ and $\beta(\boldsymbol{x})$ are either both defined, or both undefined, and if defined they are equal. Thus, for example, if f, g are functions, writing $f(x) \simeq g(x)$ is another way of saying that $f = g$; and for any number y, $f(x) \simeq y$ means that $f(x)$ is defined and $f(x) = y$ (since y is always defined).

Functions of natural numbers For most of this book we shall be concerned with functions of natural numbers; that is, functions from $\mathbb{N}^n$ to $\mathbb{N}$ for various n, most commonly $n = 1$ or 2.

A function f from $\mathbb{N}^n$ to $\mathbb{N}$ is called an *n-ary* function. The value of f at an n-tuple $(x_1, \dots, x_n) \in \mathrm{Dom}(f)$ is written $f(x_1, \dots, x_n)$, or $f(\boldsymbol{x})$, if $\boldsymbol{x}$ represents $(x_1, \dots, x_n)$. In some texts the phrase *partial function* is used to describe a function from $\mathbb{N}^n$ to $\mathbb{N}$ whose domain is not necessarily the whole of $\mathbb{N}^n$. For us the word function *means* partial function. On occasion we will, nevertheless, write *partial function* to emphasise this fact. A *total function* from $\mathbb{N}^n$ to $\mathbb{N}$ is a function whose domain is the whole of $\mathbb{N}^n$.

Particularly with number theoretic functions, we shall blur the distinction between a function and its particular values in two fairly standard and unambiguous ways. First we shall allow a phrase such as 'Let $f(x_1, \dots x_n)$ be a function ...' as a means of indicating that f is an n-ary function. Second, we shall often describe a function in terms of its general value when this is given by a formula. For instance, '*the function* x^2' means 'the unary function f whose value at any $x \in \mathbb{N}$ is x^2'; similarly, '*the function* $x + y$' is the binary function whose value at $(x, y) \in \mathbb{N}^2$ is $x + y$.

We describe the zero function $\mathbb{N} \to \mathbb{N}$ by $\mathbf{0}$; and generally, for $m \in \mathbb{N}$, we denote the function $\mathbb{N} \to \mathbb{N}$ whose value is always m by the boldface symbol $\boldsymbol{m}$.

3. Relations and predicates

If A is a set, a property $M(x_1, \ldots, x_n)$ that holds (or is true) for some n-tuples from A^n and does not hold (or is false) for all other n-tuples from A is called an n-ary *relation* or *predicate* on A.[2]

For example, the property $x<y$ is a binary relation (or predicate) on $\mathbb{N}$; $2<3$ holds (or is true) whereas $9<5$ does not hold (or is false). As another example, any n-ary function f from $\mathbb{N}^n$ to $\mathbb{N}$ gives rise to an $(n+1)$-ary predicate $M(\mathbf{x}, y)$ given by

$$M(x_1, \ldots, x_n, y) \text{ if and only if } f(x_1, \ldots, x_n) \simeq y.$$

Equivalence relations and orders (The student unfamilar with these notions may prefer to delay reading this paragraph until it is needed in chapter 9.) In chapter 9 we shall encounter two special kinds of relations on a set A.

(a) A binary relation R on a set A is called an *equivalence relation* if it has the following properties for all $x, y, z \in A$:

(i) (reflexivity) $R(x, x)$;

(ii) (symmetry) if $R(x, y)$ then $R(y, x)$;

(iii) (transitivity) if $R(x, y)$ and $R(y, z)$ then $R(x, z)$.

We think of $R(x, y)$ as saying that x, y are equivalent (in some particular sense). Then we define the *equivalence class of* x as the set $\{y: R(x, y)\}$, consisting of all things equivalent to x.

(b) A binary relation R on a set A is called a *partial order* if, for all $x, y, z \in A$,

(i) (irreflexivity) not $R(x, x)$;

(ii) (transitivity) if $R(x, y)$ and $R(y, z)$ then $R(x, z)$.

A partial order is usually denoted by the symbol $<$, and we write $x<y$ rather than $<(x, y)$. A partial order is often defined by first defining $\leq$ (meaning $<$ or $=$), with the properties

(i) $x \leq x$;

(ii) if $x \leq y$ and $y \leq x$ then $x=y$;

(iii) $\leq$ is transitive;

and then defining $x<y$ to mean $x \leq y$ and $x \neq y$.

4. Logical notation

Our logical notation and usage will be standard throughout. We use the word *iff* as an abbreviation for if and only if. The symbol $\equiv$

[2] Often an n-ary relation or predicate $M(\mathbf{x})$ on a set A is identified with the set $\{\mathbf{x}: \mathbf{x} \in A^n \text{ and } M(\mathbf{x}) \text{ holds}\}$. We do not insist on this identification here, although our exposition is consistent with this approach.

denotes definitional equivalence, while ⇒ denotes implies, and ⇔ denotes implies and is implied by. We use the symbols ∀, ∃ to mean 'for all' and 'there exists' in the standard way.

The symbol □ is used in the text to indicate the end of a proof.

5. References

Each chapter is divided into sections, and items in each section are numbered consecutively. A reference such as theorem 5-1.4 means theorem 1.4 of chapter 5: this is the fourth numbered item of § 1 in that chapter. When referring within a chapter the number of the chapter is omitted. Exercises are included in this system of numbering. Thus exercise 6-1.8(2) means the second exercise of exercises 1.8, found in chapter 6.

Reference to entries in the bibliography is made by citing the author and year of publication of the work referred to.

1
Computable functions

We begin this chapter with a discussion of the fundamental idea of an algorithm or effective procedure. In subsequent sections we describe the way in which this idea can be made precise using a kind of idealised computer; this lays the foundation for a mathematical theory of computability and computable functions.

1. Algorithms, or effective procedures

When taught arithmetic in junior school we all learnt to add and to multiply two numbers. We were not merely taught that any two numbers have a sum and a product – we were given methods or rules for finding sums and products. Such methods or rules are examples of *algorithms* or *effective procedures*. Their implementation requires no ingenuity or even intelligence beyond that needed to obey the teacher's instructions.

More generally, an *algorithm* or *effective procedure* is a mechanical rule, or automatic method, or programme for performing some mathematical operation. Some more examples of operations for which easy algorithms can be given are

(1.1) (*a*) given n, finding the nth prime number,
(*b*) differentiating a polynomial,
(*c*) finding the highest common factor of two numbers (the Euclidean algorithm),
(*d*) given two numbers x, y deciding whether x is a multiple of y.

Algorithms can be represented informally as shown in fig. 1*a*. The input is the raw data or object on which the operation is to be performed (e.g. a polynomial for (1.1) (*b*), a pair of numbers for (1.1) (*c*) and (*d*)) and the output is the result of the operation (e.g. for (1.1) (*b*), the derived polynomial, and for (1.1) (*d*), the answer yes or no). The output is produced mechanically by the black box – which could be thought of as a

Fig. 1*a*.

calculating machine, a computer, or a schoolboy correctly taught – or even a very clever dog trained appropriately. The algorithm is the procedure or method that is carried out by the black box to obtain the output from the input.

When an algorithm or effective procedure is used to calculate the values of a numerical function then the function in question is described by phrases such as *effectively calculable*, or *algorithmically computable*, or *effectively computable*, or just *computable*. For instance, the functions xy, HCF(x, y) = the highest common factor of x and y, and $f(n)$ = the nth prime number, are computable in this informal sense, as already indicated. Consider, on the other hand, the following function:

$$g(n) = \begin{cases} 1 & \text{if there is a run of exactly } n \text{ consecutive 7s} \\ & \text{in the decimal expansion of } \pi, \\ 0 & \text{otherwise.} \end{cases}$$

Most mathematicians would accept that g is a perfectly legitimate function. But is g computable? There *is* a mechanical procedure for generating successive digits in the decimal expansion of π,[1] so the following 'procedure' for computing g suggests itself.

'Given n, start generating the decimal expansion of π, one digit at a time, and watch for 7s. If at some stage a run of exactly n consecutive 7s has appeared, then stop the process and put $g(n) = 1$. If no such sequence of 7s appears put $g(n) = 0$.'

The problem with this 'procedure' is that, if for a particular n there is no sequence of exactly n consecutive 7s, then there is no stage in the process where we can stop and conclude that this is the case. For all we know at any particular stage, such a sequence of 7s could appear in the part of the expansion of π that has not yet been examined. Thus the 'procedure' will go on for ever for inputs n such that $g(n) = 0$; so it is not an *effective* procedure. (It is conceivable that there *is* an effective procedure for computing g based, perhaps, on some theoretical properties of π. At the present time, however, no such procedure is known.)

[1] This will be established in chapter 3 (example 7.1(3)).

This example pinpoints two features implicit in the idea of an effective procedure – namely, that such a procedure is carried out in a sequence of stages or steps (each completed in a finite time), and that any output should emerge after a finite number of steps.

So far we have described informally the idea of an algorithm, or effective procedure, and the associated notion of computable function. These ideas must be made precise before they can become the basis for a mathematical theory of computability – and *non*-computability.

We shall make our definitions in terms of a simple 'idealised computer' that operates programs. Clearly, the procedures that can be carried out by a real computer are examples of effective procedures. Any particular real computer, however, is limited both in the size of the numbers that it can receive as input, and in the amount of working space available; it is in these respects that our 'computer' will be idealised in accordance with the informal idea of an algorithm. The programs for our machine will be finite, and we will require that a completed computation takes only a finite number of steps. Inputs and outputs will be restricted to natural numbers; this is not a significant restriction, since operations involving other kinds of object can be coded as operations on natural numbers. (We discuss this more fully in § 5.)

2. The unlimited register machine

Our mathematical idealisation of a computer is called an *unlimited register machine* (URM); it is a slight variation of a machine first conceived by Shepherdson & Sturgis [1963]. In this section we describe the URM and how it works; we begin to explore what it can do in § 3.

The URM has an infinite number of *registers* labelled $R_1, R_2, R_3, \ldots$, each of which at any moment of time contains a natural number; we denote the number contained in R_n by r_n. This can be represented as follows

R_1	R_2	R_3	R_4	R_5	R_6	R_7	...
r_1	r_2	r_3	r_4	r_5	r_6	r_7	...

The contents of the registers may be altered by the URM in response to certain *instructions* that it can recognise. These instructions correspond to very simple operations used in performing calculations with numbers. A finite list of instructions constitutes a *program*. The instructions are of four kinds, as follows.

Zero instructions For each $n = 1, 2, 3, \ldots$ there is a *zero instruction* Z(n). The response of the URM to the instruction Z(n) is to change the contents of R_n to 0, leaving all other registers unaltered.

Example Suppose that the URM is in the following configuration

R_1	R_2	R_3	R_4	R_5	R_6	
9	6	5	23	7	0	...

and obeys the zero instruction Z(3). Then the resulting configuration is

(*) 9	6	0	23	7	0	...

The response of the URM to a zero instruction Z(n) is denoted by $0 \to R_n$, or $r_n := 0$ (this is read r_n *becomes* 0).

Successor instructions For each $n = 1, 2, 3, \ldots$ there is a *successor instruction* S(n). The response of the URM to the instruction S(n) is to increase the number contained in R_n by 1, leaving all other registers unaltered.

Example Suppose that the URM is in the configuration (*) above and obeys the successor instruction S(5). Then the new configuration is

	R_1	R_2	R_3	R_4	R_5	R_6	
(**)	9	6	0	23	8	0	...

The effect of a successor instruction S(n) is denoted by $r_n + 1 \to R_n$, or $r_n := r_n + 1$ (r_n *becomes* $r_n + 1$).

Transfer instructions For each $m = 1, 2, 3, \ldots$ and $n = 1, 2, 3, \ldots$ there is a *transfer instruction* T(m, n). The response of the URM to the instruction T(m, n) is to replace the contents of R_n by the number r_m contained in R_m (i.e. transfer r_m into R_n); all other registers (including R_m) are unaltered.

Example Suppose that the URM is in the configuration (**) above and obeys the transfer instruction T(5, 1). Then the resulting configuration is

R_1	R_2	R_3	R_4	R_5	R_6	
8	6	0	23	8	0	...

The response of the URM to a transfer instruction $T(m, n)$ is denoted by $r_m \to R_n$, or $r_n := r_m$ (r_n *becomes* r_m).

Jump instructions In the operation of an informal algorithm there may be a stage when alternative courses of action are prescribed, depending on the progress of the operation up to that stage. In other situations it may be necessary to repeat a given routine several times. The URM is able to reflect such procedures as these using *jump instructions*; these will allow jumps backwards or forwards in the list of instructions. We shall, for example, be able to use a jump instruction to produce the following response:

> 'If $r_2 = r_6$, go to the 10th instruction in the program; otherwise, go on to the next instruction in the program.'

The instruction eliciting this response will be written $J(2, 6, 10)$.

Generally, for each $m = 1, 2, 3, \ldots, n = 1, 2, 3, \ldots$ and $q = 1, 2, 3, \ldots$ there is a *jump instruction* $J(m, n, q)$. The response of the URM to the instruction $J(m, n, q)$ is as follows. Suppose that this instruction is encountered in a program P. The contents of R_m and R_n are compared, but all registers are left unaltered. Then

> if $r_m = r_n$, the URM proceeds to the qth instruction of P;
>
> if $r_m \neq r_n$, the URM proceeds to the next instruction in P.

If the jump is impossible because P has less than q instructions, then the URM stops operation.

Zero, successor and transfer instructions are called *arithmetic* instructions.

We summarise the response of the URM to the four kinds of instruction in table 1.

Computations To perform a computation the URM must be provided with a program P and an *initial configuration* – i.e. a sequence $a_1, a_2, a_3, \ldots$ of natural numbers in the registers $R_1, R_2, R_3, \ldots$. Suppose that P consists of s instructions $I_1, I_2, \ldots, I_s$. The URM begins the computation by obeying I_1, then I_2, I_3, and so on unless a jump

Table 1

Type of instruction	Instruction	Response of the URM
Zero	Z(n)	Replace r_n by 0. ($0 \rightarrow R_n$, or $r_n := 0$)
Successor	S(n)	Add 1 to r_n. ($r_n + 1 \rightarrow R_n$, or $r_n := r_n + 1$)
Transfer	T(m, n)	Replace r_n by r_m. ($r_m \rightarrow R_n$, or $r_n := r_m$)
Jump	J(m, n, q)	If $r_m = r_n$, jump to the qth instruction; otherwise go on to the next instruction in the program.

instruction, say J(m, n, q), is encountered. In this case the URM proceeds to the instruction prescribed by J(m, n, q) and the current contents of the registers R_m and R_n. We illustrate this with an example.

2.1. *Example*

Consider the following program:

I_1 J(1, 2, 6)
I_2 S(2)
I_3 S(3)
I_4 J(1, 2, 6)
I_5 J(1, 1, 2)
I_6 T(3, 1)

Let us consider the computation by the URM under this program with initial configuration

R_1	R_2	R_3	R_4	R_5	
9	7	0	0	0	...

(We are not concerned at the moment about what function this program actually computes; we wish to illustrate the way in which the URM operates programs in a purely mechanical fashion *without* needing to understand the algorithm that is being carried out.)

We can represent the progress of the computation by writing down the successive configurations that occur, together with the next instruction to be obeyed at the completion of each stage.

	R_1	R_2	R_3	R_4	R_5		Next instruction
Initial configuration	9	7	0	0	0	...	I_1
	9	7	0	0	0		I_2 (since $r_1 \neq r_2$)
	9	8	0	0	0		I_3
	9	8	1	0	0		I_4
	9	8	1	0	0		I_5 (since $r_1 \neq r_2$)
	9	8	1	0	0		I_2 (since $r_1 = r_1$)

and so on. (We shall continue this computation later.)

We can describe the operation of the URM under a program $P = I_1, I_2, \ldots, I_s$ in general as follows. The URM starts by obeying instruction I_1. At any future stage in the computation, suppose that the URM is obeying instruction I_k. Then having done so it proceeds to the *next instruction in the computation*, defined as follows:

if I_k is not a jump instruction, the *next instruction* is I_{k+1};

if $I_k = \mathrm{J}(m, n, q)$ the *next instruction* is $\begin{cases} I_q & \text{if } r_m = r_n, \\ I_{k+1} & \text{otherwise,} \end{cases}$

where r_m, r_n are the current contents of R_m and R_n.

The URM proceeds thus as long as possible; the computation *stops* when, and only when, there is no next instruction; i.e. if the URM has just obeyed instruction I_k and the 'next instruction in the computation' according to the above definition is I_v where $v > s$. This can happen in the following ways:

(i) if $k = s$ (the last instruction in P has been obeyed) and I_s is an arithmetic instruction,

(ii) if $I_k = \mathrm{J}(m, n, q)$, $r_m = r_n$ and $q > s$,

(iii) if $I_k = \mathrm{J}(m, n, q)$, $r_m \neq r_n$ and $k = s$.

We say then that the computation stops after instruction I_k; the *final configuration* is the sequence $r_1, r_2, r_3, \ldots$, the contents of the registers at this stage.

Let us now continue the computation begun in example 2.1.

Example 2.1 (continued)

	R_1	R_2	R_3	R_4	R_5		Next instruction
	9	8	1	0	0	. . .	I_2
	9	9	1	0	0		I_3
	9	9	2	0	0		I_4
	9	9	2	0	0		I_6 (since $r_1 = r_2$)
Final configuration	2	9	2	0	0		I_7: STOP.

This computation stops as indicated because there is no seventh instruction in the program.

2.2. *Exercise*

Carry out the computation under the program of example 2.1 with initial configuration 8, 4, 2, 0, 0, . . .

The essence of a program and the progress of computations under it is often conveniently described informally using a *flow diagram.* For example, a flow diagram representing the program of example 2.1 is given in fig. 1*b*. (We have indicated alongside the flow diagram the typical configuration of the registers at various stages in a computation.) Note the convention that tests or questions (corresponding to jump instructions) are placed in diamond shaped boxes.

The translation of this flow diagram into the program of exercise 2.1 is almost self-explanatory. Notice that the backwards jump on answer 'No' to the second question '$r_1 = r_2$?' is achieved by the fifth instruction J(1, 1, 2) which is an *unconditional* jump: we always have $r_1 = r_1$, so this instruction causes a jump to I_2 whenever it is encountered.

When writing a program to perform a given procedure it is often helpful to write an informal flow diagram as an intermediate step: the translation of a flow diagram into a program is then usually routine.

Fig. 1*b*. Flow diagram for the program of example 2.1.

START

$r_1 = r_2?$ — Yes

No

$r_2 := r_2 + 1$

$r_3 := r_3 + 1$

No ← $r_1 = r_2?$

Yes

$r_3 \rightarrow R_1$

STOP

Typical configuration

R_1	R_2	R_3	
x	y	z	

After k cycles round the loop in this program:

x	$y+k$	$z+k$	

If $x = y + k$:

$z+k$	$y+k$	$z+k$	

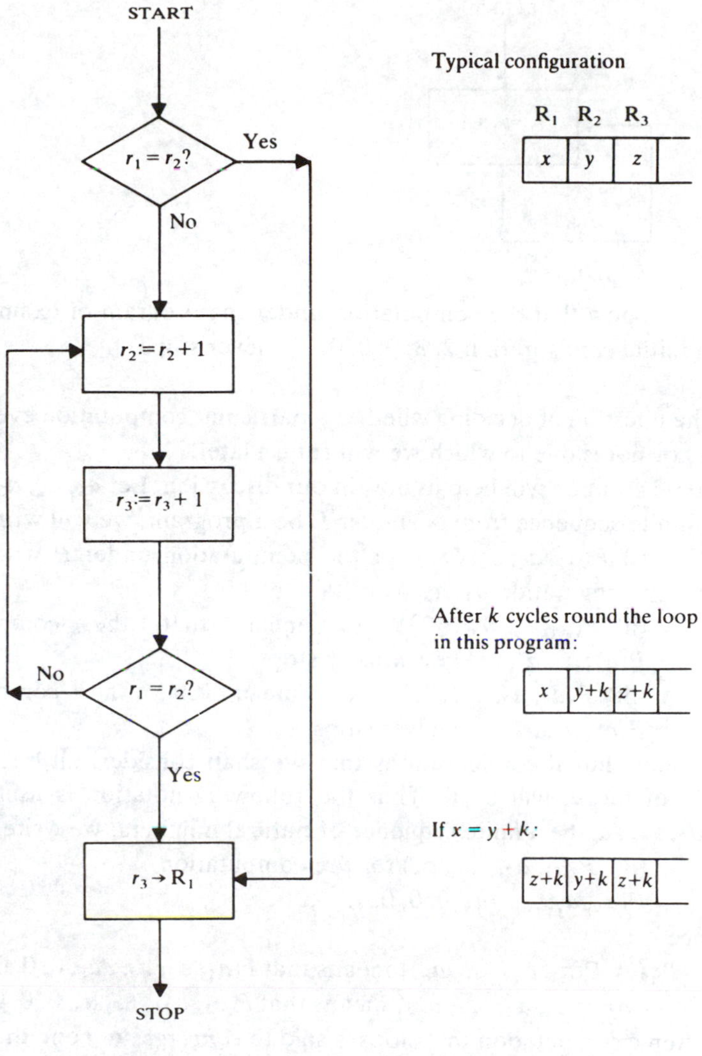

There are, of course, computations that never stop: for example, no computation under the simple program S(1), J(1, 1, 1) ever stops. Computation under this program is represented by the flow diagram in fig. 1*c*. The jump instruction invariably causes the URM to return, or loop back, to the instruction S(1).

There are more sophisticated ways in which a computation may run for ever, but always this is caused essentially by the above kind of repetition or looping back in the execution of the program.

Fig. 1*c*.

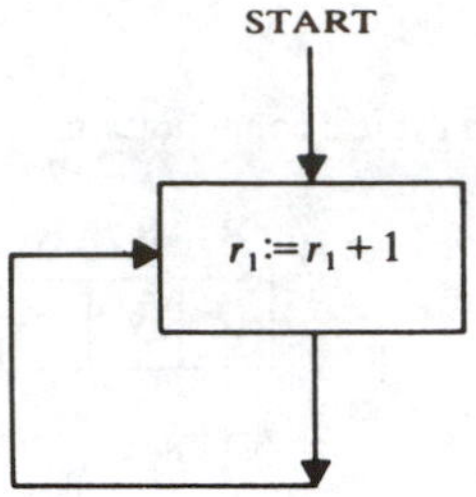

2.3 *Exercise*

Show that the computation under the program of example 2.1 with initial configuration 2, 3, 0, 0, 0, . . . never stops.

The question of deciding whether a particular computation eventually stops or not is one to which we will return later.

Some notation will help us now in our discussion. Let $a_1, a_2, a_3, \ldots$ be an infinite sequence from $\mathbb{N}$ and let P be a program; we will write

(i) $P(a_1, a_2, a_3, \ldots)$ for the computation under P with initial configuration $a_1, a_2, a_3, \ldots$;

(ii) $P(a_1, a_2, a_3, \ldots)\downarrow$ to mean that the computation $P(a_1, a_2, a_3, \ldots)$ eventually stops;

(iii) $P(a_1, a_2, a_3, \ldots)\uparrow$ to mean that the computation $P(a_1, a_2, a_3, \ldots)$ never stops.

In most initial configurations that we shall consider, all but finitely many of the a_i will be 0. Thus the following notation is useful. Let $a_1, a_2, \ldots, a_n$ be a finite sequence of natural numbers; we write

(iv) $P(a_1, a_2, \ldots, a_n)$ for the computation $P(a_1, a_2, \ldots, a_n, 0, 0, 0, \ldots)$,

Hence

(v) $P(a_1, a_2, \ldots, a_n)\downarrow$ means that $P(a_1, a_2, \ldots, a_n, 0, 0, 0, \ldots)\downarrow$;

(vi) $P(a_1, a_2, \ldots, a_n)\uparrow$ means that $P(a_1, a_2, \ldots, a_n, 0, 0, 0, \ldots)\uparrow$.

Often a computation that stops is said to *converge*, and one that never stops is said to *diverge*.

3. URM-computable functions

Suppose that f is a function from $\mathbb{N}^n$ to $\mathbb{N}$ ($n \geq 1$); what does it mean to say that f is computable by the URM? It is natural to think in terms of computing a value $f(a_1, \ldots, a_n)$ by means of a program P on initial configuration $a_1, a_2, \ldots, a_n, 0, 0, \ldots$. That is, we consider computations of the form $P(a_1, a_2, \ldots, a_n)$. If any such computation stops, we need to have a single number that we can regard as the output or result of the computation; we make the convention that this is the number r_1 finally contained in R_1. The final contents of the other registers can be regarded as rough work or jottings, that can be ignored once we have the desired result in R_1.

Since a computation $P(a_1, \ldots, a_n)$ may not stop, we can allow our definition of computability to apply to functions f from $\mathbb{N}^n$ to $\mathbb{N}$ whose domain may not be all of $\mathbb{N}^n$; i.e. partial functions. We shall require that the relevant computations stop (and give the correct result!) *precisely* for inputs from the domain of f. Thus we make the following definitions.

3.1 *Definitions*

Let f be a partial function from $\mathbb{N}^n$ to $\mathbb{N}$.

(*a*) Suppose that P is a program, and let $a_1, a_2, \ldots, a_n, b \in \mathbb{N}$.

(i) The computation $P(a_1, a_2, \ldots, a_n)$ *converges to* b if $P(a_1, a_2, \ldots, a_n)\downarrow$ and in the final configuration b is in R_1. We write this $P(a_1, \ldots, a_n)\downarrow b$;

(ii) P *URM-computes* f if, for every $a_1, \ldots, a_n, b$ $P(a_1, \ldots, a_n)\downarrow b$ if and only if $(a_1, \ldots, a_n) \in \mathrm{Dom}(f)$ and $f(a_1, \ldots, a_n) = b$. (In particular, this means that $P(a_1, \ldots, a_n)\downarrow$ if and only if $(a_1, \ldots, a_n) \in \mathrm{Dom}(f)$.)

(*b*) The function f is *URM-computable* if there is a program that URM-computes f.

The class of URM-computable functions is denoted by $\mathscr{C}$, and n-ary URM-computable functions by $\mathscr{C}_n$. From now on we will use the term *computable* to mean URM-computable, except in chapter 3 where other notions of computability are discussed.

We now consider some easy examples of computable functions.

3.2 *Examples*

(*a*) $x + y$.

We obtain $x + y$ by adding 1 to x (using the successor instruction) y times. A program to compute $x + y$ must begin on initial configuration $x, y, 0, 0, 0, \ldots$; our program will keep adding 1 to r_1, using R_3 as a counter to keep a record of how many times r_1 is thus increased. A typical configuration during the computation is

R_1	R_2	R_3	R_4	R_5	
$x + k$	y	k	0	0	...

The program will be designed to stop when $k = y$, leaving $x + y$ in R_1 as required.

The procedure we wish to embody in our program is represented by the flow diagram in fig. 1*d*. A program that achieves this is the following:

I_1 J(3, 2, 5) ←
I_2 S(1)
I_3 S(3)
I_4 J(1, 1, 1) ---

(The dotted arrow, which is *not* part of the program, is to indicate to the reader that the final instruction has the effect of always jumping back to the first instruction.) Note that the STOP has been achieved by a jump instruction to 'I_5' which does not exist. Thus, $x + y$ is computable.

Fig. 1*d*. Flow diagram for addition (example 3.2(*a*)).

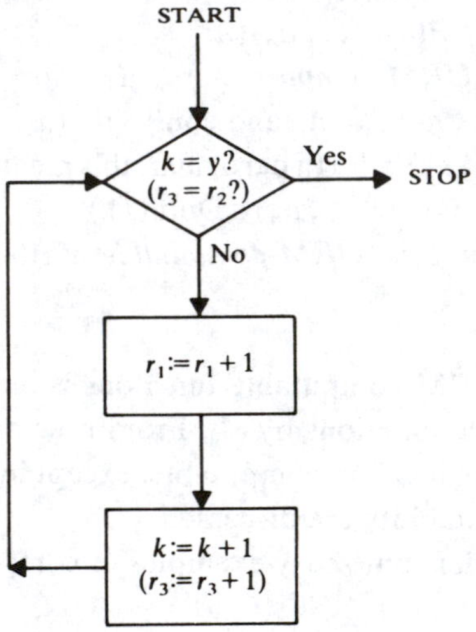

(*b*) $$x \dot{-} 1 = \begin{cases} x - 1 & \text{if } x > 0, \\ 0 & \text{if } x = 0. \end{cases}$$

(Since we are restricting ourselves to functions from ℕ to ℕ, this is the best approximation to the function $x - 1$.)

We will write a program embodying the following procedure. Given initial configuration $x, 0, 0, 0, \ldots$, first check whether $x = 0$; if so, stop; otherwise, run two counters, containing k and $k + 1$, starting with $k = 0$. A typical configuration during a computation will be

R_1	R_2	R_3	R_4	
x	k	$k+1$	0	...

Check whether $x = k+1$; if so, the required result is k; otherwise increase both counters by 1, and check again.

A flow diagram representing this procedure is given in fig. 1*e*. A program that carries out this procedure is the following:

I_1 J(1, 4, 9)
I_2 S(3)
I_3 J(1, 3, 7) ←
I_4 S(2)
I_5 S(3)
I_6 J(1, 1, 3)
I_7 T(2, 1)

Thus the function $x \dot{-} 1$ is computable.

Fig. 1*e*. Flow diagram for $x \dot{-} 1$ (example 3.2(*b*)).

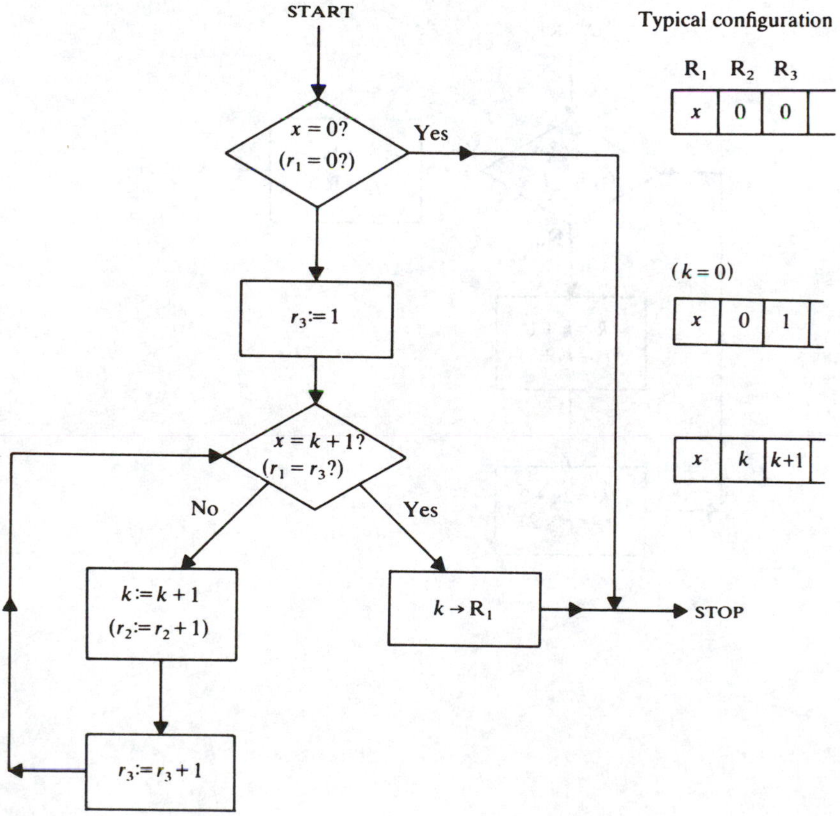

(c) $$f(x) = \begin{cases} \frac{1}{2}x & \text{if } x \text{ is even,} \\ \text{undefined} & \text{if } x \text{ is odd.} \end{cases}$$

In this example, $\mathrm{Dom}(f) = \mathbb{E}$ (the even natural numbers) so we must ensure that our program does not stop on odd inputs.

A procedure for computing $f(x)$ is as follows. Run two counters, containing k and $2k$ for $k = 0, 1, 2, 3, \ldots$; for successive values of k, check whether $x = 2k$; if so, the answer is k; otherwise increase k by one, and repeat. If x is odd, this procedure will clearly continue for ever.

The typical configuration will be

R_1	R_2	R_3	R_4	
x	$2k$	k	0	...

with $k = 0$ initially. A flow diagram for the above process is given in fig. 1f.

Fig. 1f. Flow diagram for example 3.2(c)).

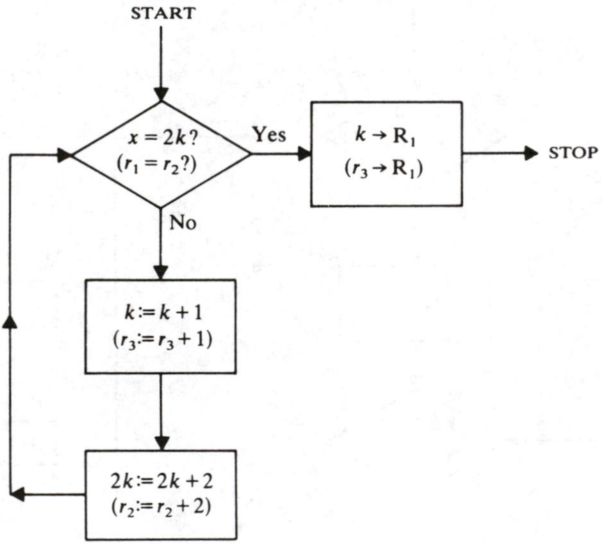

A program that executes it is

I_1 J(1, 2, 6)
I_2 S(3)
I_3 S(2)
I_4 S(2)
I_5 J(1, 1, 1)
I_6 T(3, 1)

Hence f is computable.

Note. The programs in these examples are in no sense the only programs that will compute the functions in question.

Given any program P (i.e. any finite list of instructions), and $n \geq 1$, by thinking of the effect of P on initial configurations of the form $a_1, a_2, \ldots, a_n, 0, 0, \ldots$ we see that there is a unique n-ary function that P computes, denoted by $f_P^{(n)}$. From the definition it is clear that

$$f_P^{(n)}(a_1, \ldots, a_n) = \begin{cases} \text{the unique } b \text{ such that } P(a_1, \ldots, a_n)\downarrow b, \\ \quad \text{if } P(a_1, \ldots, a_n)\downarrow; \\ \text{undefined, if } P(a_1, \ldots, a_n)\uparrow. \end{cases}$$

In a later chapter we shall consider the problem of determining $f_P^{(n)}$ for any given program P.

It is clear that a particular computable function can be computed by many different programs; for instance, any program can be altered by adding instructions that have no effect. Less trivially, there may be different informal methods for calculating a particular function, and when formalised as programs these would give different programs for the same function. In terms of the notation we have introduced, we can have different programs P_1 and P_2, with $f_{P_1}^{(n)} = f_{P_2}^{(n)}$ for some (or all) n. Later we shall consider the problem of deciding whether or not two programs compute the same functions.

3.3 *Exercises*

1. Show that the following functions are computable by devising programs that will compute them.

(*a*) $f(x) = \begin{cases} 0 & \text{if } x = 0, \\ 1 & \text{if } x \neq 0; \end{cases}$

(*b*) $f(x) = 5;$

(*c*) $f(x, y) = \begin{cases} 0 & \text{if } x = y, \\ 1 & \text{if } x \neq y; \end{cases}$

(*d*) $f(x, y) = \begin{cases} 0 & \text{if } x \leq y, \\ 1 & \text{if } x > y; \end{cases}$

(*e*) $f(x) = \begin{cases} \frac{1}{3}x \text{ if } x \text{ is a multiple of } 3, \\ \text{undefined otherwise;} \end{cases}$

(*f*) $f(x) = [2x/3]$. ($[z]$ denotes the greatest integer $\leq z$).

2. Let P be the program in example 2.1. What is $f_P^{(2)}$?
3. Suppose that P is a program without any jump instructions. Show that there is a number m such that either

$$f_P^{(1)}(x) = m, \qquad \text{for all } x,$$

or

$$f_P^{(1)}(x) = x + m, \qquad \text{for all } x.$$

4. Show that for each transfer instruction $T(m, n)$ there is a program without any transfer instructions that has exactly the same effect as $T(m, n)$ on any configuration of the URM. (Thus transfer instructions are really redundant in the formulation of our URM; it is nevertheless natural and convenient to have transfer as a basic facility of the URM.)

4. Decidable predicates and problems

In mathematics a common task is to *decide* whether numbers possess a given property. For instance, the task described in (1.1) (*d*) is to decide, given numbers x, y, whether they have the property that x is a multiple of y. An algorithm for this operation would be an effective procedure that on inputs x, y gives output Yes or No. If we adopt the convention that 1 means Yes, and 0 means No, then the operation amounts to calculation of the function

$$f(x, y) = \begin{cases} 1 & \text{if } x \text{ is a multiple of } y, \\ 0 & \text{if } x \text{ is not a multiple of } y. \end{cases}$$

Thus we can say that the property or predicate 'x is a multiple of y' is *algorithmically* or *effectively decidable*, or just *decidable* if this function f is computable.

Generally, suppose that $M(x_1, x_2, \ldots, x_n)$ is an n-ary predicate of natural numbers. The *characteristic function* $c_M(\boldsymbol{x})$ (setting $\boldsymbol{x} = (x_1, \ldots, x_n)$) is given by

$$c_M(\boldsymbol{x}) = \begin{cases} 1 & \text{if } M(\boldsymbol{x}) \text{ holds}, \\ 0 & \text{if } M(\boldsymbol{x}) \text{ doesn't hold}. \end{cases}$$

4.1 *Definition*

The predicate $M(\mathbf{x})$ is *decidable* if the function c_M is computable; $M(\mathbf{x})$ is *undecidable* if $M(\mathbf{x})$ is not decidable.

4.2 *Examples*

The following predicates are decidable:

(*a*) '$x \neq y$': the function f of exercise 3.3 (1*c*) is the characteristic function of this predicate.

(*b*) '$x = 0$': the characteristic function is given by

$$g(x) = \begin{cases} 1 & \text{if } x = 0, \\ 0 & \text{if } x \neq 0. \end{cases}$$

The following simple program computes g:

```
J(1, 2, 3)
J(1, 1, 4)
S(2)
T(2, 1)
```

(*c*) 'x is a multiple of y': it is possible to write a program for the characteristic function, but this would be somewhat lengthy and complicated. A simpler demonstration that this predicate is decidable will emerge from the next chapter, where techniques for generating more complex computable functions are developed.

Note that when discussing decidability (or undecidability) we are always concerned with the computability (or non-computability) of *total* functions.

In the context of decidability, properties or predicates are sometimes described as *problems.* Thus we might say that the problem '$x \neq y$' is decidable. In chapter 6 we will study undecidable problems.

4.3 *Exercise*

Show that the following predicates are decidable.

(*a*) '$x < y$',

(*b*) '$x \neq 3$',

(*c*) 'x is even'.

5. Computability on other domains

Since the URM handles only natural numbers, our definition of computability and decidability applies only to functions and predicates of natural numbers. These notions are easily extended to other kinds of object (e.g. integers, polynomials, matrices, etc.) by means of coding, as follows.

A *coding* of a domain D of objects is an explicit and effective injection $\alpha: D \to \mathbb{N}$. We say that an object $d \in D$ is *coded* by the natural number $\alpha(d)$. Suppose now that f is a function from D to D; then f is naturally coded by the function f^* from $\mathbb{N}$ to $\mathbb{N}$ that maps the code of an object $d \in \mathrm{Dom}(f)$ to the code of $f(d)$. Explicitly we have

$$f^* = \alpha \circ f \circ \alpha^{-1}.$$

Now we may extend the definition of URM-computability to D by saying that f is *computable* if f^* is a computable function of natural numbers.

5.1 *Example*

Consider the domain $\mathbb{Z}$. An explicit coding is given by the function α where

$$\alpha(n) = \begin{cases} 2n & \text{if } n \geq 0, \\ -2n-1 & \text{if } n < 0. \end{cases}$$

Then α^{-1} is given by

$$\alpha^{-1}(m) = \begin{cases} \tfrac{1}{2}m & \text{if } m \text{ is even,} \\ -\tfrac{1}{2}(m+1) & \text{if } m \text{ is odd.} \end{cases}$$

Consider now the function $x-1$ on $\mathbb{Z}$; if we call this function f, then $f^*: \mathbb{N} \to \mathbb{N}$ is given by

$$f^*(x) = \begin{cases} 1 & \text{if } x = 0 \text{ (i.e. } x = \alpha(0)), \\ x-2 & \text{if } x > 0 \text{ and } x \text{ is even (i.e. } x = \alpha(n), n > 0), \\ x+2 & \text{if } x \text{ is odd. (i.e. } x = \alpha(n), n < 0). \end{cases}$$

It is a routine exercise to write a program that computes f^*; hence $x-1$ is a computable function on $\mathbb{Z}$.

The definitions of computable n-ary function on a domain D and decidable predicate on D are obtained by the obvious extension of the above idea.

5.2 *Exercises*

1. Show that the function $2x$ on $\mathbb{Z}$ is computable.
2. Show that the predicate '$x \geq 0$' is a decidable predicate on $\mathbb{Z}$.

2
Generating computable functions

In this chapter we shall see that various methods of combining computable functions give rise to other computable functions. This will enable us to show quite rapidly that many commonly occurring functions are computable, without writing a program each time – a task that would be rather laborious and tedious.

1. The basic functions

First we note that some particularly simple functions are computable; from these *basic functions* (defined in lemma 1.1 below) we shall then build more complicated computable functions using the techniques developed in subsequent sections.

1.1. *Lemma*

The following basic functions are computable:

(*a*) *the zero function* $\mathbf{0}$($\mathbf{0}(x) = 0$ for all x);

(*b*) *the successor function* $x+1$;

(*c*) *for each* $n \geq 1$ and $1 \leq i \leq n$, *the projection function* U_i^n *given by* $U_i^n(x_1, x_2, \ldots, x_n) = x_i$.

Proof. These functions correspond to the arithmetic instructions for the URM. Specifically, programs are as follows:

(*a*) $\mathbf{0}$: program Z(1);

(*b*) $x+1$: program S(1);

(*c*) U_i^n: program T(i, 1). □

2. Joining programs together

In each of §§ 3–5 below we need to write programs that incorporate other programs as *subprograms* or *subroutines*. In this section we deal with some technical matters so as to make the program writing of later sections as straightforward as possible.

A simple example of program building is when we have programs P and Q, and we wish to write a program for the composite procedure: first do P, and then do Q. Our instinct is to simply write down the instructions in P followed by the instructions in Q. But there are two technical points to consider.

Suppose that $P = I_1, I_2, \ldots, I_s$. A computation under P is completed when the 'next instruction for the computation' is I_v for some $v > s$; we then require the computation under our composite program to proceed to the *first* instruction of Q. This will happen automatically if $v = s+1$, but not otherwise. Thus for building composite programs we must confine our attention to programs that invariably stop because the next instruction is I_{s+1}. Such programs are said to be in *standard form*. Clearly it is only jump instructions that can cause a program to stop in non-standard fashion. Thus we have the following definition.

2.1. *Definition*

A program $P = I_1, I_2, \ldots, I_s$ is in *standard form* if, for every jump instruction $J(m, n, q)$ in P we have $q \leq s+1$.

Examples. In examples 1-3.2 the programs for (a) and (c) are in standard form, whereas the program in (b) is not.

Insisting on standard form if necessary is no restriction, as we now see.

2.2. *Lemma*

For any program P there is a program P^* in standard form such that any computation under P^* is identical to the corresponding computation under P, except possibly in the manner of stopping. In particular, for any $a_1, \ldots, a_n, b$,

$$P(a_1, \ldots, a_n)\downarrow b \text{ if and only if } P^*(a_1, \ldots, a_n)\downarrow b,$$

and hence $f_P^{(n)} = f_{P^*}^{(n)}$ for every $n > 0$.

Proof. Suppose that $P = I_1, I_2, \ldots, I_s$. To obtain P^* from P simply change the jump instructions so that all jump stops occur because the jump is to I_{s+1}. Explicitly, put $P^* = I_1^*, I_2^*, \ldots, I_s^*$ where

if I_k is not a jump instruction, then $I_k^* = I_k$;

if $I_k = J(m, n, q)$, then $I_k^* = \begin{cases} I_k & \text{if } q \leq s+1, \\ J(m, n, s+1) & \text{if } q > s+1. \end{cases}$

Then clearly P^* is as required. □

Let us assume now that the programs P and Q are in standard form. The second problem when joining P and Q concerns the jump instructions in Q. A jump $J(m, n, q)$ occurring in Q commands a jump to the qth instruction of Q (if $r_m = r_n$). But the qth instruction of Q will become the $s+q$th instruction in the composite program; thus each jump $J(m, n, q)$ in Q must be modified to become $J(m, n, s+q)$ in the composite program if the sense is to be preserved.

Now without any further worry we can define the *join* or *concatenation* of two programs in standard form:

2.3. *Definition*

Let P and Q be programs of lengths s, t respectively, in standard form. The *join* or *concatenation* of P and Q, written PQ or $\begin{matrix}P\\Q\end{matrix}$, is the program $I_1, I_2, \ldots, I_s, I_{s+1} \ldots, I_{s+t}$ where $P = I_1, \ldots, I_s$, and the instructions $I_{s+1}, \ldots, I_{s+t}$ are the instructions of Q with each jump $J(m, n, q)$ replaced by $J(m, n, s+q)$.

With this definition it is clear that the effect of PQ is as desired: any computation under PQ is identical to the corresponding computation under P followed by the computation under Q whose initial configuration is the final configuration from the computation under P.

There are two further considerations before we can proceed to the major tasks of this chapter. Suppose that we wish to compose a program Q having a given program P as a subroutine. To write Q it is often important to be able to find some registers that are unaffected by computations under P. This can be done as follows.

Since P is finite, there is a smallest number u such that none of the registers R_v for $v > u$ is mentioned in P; i.e. if $Z(n)$, or $S(n)$, or $T(m, n)$, or $J(m, n, q)$ is an instruction in P, then $m, n \leq u$. Clearly, during any computation under P, the contents of R_v for $v > u$ remain unaltered, and have no effect on the values of $r_1, \ldots, r_u$. Thus when writing our new program Q the registers R_v for $v > u$ can be used, for example, to store information without affecting any computation under the subroutine P. We denote the number u by $\rho(P)$.

Finally, we introduce some notation that will greatly simplify the main proofs of this chapter. Suppose that P is a program in standard form designed to compute a function $f(x_1, \ldots, x_n)$. Often when using P as a subroutine in a larger program the inputs $x_1, \ldots, x_n$ for which $f(x_1, \ldots, x_n)$ is desired may be held in registers $R_{l_1}, \ldots, R_{l_n}$ rather than $R_1, \ldots, R_n$ as the program P requires; further, the output $f(x_1, \ldots, x_n)$ may be required for future purposes to be in some register R_l rather than the conventional R_1; and finally the working registers $R_1, \ldots, R_{\rho(P)}$ for P may contain all kinds of unwanted information. We can modify P to take account of all of these points as follows.

We write $P[l_1, \ldots, l_n \to l]$ for the program in fig. 2*a* that translates the flow diagram alongside. The program $P[l_1, \ldots, l_n \to l]$ has the effect of computing $f(r_{l_1}, \ldots, r_{l_n})$ and placing the result in R_l. Moreover, the only registers affected by this program are (at most) $R_1, R_2, \ldots, R_{\rho(P)}$ and R_l. (We have assumed in defining $P[l_1, \ldots, l_n \to l]$ that $R_{l_1}, \ldots, R_{l_n}$ are distinct from $R_1, \ldots, R_n$; this will be the case in all our uses of this notation. The reader should be able to modify the definition for situations where this is not the case.)

Fig. 2*a*. Flow diagram for $P[l_1, \ldots, l_n \to l]$.

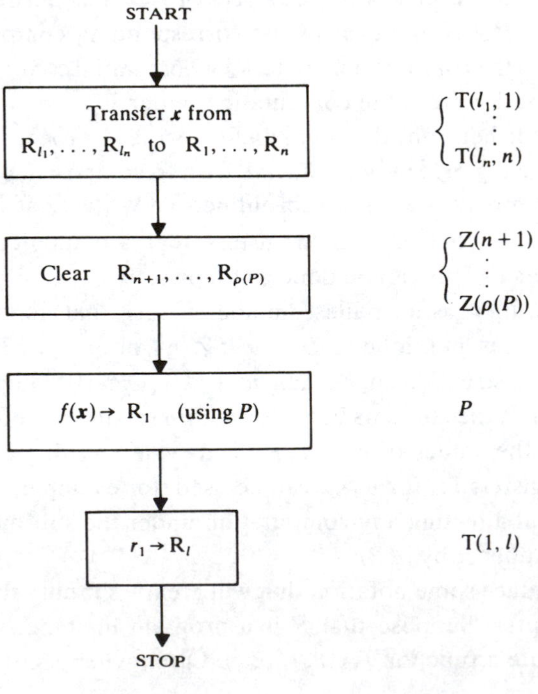

3. Substitution

A common way of manufacturing new functions from old is to substitute functions into other functions, otherwise known as composition of functions. In the following theorem we show that when this process is applied to computable functions, the resulting functions are also computable. In short, we say that $\mathscr{C}$ is *closed* under the operation of substitution.

3.1. *Theorem*

Suppose that $f(y_1, \ldots, y_k)$ *and* $g_1(\boldsymbol{x}), \ldots, g_k(\boldsymbol{x})$ *are computable functions, where* $\boldsymbol{x} = (x_1, \ldots, x_n)$. *Then the function* $h(\boldsymbol{x})$ *given by*

$$h(\boldsymbol{x}) \simeq f(g_1(\boldsymbol{x}), \ldots, g_k(\boldsymbol{x}))$$

is computable.

(*Note.* $h(\boldsymbol{x})$ *is defined if and only if* $g_1(\boldsymbol{x}), \ldots, g_k(\boldsymbol{x})$ *are all defined and* $(g_1(\boldsymbol{x}), \ldots, g_k(\boldsymbol{x})) \in \mathrm{Dom}(f)$; *thus,* if f *and* $g_1, \ldots, g_k$ *are all total functions, then* h *is total.*)

Proof. Suppose that $F, G_1, \ldots, G_k$ are programs in standard form which compute $f, g_1, \ldots, g_k$ respectively. We will write a program H that embodies the following natural procedure for computing h. 'Given $\boldsymbol{x}$, use the programs $G_1, \ldots, G_k$ to compute in succession $g_1(\boldsymbol{x}), g_2(\boldsymbol{x}), \ldots, g_k(\boldsymbol{x})$, making a note of these values as they are obtained. Then use the program F to compute $f(g_1(\boldsymbol{x}), \ldots, g_k(\boldsymbol{x}))$.'

We must take a little care to avoid losing information needed at later stages in the procedure, namely $\boldsymbol{x}$ and those values $g_i(\boldsymbol{x})$ already obtained. Putting $m = \max(n, k, \rho(F), \rho(G_1), \ldots, \rho(G_k))$, we shall begin by storing $\boldsymbol{x}$ in $R_{m+1}, \ldots, R_{m+n}$; the registers $R_{m+n+1}, \ldots, R_{m+n+k}$ will be used to store the values $g_i(\boldsymbol{x})$ as they are computed for $i = 1, 2, \ldots, k$. These registers are completely ignored by computations under $F, G_1, \ldots, G_k$. A typical configuration during computation under H will be

	Storage registers							
$R_1 \ldots R_m$	$R_{m+1} \ldots R_{m+n}$	R_{m+n+1}	R_{m+n+2}	$\ldots$	R_{m+n+i}			
$\ldots$	$\boldsymbol{x}$	$g_1(\boldsymbol{x})$	$g_2(\boldsymbol{x})$	$\ldots$	$g_i(\boldsymbol{x})$	0	0	$\ldots$

An informal flow diagram for computing h is given in fig. 2*b*. This is easily translated into the following program H that computes h:

$T(1, m+1)$

$\vdots$

$T(n, m+n)$

$G_1[m+1, m+2, \ldots, m+n \rightarrow m+n+1]$ (Recall the meaning of this notation from § 2.)

$\vdots$

$G_k[m+1, m+2, \ldots, m+n \rightarrow m+n+k]$

$F[m+n+1, \ldots, m+n+k \rightarrow 1]$

Fig. 2*b*. Substitution (theorem 3.1).

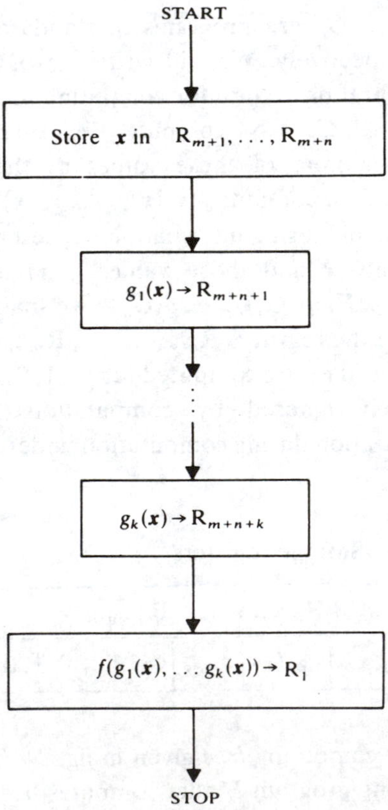

Clearly a computation $H(\boldsymbol{x})$ will stop if and only if each computation $G_i(\boldsymbol{x})$ stops $(1 \leq i \leq k)$ and the computation $F(g_1(\boldsymbol{x}), \ldots, g_k(\boldsymbol{x}))$ stops, which is exactly as required. □

New functions can be obtained from any given function by rearranging or identifying its variables, or by adding new dummy variables; for instance, from a function $f(y_1, y_2)$ we can obtain

$$h_1(x_1, x_2) \simeq f(x_2, x_1) \quad \text{(rearrangement)},$$
$$h_2(x) \simeq f(x, x) \quad \text{(identification)},$$
$$h_3(x_1, x_2, x_3) \simeq f(x_2, x_3) \quad \text{(adding dummy variables)}.$$

The following application of theorem 3.1 shows that any of these operations (or a combination of them) transforms computable functions into computable functions.

3.2. *Theorem*

Suppose that $f(y_1, \ldots, y_k)$ is a computable function and that $x_{i_1}, x_{i_2}, \ldots, x_{i_k}$ is a sequence of k of the variables $x_1, \ldots, x_n$ (possibly with repetitions). Then the function h given by

$$h(x_1, \ldots, x_n) \simeq f(x_{i_1}, \ldots, x_{i_k})$$

is computable.

Proof. Writing $\boldsymbol{x} = (x_1, \ldots, x_n)$ we have that

$$h(\boldsymbol{x}) \simeq f(\mathrm{U}^n_{i_1}(\boldsymbol{x}), \mathrm{U}^n_{i_2}(\boldsymbol{x}), \ldots, \mathrm{U}^n_{i_k}(\boldsymbol{x}))$$

which is computable, by Lemma 1.1(*c*) and theorem 3.1. □

Using this result we can see that theorem 3.1 also holds when the functions $g_1, \ldots, g_k$ substituted into f are not necessarily functions of all of the variables $x_1, \ldots, x_n$, as in the following example.

3.3. *Example*

The function $f(x_1, x_2, x_3) = x_1 + x_2 + x_3$ is computable; this can be deduced from the fact that $x + y$ is computable (example 1-3.2(*a*)), by substituting $x_1 + x_2$ for x, and x_3 for y in $x + y$.

Substitution combined with the principle described in the next section gives a powerful method of generating computable functions.

3.4. *Exercises*

1. Without writing any programs, show that for every $m \in \mathbb{N}$ the following functions are computable:
   (*a*) $\boldsymbol{m}$ (recall that $\boldsymbol{m}(x) = m$, for all x),
   (*b*) mx.
2. Suppose that $f(x, y)$ is computable, and $m \in \mathbb{N}$. Show that the function
   $h(x) \simeq f(x, m)$
   is computable.
3. Suppose that $g(x)$ is a total computable function. Show that the predicate $M(x, y)$ given by
   $M(x, y) \equiv$ '$g(x) = y$'
   is decidable.

4. Recursion

Recursion is a method of defining a function by specifying each of its values in terms of previously defined values, and possibly using other already defined functions.

To be precise, suppose that $f(\boldsymbol{x})$ and $g(\boldsymbol{x}, y, z)$ are functions (not necessarily total or computable). Consider the following 'definition' of a new function $h(\boldsymbol{x}, y)$:

(4.1) (i) $h(\boldsymbol{x}, 0) \simeq f(\boldsymbol{x})$,

(ii) $h(\boldsymbol{x}, y+1) \simeq g(\boldsymbol{x}, y, h(\boldsymbol{x}, y))$.

At first sight this may seem a little dubious as a definition, for in the second line it appears that h is being defined in terms of itself – a circular definition! However, with a little thought we can convince ourselves that this is a valid definition: to find the value of $h(\boldsymbol{x}, 3)$ for instance, first find $h(\boldsymbol{x}, 0)$ using (4.1)(i); then, knowing $h(\boldsymbol{x}, 0)$, use (4.1)(ii) to obtain $h(\boldsymbol{x}, 1)$; similarly, obtain $h(\boldsymbol{x}, 2)$, and finally $h(\boldsymbol{x}, 3)$ by further applications of (4.1)(ii). Thus, circularity is avoided by thinking of the values of $h(\boldsymbol{x}, y)$ as being defined one at a time, always in terms of a value already obtained.

A function h defined thus is said to be defined by *recursion* from the functions f and g; the equations 4.1 are known as *recursion equations.* Unless both f and g are total, then h as defined by (4.1) may not be total; the domain of h will satisfy the conditions

$$(\boldsymbol{x}, 0) \in \mathrm{Dom}(h) \quad \text{iff} \quad \boldsymbol{x} \in \mathrm{Dom}(f),$$

$$(\boldsymbol{x}, y+1) \in \mathrm{Dom}(h) \quad \text{iff} \quad (\boldsymbol{x}, y) \in \mathrm{Dom}(h) \text{ and } (\boldsymbol{x}, y, h(\boldsymbol{x}, y)) \in \mathrm{Dom}(g).$$

Let us summarise the above discussion in a theorem, whose proof we omit.

4.2. *Theorem*

Let $\boldsymbol{x} = (x_1, \ldots, x_n)$, *and suppose that* $f(\boldsymbol{x})$ *and* $g(\boldsymbol{x}, y, z)$ *are functions; then there is a unique function* $h(\boldsymbol{x}, y)$ *satisfying the recursion equations*

$$h(\boldsymbol{x}, 0) \simeq f(\boldsymbol{x}),$$

$$h(\boldsymbol{x}, y+1) \simeq g(\boldsymbol{x}, y, h(\boldsymbol{x}, y)).$$

Note. When $n = 0$ (i.e. the parameters $\boldsymbol{x}$ do not appear) the recursion equations take the form

$$h(0) = a,$$

$$h(y+1) \simeq g(y, h(y)),$$

where $a \in \mathbb{N}$.

4.3. *Examples*

(*a*) Addition: for any x, y we have

$$x + 0 = x,$$

$$x + (y+1) = (x+y) + 1.$$

Thus addition (i.e. the function $h(x, y) = x + y$) is defined by recursion from the functions $f(x) = x$ and $g(x, y, z) = z + 1$.

(*b*) $y!$: with the convention that $0! = 1$, we have that

$$0! = 1,$$

$$(y+1)! = y!(y+1).$$

Thus the function $y!$ is defined by recursion from 1 and the function $g(y, z) = z(y+1)$.

There are forms of definition by recursion that are more general than the one we have discussed; we shall encounter an example of this in § 5, and a fuller discussion of this topic is included in chapter 10. In contexts where general kinds of recursion are being considered, the particularly simple kind of definition given by (4.1) is called *primitive recursion.*

Many commonly occurring functions have easy definitions by (primitive) recursion, so for establishing computability the next theorem is extremely useful. Briefly, it shows that $\mathscr{C}$ is closed under definition by recursion.

4.4. *Theorem*

Suppose that $f(\boldsymbol{x})$ *and* $g(\boldsymbol{x}, y, z)$ *are computable functions, where* $\boldsymbol{x} = (x_1, \ldots, x_n)$; *then the function* $h(\boldsymbol{x}, y)$ *obtained from* f *and* g *by recursion is computable.*

Proof. Let F and G be programs in standard form which compute the functions $f(\boldsymbol{x})$ and $g(\boldsymbol{x}, y, z)$. We will devise a program H for the function $h(\boldsymbol{x}, y)$ given by the recursion equations 4.1. Given an initial configuration $x_1, \ldots, x_n, y, 0, 0, 0 \ldots$ H will first compute $h(\boldsymbol{x}, 0)$ (using F); then, if $y \neq 0$, H will use G to compute successively $h(\boldsymbol{x}, 1)$, $h(\boldsymbol{x}, 2), \ldots, h(\boldsymbol{x}, y)$, and then stop.

Let $m = \max(n+2, \rho(F), \rho(G))$; we begin by storing $\boldsymbol{x}, y$ in $R_{m+1}, \ldots, R_{m+n+1}$; the next two registers will be used to store the current value of the numbers k and $h(\boldsymbol{x}, k)$ for $k = 0, 1, 2, \ldots, y$. Writing t for $m+n$, a typical configuration during the procedure will thus be

	$R_1 \ldots R_m$	Storage registers: $R_{m+1} \ldots R_t$	R_{t+1}	R_{t+2}	R_{t+3}	
(*)	...	$\boldsymbol{x}$	y	k	$h(\boldsymbol{x}, k)$	...

with $k = 0$ initially.

An informal flow diagram for the procedure is given in fig. 2*c*. This flow diagram translates easily into the following program H that computes h:

$$
\begin{array}{ll}
 & T(1, m+1) \\
 & \vdots \\
 & T(n+1, m+n+1) \\
 & F[1, 2, \ldots, n \rightarrow t+3] \\
I_q & J(t+2, t+1, p) \\
 & G[m+1, \ldots, m+n, t+2, t+3 \rightarrow t+3] \\
 & S(t+2) \\
 & J(1, 1, q) \\
I_p & T(t+3, 1)
\end{array}
$$

Hence h is computable. □

Fig. 2c. Recursion (theorem 4.4).

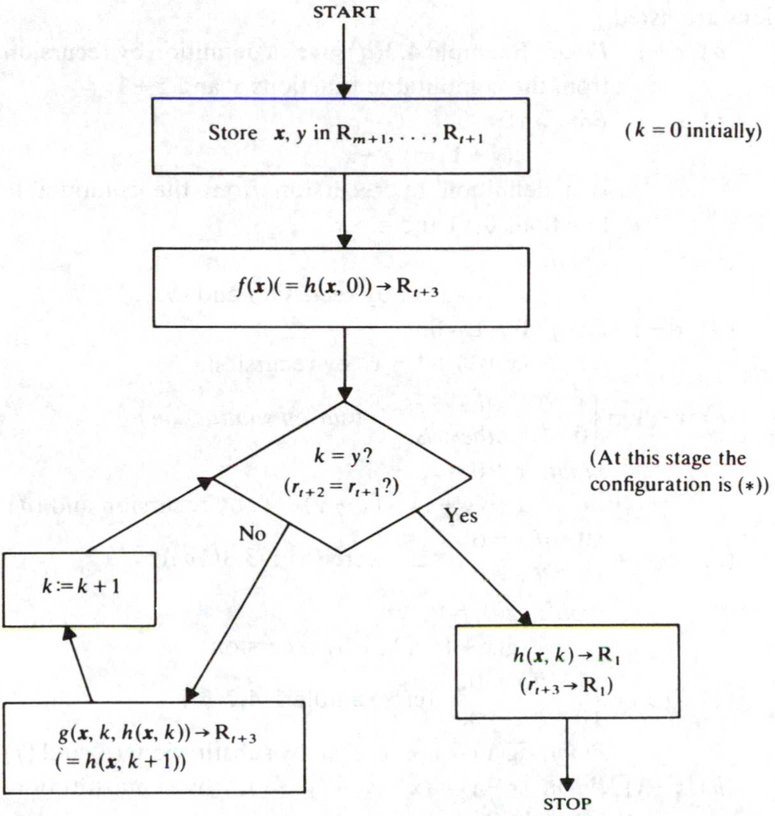

We now proceed to use theorems 3.1 and 4.4 to compile a collection of computable functions. The collection is potentially infinite, so our choice is influenced by (i) the needs of subsequent development of our theory, and (ii) the desire to give credence to the thesis that all functions that we would regard as computable in the informal sense are indeed URM-computable. For reasons which will become apparent later we shall include some functions such as $x + y$ and $x \dot{-} 1$ for which we have already written programs.

We shall use repeatedly the fact that, by theorem 3.2, in a definition by recursion such as (4.1), the computable functions f and g need not be functions of all of the named variables for the function h to be computable.

4.5. *Theorem*

The following functions are computable. (Proofs are given as the functions are listed.)

(*a*) $x+y$ *Proof.* Example 4.3(*a*) gives a definition by recursion from the computable functions x and $z+1$.

(*b*) xy *Proof.* $x0=0$,

$x(y+1)=xy+x$,

is a definition by recursion from the computable functions $\mathbf{0}(x)$ and $z+x$.

(*c*) x^y *Proof.* $x^0=1$,

$x^{y+1}=x^y x$; by recursion and (*b*).

(*d*) $x\dot{-}1$ *Proof.* $0\dot{-}1=0$,

$(x+1)\dot{-}1=x$; by recursion.

(*e*) $x\dot{-}y=\begin{cases} x-y & \text{if } x\geq y,\\ 0 & \text{otherwise.}\end{cases}$ (*cut-off subtraction*)

Proof. $x\dot{-}0=x$,

$x\dot{-}(y+1)=(x\dot{-}y)\dot{-}1$; by recursion and (*d*).

(*f*) $\mathrm{sg}(x)=\begin{cases} 0 & \text{if } x=0,\\ 1 & \text{if } x\neq 0.\end{cases}$ (cf. exercises 1-3.3(1*a*))

Proof. $\mathrm{sg}(0)=0$,

$\mathrm{sg}(x+1)=1$; by recursion.

(*g*) $\overline{\mathrm{sg}}(x)=\begin{cases} 1 & \text{if } x=0,\\ 0 & \text{if } x\neq 0.\end{cases}$ (cf. example 1-4.2(*b*))

Proof. $\overline{\mathrm{sg}}(x)=1\dot{-}\mathrm{sg}(x)$; by substitution, (*e*) and (*f*).

(*h*) $|x-y|$ *Proof.* $|x-y|=(x\dot{-}y)+(y\dot{-}x)$; by substitution, (*a*) and (*e*).

(*i*) $x!$ *Proof.* Example 4.3(*b*) gives a definition by recursion from computable functions.

(*j*) $\min(x,y)=$ *minimum of x and y.*

Proof. $\min(x,y)=x\dot{-}(x\dot{-}y)$; by substitution.

(*k*) $\max(x,y)=$ *maximum of x and y.*

Proof. $\max(x,y)=x+(y\dot{-}x)$; by substitution.

(*l*) $\mathrm{rm}(x,y)=$ *remainder when y is divided by x* (*to obtain a total function, we adopt the convention* $\mathrm{rm}(0,y)=y$).

Proof. We have

$$\mathrm{rm}(x,y+1)=\begin{cases} \mathrm{rm}(x,y)+1 & \text{if } \mathrm{rm}(x,y)+1\neq x,\\ 0 & \text{if } \mathrm{rm}(x,y)+1=x.\end{cases}$$

This gives the following definition by recursion:

$\mathrm{rm}(x,0)=0$,

$\mathrm{rm}(x,y+1)=(\mathrm{rm}(x,y)+1)\,\mathrm{sg}(|x-(\mathrm{rm}(x,y)+1)|)$.

The second equation can be written

$\mathrm{rm}(x, y+1) = g(x, \mathrm{rm}(x, y))$

where $g(x, z) = (z+1)\,\mathrm{sg}(|x-(z+1)|)$; and g is computable by several applications of substitution. Hence $\mathrm{rm}(x, y)$ is computable.

(*m*) $\mathrm{qt}(x, y)$ = *quotient when y is divided by x (to obtain a total function we define* $\mathrm{qt}(0, y) = 0$).

Proof. Since

$$\mathrm{qt}(x, y+1) = \begin{cases} \mathrm{qt}(x, y)+1 & \text{if } \mathrm{rm}(x, y)+1 = x, \\ \mathrm{qt}(x, y) & \text{if } \mathrm{rm}(x, y)+1 \neq x, \end{cases}$$

we have the following definition by recursion from computable functions:

$\mathrm{qt}(x, 0) = 0,$

$\mathrm{qt}(x, y+1) = \mathrm{qt}(x, y) + \overline{\mathrm{sg}}(|x-(\mathrm{rm}(x, y)+1)|).$

(*n*) $\mathrm{div}(x, y) = \begin{cases} 1 & \textit{if } x \mid y \ (x \textit{ divides } y), \\ 0 & \textit{if } x \nmid y. \end{cases}$

(*We adopt the convention that* $0 \mid 0$ *but* $0 \nmid y$ *if* $y \neq 0$.) *Hence* $x \mid y$ *is decidable* (recall definition 1-4.1).

Proof. $\mathrm{div}(x, y) = \overline{\mathrm{sg}}(\mathrm{rm}(x, y))$, computable by substitution. □

The following are useful corollaries involving decidable predicates.

4.6. *Corollary* (Definition by cases)

Suppose that $f_1(\boldsymbol{x}), \ldots, f_k(\boldsymbol{x})$ *are total computable functions, and* $M_1(\boldsymbol{x}), \ldots, M_k(\boldsymbol{x})$ *are decidable predicates, such that for every* $\boldsymbol{x}$ *exactly one of* $M_1(\boldsymbol{x}), \ldots, M_k(\boldsymbol{x})$ *holds. Then the function* $g(\boldsymbol{x})$ *given by*

$$g(\boldsymbol{x}) = \begin{cases} f_1(\boldsymbol{x}) & \textit{if } M_1(\boldsymbol{x}) \textit{ holds}, \\ f_2(\boldsymbol{x}) & \textit{if } M_2(\boldsymbol{x}) \textit{ holds}, \\ \vdots & \quad \vdots \\ f_k(\boldsymbol{x}) & \textit{if } M_k(\boldsymbol{x}) \textit{ holds}, \end{cases}$$

is computable.

Proof. $g(\boldsymbol{x}) = c_{M_1}(\boldsymbol{x})f_1(\boldsymbol{x}) + \ldots + c_{M_k}(\boldsymbol{x})f_k(\boldsymbol{x})$, computable by substitution using addition and multiplication. □

4.7. *Corollary* (Algebra of decidability)

Suppose that $M(\boldsymbol{x})$ *and* $Q(\boldsymbol{x})$ *are decidable predicates; then the following are also decidable.*

(*a*) '*not* $M(\boldsymbol{x})$'

(*b*) '$M(\boldsymbol{x})$ *and* $Q(\boldsymbol{x})$'
(*c*) '$M(\boldsymbol{x})$ *or* $Q(\boldsymbol{x})$'

Proof. The characteristic functions of these predicates are as follows:
(*a*) 'not $M(\boldsymbol{x})$': $1 \dot{-} c_M(\boldsymbol{x})$,
(*b*) '$M(\boldsymbol{x})$ and $Q(\boldsymbol{x})$': $c_M(\boldsymbol{x})\, c_Q(\boldsymbol{x})$,
(*c*) '$M(\boldsymbol{x})$ or $Q(\boldsymbol{x})$': $\max(c_M(\boldsymbol{x}), c_Q(\boldsymbol{x}))$ (where we take 'or' in the inclusive sense).

Each of the functions on the right is computable provided c_M and c_Q are, by substitution in functions from theorem 4.5. □

Recursion can be used to establish the computability of functions obtained by other function building techniques, which we now describe. First, we introduce some notation.

Suppose that $f(\boldsymbol{x}, z)$ is any function; the *bounded sum* $\sum_{z<y} f(\boldsymbol{x}, z)$ and the *bounded product* $\prod_{z<y} f(\boldsymbol{x}, z)$ are the functions of $\boldsymbol{x}$, y given by the following recursion equations.

$$(4.8) \quad \begin{cases} \sum_{z<0} f(\boldsymbol{x}, z) = 0, \\ \sum_{z<y+1} f(\boldsymbol{x}, z) = \sum_{z<y} f(\boldsymbol{x}, z) + f(\boldsymbol{x}, y), \end{cases}$$

$$(4.9) \quad \begin{cases} \prod_{z<0} f(\boldsymbol{x}, z) = 1, \\ \prod_{z<y+1} f(\boldsymbol{x}, z) = \left(\prod_{z<y} f(\boldsymbol{x}, z)\right) \cdot f(\boldsymbol{x}, y). \end{cases}$$

4.10. *Theorem*

Suppose that $f(\boldsymbol{x}, z)$ *is a total computable function; then the functions* $\sum_{z<y} f(\boldsymbol{x}, z)$ *and* $\prod_{z<y} f(\boldsymbol{x}, z)$ *are computable.*

Proof. The equations 4.8 and 4.9 are definitions by recursion from computable functions. □

It is easily seen that if the bound on z in a bounded sum or product is given by any computable function, the result is still computable, as follows.

4.11. *Corollary*

Suppose that $f(\boldsymbol{x}, z)$ *and* $k(\boldsymbol{x}, \boldsymbol{w})$ *are total computable functions; then so are the functions* $\sum_{z<k(\boldsymbol{x},\boldsymbol{w})} f(\boldsymbol{x}, z)$ *and* $\prod_{z<k(\boldsymbol{x},\boldsymbol{w})} f(\boldsymbol{x}, z)$ *(both functions of* $\boldsymbol{x}$, $\boldsymbol{w}$*).*

Proof. By substitution of $k(\mathbf{x}, \mathbf{w})$ for y in the bounded sum $\sum_{z<y} f(\mathbf{x}, z)$ and the bounded product $\prod_{z<y} f(\mathbf{x}, z)$. □

We now describe another useful function building technique which yields computable functions. We write

$$\mu z<y(\ldots)$$

for 'the least z less than y such that . . . '. In order that this expression be totally defined, we give it the value y when no such z exists. Then, for example, given a function $f(\mathbf{x}, z)$ we can define a new function g by

$$g(\mathbf{x}, y) = \mu z<y(f(\mathbf{x}, z)=0)$$

$$= \begin{cases} \text{the least } z<y & \text{such that } f(\mathbf{x}, z)=0, \text{ if such a } z \text{ exists;} \\ y & \text{if there is no such } z. \end{cases}$$

The operator $\mu z<y$ is called a *bounded minimalisation operator*, or *bounded μ-operator.*

4.12. *Theorem*

Suppose that $f(\mathbf{x}, y)$ is a total computable function; then so is the function $\mu z<y(f(\mathbf{x}, z)=0)$.

Proof. Consider the function

$$h(\mathbf{x}, v) = \prod_{u \le v} \operatorname{sg}(f(\mathbf{x}, u)),$$

which is computable by corollary 4.11. For a given $\mathbf{x}$, y, suppose that $z_0 = \mu z<y(f(\mathbf{x}, z)=0)$. It is easy to see that

if $v<z_0$, then $h(\mathbf{x}, v)=1$;

if $z_0 \le v < y$, then $h(\mathbf{x}, v)=0$.

Thus

$$z_0 = \text{the number of } v\text{s less than } y \text{ such that } h(\mathbf{x}, v)=1,$$

$$= \sum_{v<y} h(\mathbf{x}, v).$$

Hence

$$\mu z<y(f(\mathbf{x}, z)=0) = \sum_{v<y}\left(\prod_{u\le v} \operatorname{sg}(f(\mathbf{x}, u))\right),$$

and is computable by theorem 4.10. □

As with bounded sums and products, the bound in bounded minimalisation can be given by any computable function:

4.13. *Corollary*

If $f(\mathbf{x}, z)$ and $k(\mathbf{x}, \mathbf{w})$ are total computable functions, then so is the function

$$\mu z < k(\mathbf{x}, \mathbf{w})(f(\mathbf{x}, z) = 0).$$

Proof. By substitution of $k(\mathbf{x}, \mathbf{w})$ for y in the computable function $\mu z < y(f(\mathbf{x}, z) = 0)$. □

Theorems 4.10 and 4.12 give us the following applications involving decidable predicates.

4.14. *Corollary*

Suppose that $R(\mathbf{x}, y)$ is a decidable predicate: then

(*a*) *the function $f(\mathbf{x}, y) = \mu z < y\, R(\mathbf{x}, z)$ is computable.*

(*b*) *the following predicates are decidable:*

(i) $M_1(\mathbf{x}, y) \equiv \forall z < y\, R(\mathbf{x}, z)$,

(ii) $M_2(\mathbf{x}, y) \equiv \exists z < y\, R(\mathbf{x}, z)$.

Proof.

(*a*) $f(\mathbf{x}, y) = \mu z < y(\overline{\text{sg}}(c_R(\mathbf{x}, z)) = 0)$.

(*b*) (i) $c_{M_1}(\mathbf{x}, y) = \prod_{z<y} c_R(\mathbf{x}, z)$.

(ii) $M_2(\mathbf{x}, y) \equiv \text{not}\ (\forall z < y\ (\text{not}\ R(\mathbf{x}, z)))$

which is decidable by (*b*)(i) and 4.7(*a*). □

Note. As in 4.11 and 4.13, the bound on z in this corollary could be any total computable function.

We now use the above techniques to enlarge our collection of particular computable functions and decidable properties.

4.15. *Theorem*

The following functions are computable.

(*a*) $\mathrm{D}(x)$ = *the number of divisors of x (convention: $\mathrm{D}(0) = 1$),*

(*b*) $\Pr(x) = \begin{cases} 1 & \textit{if } x \textit{ is prime,} \\ 0 & \textit{if } x \textit{ is not prime} \end{cases}$

(*i.e. 'x is prime' is decidable*).

(*c*) p_x = *the* xth *prime number (as a convention we set $\mathrm{p}_0 = 0$, then $\mathrm{p}_1 = 2$, $\mathrm{p}_2 = 3$, etc.)*

(*d*) $(x)_y = \begin{cases} \textit{the exponent of } p_y \textit{ in the prime factorisation of } x, \textit{ for} \\ x, y > 0, \\ 0 \quad \textit{if } x = 0 \textit{ or } y = 0. \end{cases}$

Proof.

(*a*) $D(x)=\sum_{y\le x}\mathrm{div}(y, x)$ (where div is as in theorem 4.5(*n*)).

(*b*) $\Pr(x)=\begin{cases}1 & \text{if } D(x)=2 \text{ (i.e. } x>1 \text{ and the only divisors of } x \text{ are 1 and } x\text{)},\\ 0 & \text{otherwise}\end{cases}$

$=\overline{\mathrm{sg}}(|D(x)-2|)$.

(*c*) $p_0=0$,

$p_{x+1}=\mu z\le(p_x!+1)(z>p_x \text{ and } z \text{ is prime})$,

which is a definition by recursion; the predicate '$z>y$ and z is prime' is decidable, so using corollary 4.14 (and the note following) we have a computable function.

(*d*) $(x)_y=\mu z<x(p_y^{z+1}\nmid x)$, which is computable since the predicate '$p_y^{z+1}\nmid x$' is decidable. □

Note. The function $(x)_y$ is needed in the following kind of situation. A sequence $s=(a_1, a_2, a_3, \ldots, a_n)$ from $\mathbb{N}$ can be coded by the single number $b=p_1^{a_1+1}p_2^{a_2+1}\ldots p_n^{a_n+1}$; then the length n of s and the numbers a_i can be recovered effectively from b as follows:

$n=\mu z<b((b)_{z+1}=0)$,

$a_i=(b)_i\dot{-}1$ for $1\le i\le n$.

Alternative ways of coding pairs and sequences are indicated in exercises 4.16 (2, 5) below.

4.16. *Exercises*

1. Show that the following functions are computable:
   (*a*) Any polynomial function $a_0+a_1x+\ldots+a_nx^n$, where $a_0, a_1, \ldots, a_n\in\mathbb{N}$,
   (*b*) $[\sqrt{x}]$,
   (*c*) $\mathrm{LCM}(x, y)$ = the least common multiple of x and y,
   (*d*) $\mathrm{HCF}(x, y)$ = the highest common factor of x and y,
   (*e*) $f(x)$ = number of prime divisors of x,
   (*f*) $\phi(x)$ = the number of positive integers less than x which are relatively prime to x. (*Euler's function*) (We say that x, y are *relatively prime* if $\mathrm{HCF}(x, y)=1$.)
2. Let $\pi(x, y)=2^x(2y+1)-1$. Show that π is a computable bijection from $\mathbb{N}^2$ to $\mathbb{N}$, and that the functions π_1, π_2 such that $\pi(\pi_1(z), \pi_2(z))=z$ for all z are computable.
3. Suppose $f(x)$ is defined by
   $f(0)=1$,

$f(1)=1$,
$f(x+2)=f(x)+f(x+1)$.
($f(x)$ is the *Fibonacci* sequence.)
Show that f is computable. (*Hint:* first show that the function $g(x)=2^{f(x)}3^{f(x+1)}$ is computable, using recursion.)

4. Show that the following problems are decidable:
   (*a*) x is odd,
   (*b*) x is a power of a prime number,
   (*c*) x is a perfect cube.
5. Any number $x\in\mathbb{N}$ has a unique expression as
   (1) $x=\sum_{i=0}^{\infty}\alpha_i 2^i$, with $\alpha_i=0$ or 1, all i. Hence, if $x>0$, there are unique expressions for x in the forms
   (2) $x=2^{b_1}+2^{b_2}+\ldots+2^{b_l}$, with $0\le b_1<b_2<\ldots<b_l$ and $l\ge 1$.
   and
   (3) $x=2^{a_1}+2^{a_1+a_2+1}+\ldots+2^{a_1+a_2+\ldots+a_k+k-1}$.
   Putting
   $\alpha(i,x)=\alpha_i$ as in the expression (1);
   $$l(x)=\begin{cases} l \text{ as in (2),} & \text{if } x>0,\\ 0 & \text{otherwise;}\end{cases}$$
   $$b(i,x)=\begin{cases} b_i, \text{ as in (2),} & \text{if } x>0 \text{ and } 1\le i\le l,\\ 0 & \text{otherwise;}\end{cases}$$
   $$a(i,x)=\begin{cases} a_i, \text{ as in (3),} & \text{if } x>0 \text{ and } 1\le i\le l,\\ 0 & \text{otherwise;}\end{cases}$$
   show that each of the functions α, l, b, a is computable. (The expression (3) is a way of regarding x as coding the sequence $(a_1, a_2, \ldots, a_l)$ of numbers, and will be used in chapter 5.)

5. Minimalisation

In the previous section we have seen that a large collection of functions can be shown to be computable using the operations of substitution and recursion, and operations derived from these. There is a third important operation which generates further computable functions, namely *unbounded minimalisation*, or just *minimalisation*, which we now describe.

Suppose that $f(\mathbf{x}, y)$ is a function (not necessarily total) and we wish to define a function $g(\mathbf{x})$ by

$$g(\mathbf{x})=\text{the least } y \text{ such that } f(\mathbf{x}, y)=0,$$

in such a way that if f is computable then so is g. Two problems can arise. First, for some $\boldsymbol{x}$ there may not be any y such that $f(\boldsymbol{x}, y)=0$. Second, assuming that f is computable, consider the following natural algorithm for computing $g(\boldsymbol{x})$. 'Compute $f(\boldsymbol{x}, 0), f(\boldsymbol{x}, 1), \ldots$ until y is found such that $f(\boldsymbol{x}, y)=0$'. This procedure may not terminate if f is not total, even if such a y exists; for instance, if $f(\boldsymbol{x}, 0)$ is undefined but $f(\boldsymbol{x}, 1)=0$.

Thus we are led to the following definition of the *minimalisation operator* μ, which yields computable functions from computable functions.

5.1. *Definition*

For any function $f(\boldsymbol{x}, y)$

$$\mu y(f(\boldsymbol{x}, y)=0)=\begin{cases} \text{the least } y \text{ such that} & \\ \qquad \text{(i) } f(\boldsymbol{x}, z) \text{ is defined, all } z \leq y, \text{ and} & \\ \qquad \text{(ii) } f(\boldsymbol{x}, y)=0, & \text{if such a } y \text{ exists,} \\ \text{undefined,} & \text{if there is no such } y. \end{cases}$$

$\mu y(\ldots)$ is read 'the least y such that . . .'. This operator is sometimes called simply the *μ-operator.*

The next theorem shows that $\mathscr{C}$ is closed under minimalisation.

5.2. *Theorem*

Suppose that $f(\boldsymbol{x}, y)$ is computable; then so is the function $g(\boldsymbol{x})= \mu y(f(\boldsymbol{x}, y)=0)$.

Proof. Suppose that $\boldsymbol{x}=(x_1, \ldots, x_n)$ and that F is a program in standard form that computes the function $f(\boldsymbol{x}, y)$. Let $m=\max(n+1, \rho(F))$. We write a program G that embodies the natural algorithm for g: for $k=0, 1, 2 \ldots,$ compute $f(\boldsymbol{x}, k)$ until a value of k is found such that $f(\boldsymbol{x}, k)=0$; this value of k is the required output.

The value of $\boldsymbol{x}$ and the current value of k will be stored in registers $R_{m+1}, \ldots, R_{m+n+1}$ before computing $f(\boldsymbol{x}, k)$: thus the typical configuration will be

Storage registers ($R_{m+1} \ldots R_{m+n+1}$)

$R_1 \ldots R_m$	$R_{m+1} \ldots R_{m+n}$	R_{m+n+1}	R_{m+n+2}	
. . .	$\boldsymbol{x}$	k	0	

with $k=0$ initially. Note that r_{m+n+2} is always 0.

A flow diagram that carries out the above procedure for g is given in fig. 2d. This translates easily into the following program G for g:

$$
\begin{array}{ll}
 & T(1, m+1) \\
 & \vdots \\
 & T(n, m+n) \\
I_p & F[m+1, m+2, \ldots, m+n+1 \to 1] \\
 & J(1, m+n+2, q) \\
 & S(m+n+1) \\
 & J(1, 1, p) \\
I_q & T(m+n+1, 1)
\end{array}
$$

(I_p is the first instruction of the subroutine $F[m+1, m+2, \ldots \to 1]$.) □

Fig. 2d. Minimalisation (theorem 5.2).

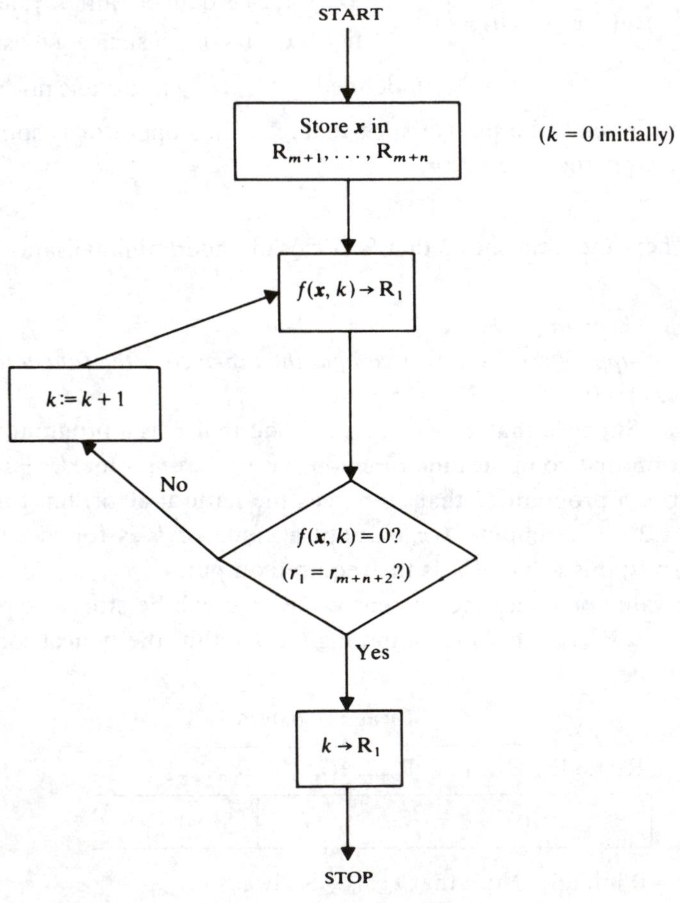

5.3. *Corollary*

Suppose that $R(\boldsymbol{x}, y)$ is a decidable predicate; then the function

$$g(\boldsymbol{x}) = \mu y\, R(\boldsymbol{x}, y)$$
$$= \begin{cases} \textit{the least } y \textit{ such that } R(\boldsymbol{x}, y) \textit{ holds,} & \textit{if there is such a } y, \\ \textit{undefined} & \textit{otherwise,} \end{cases}$$

is computable

Proof. $g(\boldsymbol{x}) = \mu y(\overline{\mathrm{sg}}(c_R(\boldsymbol{x}, y)) = 0)$. □

In view of this corollary, the μ-operator is often called a *search operator.* Given a decidable predicate $R(\boldsymbol{x}, y)$ the function $g(\boldsymbol{x})$ searches for a y such that $R(\boldsymbol{x}, y)$ holds, and moreover, finds the least such y if there is one.

The μ-operator may generate a non-total computable function from a total computable function; for instance, putting $f(x, y) = |x - y^2|$, and $g(x) \simeq \mu y(f(x, y) = 0)$, we have that g is the non-total function

$$g(x) = \begin{cases} \sqrt{x} & \text{if } x \text{ is a perfect square,} \\ \text{undefined} & \text{otherwise.} \end{cases}$$

Thus, in a trivial sense, using the μ-operator together with substitution and recursion, we can generate from the basic functions more functions than can be obtained using only substitution and recursion (since these operations always yield total functions from total functions). There are also, however, *total* functions for which the use of the μ-operator is essential. Example 5.5 below gives one such function; we present another example in chapter 5. Thus we see that, in a strong sense, minimalisation, unlike bounded minimalisation, cannot be defined in terms of substitution and recursion. It turns out, nevertheless, that most commonly occurring computable total functions can be built up from the basic functions using substitution and recursion only: such functions are called *primitive recursive*, and are discussed further in chapter 3 § 3. In practice, of course, we might establish the computability of these functions by what amounts to a non-essential use of minimalisation, if this makes the task easier.

5.4. *Exercises*

1. Suppose that $f(x)$ is a total injective computable function; prove that f^{-1} is computable.
2. Suppose that $p(x)$ is a polynomial with integer coefficients; show that the function

$f(a) =$ least non-negative integral root of $p(x) - a (a \in \mathbb{N})$ is computable ($f(a)$ is undefined if there is no such root).

3. Show that the function

$$f(x, y) = \begin{cases} x/y & \text{if } y \neq 0 \text{ and } y \mid x, \\ \text{undefined} & \text{otherwise,} \end{cases}$$

is computable.

We conclude this chapter with an example of a function that makes essential use of the μ-operator; it also shows how this operator can be used not only to search for a single number possessing a given property, but to search for finite sequences or sets of numbers, or other objects coded by a single number. The function is a modification by Péter of an example due to Ackermann, after whom it is named. It is rather more complicated than any function we have considered so far.

5.5. *Example* (The Ackermann function)

The function $\psi(x, y)$ given by the following equations is computable:

$$\psi(0, y) = y + 1,$$
$$\psi(x+1, 0) \simeq \psi(x, 1),$$
$$\psi(x+1, y+1) \simeq \psi(x, \psi(x+1, y)).$$

This definition involves a kind of double recursion that is stronger than the primitive recursion discussed in § 3. To see, nevertheless, that these equations do unambiguously define a function, notice that any value $\psi(x, y)$ $(x > 0)$ is defined in terms of 'earlier' values $\psi(x_1, y_1)$ with $x_1 < x$ or $x_1 = x$ and $y_1 < y$. In fact, $\psi(x, y)$ can be obtained by using only a *finite* number of such earlier values: this is easily established by induction on x and y. Hence ψ is computable in the informal sense. For instance, it is easy to calculate that $\psi(1, 1) = 3$ and $\psi(2, 1) = 5$.

To show rigorously that ψ is computable is quite difficult. We sketch a proof using the idea of a *suitable* set of triples S. The essential property of a suitable set S (defined below) is that if $(x, y, z) \in S$, then

(5.6) (i) $z = \psi(x, y)$,

(ii) S contains all the earlier triples $(x_1, y_1, \psi(x_1, y_1))$ that are needed to calculate $\psi(x, y)$.

Definition

A finite set of triples S is said to be *suitable* if the following conditions are satisfied:

(*a*) if $(0, y, z) \in S$ then $z = y+1$,

(*b*) if $(x+1, 0, z) \in S$ then $(x, 1, z) \in S$,

(*c*) if $(x+1, y+1, z) \in S$ then there is u such that $(x+1, y, u) \in S$ and $(x, u, z) \in S$.

These three conditions correspond to the three clauses in the definition of ψ: for instance, (*a*) corresponds to the statement: if $z = \psi(0, y)$, then $z = y+1$; (*c*) corresponds to the statement: if $z = \psi(x+1, y+1)$, then there is u such that $u = \psi(x+1, y)$ and $z = \psi(x, u)$.

The definition of a suitable set S ensures that (5.6) is satisfied. Moreover, for any particular pair of numbers (m, n) there is a suitable set S such that $(m, n, \psi(m, n)) \in S$; for example, let S be the set of triples $(x, y, \psi(x, y))$ that are used in the calculation of $\psi(m, n)$.

Now a triple (x, y, z) can be coded by the single positive number $u = 2^x 3^y 5^z$; a finite set of positive numbers $\{u_1, \ldots, u_k\}$ can be coded by the single number $p_{u_1} p_{u_2} \ldots p_{u_k}$. Hence a finite set of triples can be coded by a single number v say. Let S_v denote the set of triples coded by the number v. Then we have

$$(x, y, z) \in S_v \Leftrightarrow p_{2^x 3^y 5^z} \text{ divides } v,$$

so '$(x, y, z) \in S_v$' is a decidable predicate of x, y, z, v; and if it holds, then $x, y, z < v$. Hence, using the techniques and functions of earlier sections we can show that the following predicate is decidable:

$$R(x, y, v) \equiv \text{'}v \text{ is the code number of a suitable set of triples and } \exists z < v\ ((x, y, z) \in S_v).\text{'}$$

Thus the function

$$f(x, y) = \mu v R(x, y, v)$$

is a computable function that searches for the code of a suitable set containing (x, y, z) for some z. Hence

$$\psi(x, y) = \mu z ((x, y, z) \in S_{f(x,y)})$$

which shows that ψ is computable.

A more sophisticated proof that ψ is computable will be given in chapter 10 as an application of more advanced theoretical results.

We do not prove here that ψ cannot be shown to be computable using substitution and recursion alone. This matter is further discussed in § 3 of the next chapter.

3

Other approaches to computability: Church's thesis

Over the past fifty years there have been many proposals for a precise mathematical characterisation of the intuitive idea of effective computability. The URM approach is one of the more recent of these. In this chapter we pause in our investigation of URM-computability itself to consider two related questions.

1. How do the many different approaches to the characterisation of computability compare with each other, and in particular with URM-computability?
2. How well do these approaches (particularly the URM approach) characterise the informal idea of effective computability?

The first question will be discussed in §§ 1–6; the second will be taken up in § 7. The reader interested only in the technical development of the theory in this book may omit §§ 3–6; none of the development in later chapters depends on these sections.

1. Other approaches to computability

The following are some of the alternative characterisations that have been proposed:

(*a*) *Gödel–Herbrand–Kleene* (1936). General recursive functions defined by means of an equation calculus. (Kleene [1952], Mendelson [1964].)

(*b*) *Church* (1936). λ-definable functions. (Church [1936] or [1941].)

(*c*) *Gödel–Kleene* (1936). μ-recursive functions and partial recursive functions (§ 2 of this chapter.).

(*d*) *Turing* (1936). Functions computable by finite machines known as Turing machines. (Turing [1936]; § 4 of this chapter.)

(*e*) *Post* (1943). Functions defined from canonical deduction systems. (Post [1943], Minsky [1967]; § 5 of this chapter.)

(*f*) *Markov* (1951). Functions given by certain algorithms over a finite alphabet. (Markov [1954], Mendelson [1964]; § 5 of this chapter.)

(*g*) *Shepherdson–Sturgis* (1963). URM-computable functions. (Shepherdson & Sturgis [1963].)

There is great diversity among these various approaches; each has its own rationale for being considered a plausible characterisation of computability. The remarkable result of investigation by many researchers is the following:

1.1. *The Fundamental result*

Each of the above proposals for a characterisation of the notion of effective computability gives rise to the same class of functions, the class that we have denoted $\mathscr{C}$.

Thus we have the simplest possible answer to the first question posed above. Before discussing the second question, we shall examine briefly the approaches of Gödel–Kleene, Turing, Post and Markov, mentioned above, and we will sketch some of the proofs of the equivalence of these with the URM approach. The reader interested to discover full details of these and other approaches, and proofs of all the equivalences in the Fundamental result, may consult the references indicated.

2. Partial recursive functions (Gödel–Kleene)

2.1. *Definition*

The class $\mathscr{R}$ of *partial recursive functions* is the smallest class of partial functions that contains the basic functions $\mathbf{0}$, $x+1$, U_i^n (lemma 2-1.1) and is closed under the operations of substitution, recursion and minimalisation. (Equivalently, $\mathscr{R}$ is the class of partial functions that can be built up from the basic functions by a finite number of operations of substitution, recursion or minimalisation.)

Note that in the definition of the class $\mathscr{R}$, no restriction is placed on the use of the μ-operator, so that $\mathscr{R}$ contains non-total functions. Gödel and Kleene originally confined their attention to *total* functions; the class of functions first considered was the class $\mathscr{R}_0$ of *μ-recursive functions*, defined like $\mathscr{R}$ above, except that applications of the μ-operator are allowed only if a *total* function results. Thus $\mathscr{R}_0$ is a class of total functions, and clearly $\mathscr{R}_0 \subseteq \mathscr{R}$. In fact, $\mathscr{R}_0$ contains all of the total functions that are in $\mathscr{R}$, although this is not immediately obvious; see corollary 2.3 below for a proof. Hence $\mathscr{R}$ is a natural extension of $\mathscr{R}_0$ to a class of partial functions.

The term *recursive function* is used nowadays to describe μ-recursive functions; so a recursive function is always total – it is a totally defined partial recursive function. The term *general recursive* function is sometimes used to describe μ-recursive functions, although historically, this was the name Kleene gave to the total functions given by his equation calculus approach ((*a*) in § 1). It was Kleene who proved the equivalence of general recursive functions (given by the equation calculus) and μ-recursive functions.

We now outline a proof of

2.2. *Theorem*
$\mathscr{R} = \mathscr{C}$.

Proof. From the main results of chapter 2 (lemma 1.1, theorems 3.1, 4.4, 5.2) it follows that $\mathscr{R} \subseteq \mathscr{C}$.

For the converse, suppose that $f(\boldsymbol{x})$ is a URM-computable function, computed by a program $P = I_1, \ldots, I_s$. By a *step* in a computation $P(\boldsymbol{x})$ we mean the implementation of one instruction. Consider the following functions connected with computations under P.

$$c(\boldsymbol{x}, t) = \begin{cases} \text{contents of } R_1 \text{ after } t \text{ steps in the computation} \\ P(\boldsymbol{x}), \text{ if } P(\boldsymbol{x}) \text{ has not already stopped;} \\ \\ \text{the final contents of } R_1 \text{ if } P(\boldsymbol{x}) \text{ has stopped} \\ \text{after fewer than } t \text{ steps.} \end{cases}$$

$$j(\boldsymbol{x}, t) = \begin{cases} \text{number of the next instruction, when } t \text{ steps of} \\ \text{the computation } P(\boldsymbol{x}) \text{ have been performed,} \\ \qquad \text{if } P(\boldsymbol{x}) \text{ has not stopped after } t \text{ steps or fewer;} \\ \\ 0 \quad \text{if } P(\boldsymbol{x}) \text{ has stopped after } t \text{ steps or fewer.} \end{cases}$$

Clearly c and j are total functions.

If $f(\boldsymbol{x})$ is defined, then $P(\boldsymbol{x})$ converges after exactly t_0 steps, where

$$t_0 = \mu t(j(\boldsymbol{x}, t) = 0),$$

and then

$$f(\boldsymbol{x}) = c(\boldsymbol{x}, t_0).$$

If, on the other hand, $f(\boldsymbol{x})$ is not defined, then $P(\boldsymbol{x})$ diverges, and so $j(\boldsymbol{x}, t)$ is never zero. Thus $\mu t(j(\boldsymbol{x}, t) = 0)$ is undefined. Hence, in either case, we have

$$f(\mathbf{x}) \simeq c(\mathbf{x}, \mu t(j(\mathbf{x}, t) = 0)).$$

So, to show that f is partial recursive, it is sufficient to show that c and j are recursive functions. It is clear that these functions are computable in the informal sense – we can simply simulate the computation $P(\mathbf{x})$ for up to t steps. By a detailed analysis of computations $P(\mathbf{x})$ and utilising many of the functions obtained in chapter 2, it is not difficult, though rather tedious, to show that c and j are recursive; in fact, they can be obtained from the basic functions without the use of minimalisation (so they are *primitive recursive* – see § 3 of this chapter). (A detailed proof of rather more than this will be given in chapter 5 – theorem 1.2 and Appendix). Hence f is partial recursive. □

2.3. *Corollary*

Every total function in $\mathscr{R}$ belongs to $\mathscr{R}_0$.

Proof. Suppose that $f(\mathbf{x})$ is a total function in $\mathscr{R}$; then f is URM-computable by a program P. Let c and j be the functions defined in the proof of theorem 2.2; as noted there, these can be obtained without any use of minimalisation, so in particular they are in $\mathscr{R}_0$. Further, since f is total, $P(\mathbf{x})$ converges for every $\mathbf{x}$, so the function $\mu t(j(\mathbf{x}, t) = 0)$ is total and belongs to $\mathscr{R}_0$. Now

$$f(\mathbf{x}) = c(\mathbf{x}, \mu t(j(\mathbf{x}, t) = 0)),$$

so f also is in $\mathscr{R}_0$. □

A predicate $M(\mathbf{x})$ whose characteristic function c_M is recursive is called a *recursive predicate*. In view of theorem 2.2, a recursive predicate is the same as a decidable predicate.

3. A digression: the primitive recursive functions

This is a natural point to mention an important subclass of $\mathscr{R}$, the class of *primitive recursive functions*, although they do not form part of the main line of thought in this chapter. These functions were referred to in chapter 2 § 5.

3.1. *Definition*

(*a*) The class $\mathscr{PR}$ of *primitive recursive functions* is the smallest class of functions that contains the basic functions $\mathbf{0}$, $x+1$, U_i^n, and is closed under the operations of substitution and recursion.

(*b*) A *primitive recursive predicate* is one whose characteristic function is primitive recursive.

All of the particular computable functions obtained in §§ 1, 3, 4 of chapter 2 are primitive recursive, since minimalisation was not used there. We have already noted that the functions c and j used in the proof of theorem 2.2 are primitive recursive. Further, from theorems 2-4.10 and 2-4.12 we see that $\mathcal{PR}$ is closed under bounded sums and products, and under bounded minimalisation. Thus the class of primitive recursive functions is quite extensive.

There are nevertheless recursive functions (or, equivalently, total computable functions) that are not primitive recursive. Indeed, the Ackermann function ψ of example 2-5.5 was given as an instance of such a function. A detailed proof that the Ackermann function is not primitive recursive is rather lengthy, and we refer the reader to Péter [1967, chapter 9] or Mendelson [1964, p. 250, exercise 11]. Essentially one shows that ψ grows faster than any given primitive recursive function. (To see how fast ψ grows try to calculate a few simple values.)

In chapter 5 we will be able to give an example of a total computable (i.e. recursive) function that we shall prove is not primitive recursive.

Our conclusion is that although the primitive recursive functions form a natural and very extensive class, they do *not* include all computable functions and thus fall short as a possible characterisation of the informal notion of computability.

4. Turing-computability

The definition of computability proposed by A. M. Turing [1936] is based on an analysis of a human agent's implementation of an algorithm, using pen and paper. Turing viewed this as a succession of very simple acts of the following kinds

(*a*) writing or erasing a single symbol.

(*b*) transferring attention from one part of the paper to another.

At each stage the algorithm specifies the action to be performed next. This depends only on (i) the symbol on the part of the paper currently being scrutinised by the agent, and (ii) the current state (of mind) of the agent. For the purposes of implementing the algorithm this is assumed to be determined entirely by the algorithm and the history of the operation so far. It may incorporate a partial record of what has happened to date, but it will not reflect the mood or intelligence of the agent, or the state of his indigestion. Moreover, there are only finitely many distinguishable states in which the agent can be, because he is finite. The state of the agent may, of course, change as a result of the action taken at this stage.

Turing devised finite machines that carry out algorithms conceived in this way. There is a different machine for each algorithm. We shall briefly describe these machines, which have become known as *Turing machines*.

4.1. *Turing machines.*

A Turing machine M is a finite device, which performs operations on a paper tape. This tape is infinite in both directions, and is divided into single squares along its length. (The tape represents the paper used by a human agent implementing an algorithm; each square represents a portion of the paper capable of being viewed in a given instant. In any particular terminating computation under M only a finite part of the tape will be used, although we may not know in advance how much will be needed. The tape is nevertheless infinite, corresponding to the human situation where we envisage an unlimited supply of clean paper.)

At any given time each square of the tape is either blank or contains a single symbol from a fixed finite list of symbols $s_1, s_2, \ldots, s_n$, the *alphabet* of M. We will let B denote a blank, and count it as the symbol s_0 belonging to M's alphabet.

M has a *reading head* which at any given time scans or reads a single square of the tape. We can visualise this as shown in fig. 3a.

M is capable of three kinds of simple operation on the tape, namely:

Fig. 3a. A Turing machine.

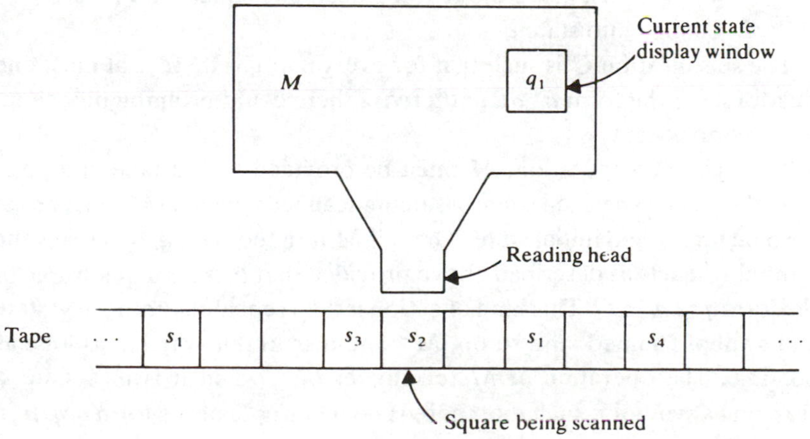

(*a*) erase the symbol in the square being scanned and replace it by another symbol from the alphabet of M;
(*b*) move the reading head one square to the right of that being scanned (or, equivalently, move the tape one square to the left);
(*c*) move the reading head one square to the left of that being scanned (or, equivalently, move the tape one square to the right).

At any given time M is in one of a fixed finite number of states, represented by symbols $q_1, \ldots, q_m$. During operation the state of M can change. We may envisage the symbol for the current state as being displayed in a window on the exterior of M (as in fig. 3*a*), and think of this as a partial guide to what has happened to date and what will happen in the future.

The action that M takes at any instant depends on the current state of M and on the symbol currently being scanned. This dependence is described in M's *specification* which consists of a finite set Q of quadruples, each of which takes one of the following forms

$$\begin{matrix} q_is_js_kq_l & \\ q_is_jRq_l & \begin{pmatrix} 1 \leq i, l \leq m \\ 0 \leq j, k \leq n \end{pmatrix} \\ q_is_jLq_l & \end{matrix}$$

A quadruple $q_is_j\alpha q_l$ in Q specifies the action to be taken by M when it is in the state q_i and scanning the symbol s_j, as follows:

1. Operate on the tape thus:
   (*a*) if $\alpha = s_k$, erase s_j and write s_k in the square being scanned;
   (*b*) if $\alpha = R$, move the reading head one square to the right;
   (*c*) if $\alpha = L$, move the reading head one square to the left;
2. Change into state q_l.

The specification Q is such that for every pair q_is_j there is at most one quadruple of the form $q_is_j\alpha\beta$; otherwise there could be ambiguity about what M does next.

To begin a computation, M must be provided with a tape and positioned so that a specified square is being scanned; further, M must be set in some prescribed initial state. Then, if M is in the state q_i and scans the symbol s_j, it acts as described above provided that there is a quadruple of the form $q_is_j\alpha q_l$ in Q. This kind of action is then repeated for the new state and symbol scanned, and so on. M continues in this way for as long as possible. The operation of M terminates only when it is in a state q_i scanning a symbol s_j such that there is no quadruple of the form $q_is_j\alpha\beta$ in

Q; i.e. there is no quadruple in Q that specifies what to do next. (It is possible that this never happens.)

4.2. *Example*

Let M be a Turing machine whose alphabet consists of the symbols 0, 1, (and a blank of course) and whose possible states are q_1 and q_2. The specification of M is

$q_1 0 R q_1$

$q_1 1 0 q_2$

$q_2 0 R q_2$

$q_2 1 R q_1$

Suppose that M is provided with the tape

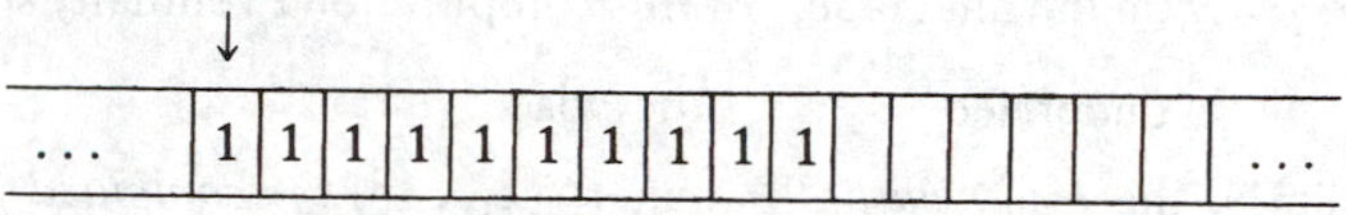

scanning the square marked ↓, and initially in state q_1. It is easy to see that M's action is to work from left to right along the tape, replacing alternate 1s by the symbol 0; M stops when it scans the first blank square since there is no quadruple that specifies what it should do. The resulting tape is

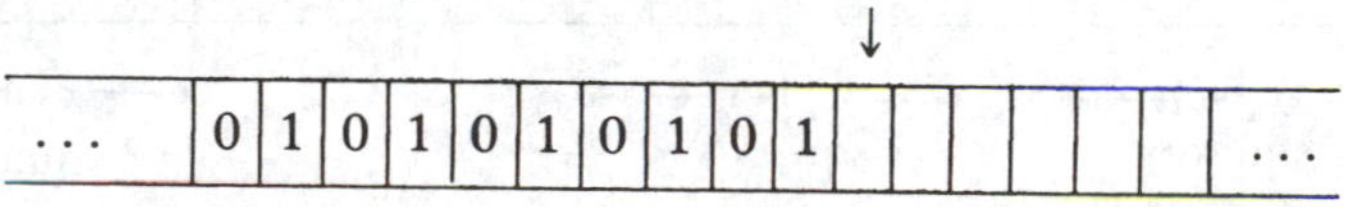

with the square marked ↓ being scanned, and M is in state q_1.

On the other hand, if M is provided with a tape such that every square contains the symbol 0 or 1, then the operation of M never stops.

It is clear from this example that a Turing machine M is a device for effecting an algorithm that operates on tapes. Complete details of the algorithm are contained in the specification Q of M. Thus, for the mathematician, a Turing machine is *defined* to be the set of quadruples that specify it. It is not usual to build physical Turing machines, except for illustrative purposes.

4.3. *Turing-computable functions*

In order to regard a Turing machine M as computing a numerical function, we must use some convention for representing numbers on a tape. One way is as follows: suppose, for convenience of exposition, that the symbol s_1 of M's alphabet is 1. We use 1 as a 'tally symbol', and then represent a number x on the tape as follows (ignore the marker ↓ for the moment):

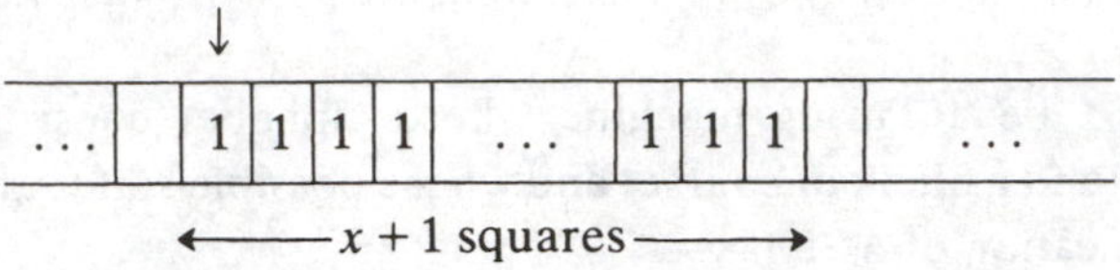

We use $x+1$ tallys to represent x, so as to distinguish 0 from a blank tape.

The *partial function* $f(x)$ *computed by* M is defined as follows. Consider the computation by M on the above tape, starting in state q_1, and initially scanning the square marked ↓. Then

$$f(x) = \begin{cases} \text{the total number of occurrences of the symbol 1} \\ \text{on the final tape,} \quad \text{if this computation eventually stops;} \\ \text{undefined} \qquad\qquad \text{otherwise.} \end{cases}$$

Similarly, the n-ary *partial function* $f(x_1, \ldots, x_n)$ *computed by* M is defined by counting the number of 1s on the final tape when M is started in state q_1 and scanning the square marked ↓ on the following tape:

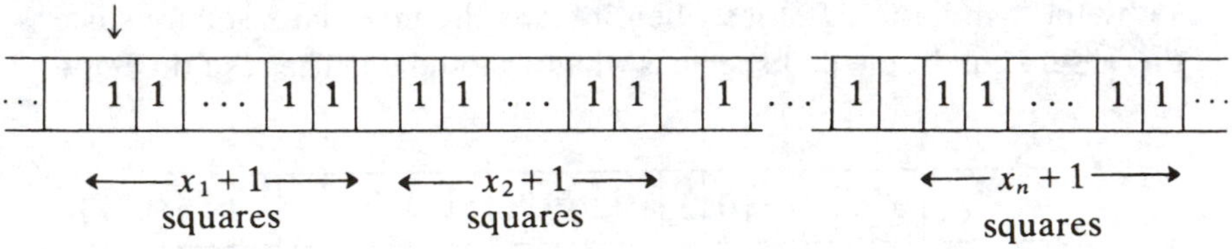

4.4. *Definition*

A partial function is *Turing-computable* if there is a Turing machine that computes it. The class of all Turing-computable functions is denoted $\mathscr{TC}$.

4.5. *Example*

The function $x+y$ is Turing-computable; the Turing machine given by the following specification Turing-computes this function.

$q_1 1 B q_1$

$q_1 B R q_2$

$q_2 1 B q_3$

$q_2 B R q_2$

The tape representation of (x, y) contains $x+y+2$ occurrences of the symbol 1, so the machine M is designed to erase the first two of these occurrences starting from the left. The details are easy to check by trying a few particular values for x, y.

4.6. *Exercises*

1. What unary function is Turing-computed by the machine in example 4.2?
2. Devise Turing machines that will Turing-compute the functions (*a*) $x \dot{-} 1$ (*b*) $2x$.

It is not our purpose here to develop the theory of Turing machines and Turing-computable functions; the interested reader should consult the books by Davis [1958] or Minsky [1967] listed in the bibliography.

The fundamental result linking Turing-computability with partial recursive functions and URM-computability is the following.

4.7. *Theorem*

$\mathscr{R} = \mathscr{TC} = \mathscr{C}$.

Proof. There are various ways of establishing this result, which we indicate in barest outline.

A direct proof that $\mathscr{TC} \subseteq \mathscr{R}$ is somewhat similar to the proof that $\mathscr{C} \subseteq \mathscr{R}$ (theorem 2.2). The tape configurations and states of a Turing machine during a computation can be coded by natural numbers, and the operation of the machine is then represented by recursive functions of these numbers.

For the converse inclusion, $\mathscr{R} \subseteq \mathscr{TC}$, one can show directly that $\mathscr{TC}$ contains the basic functions and is closed under substitution, recursion, and minimalisation. This is done in detail in Davis [1958]. Alternatively, one can show that $\mathscr{C} \subseteq \mathscr{TC}$ by showing that URMs are equivalent in power to a succession of simpler machines, ending with Turing machines. This is the proof given in their original paper by Shepherdson & Sturgis [1963]. □

5. Symbol manipulation systems of Post and Markov

E. L. Post and A. A. Markov formulated their ideas of effectiveness in terms of strings of symbols. They recognised that objects (including numbers) to which effective processes apply can always be represented as strings of symbols; in fact, in contexts such as symbolic logic, abstract algebra and the analysis of languages the objects actually are strings of symbols. Both Post and Markov, from different points of view, considered that effective operations on strings of symbols are those that are built up from very simple manipulations of the strings themselves.

Post's central idea was that of a *canonical system*, which we describe below. Such systems do not compute functions; they generate sets of strings. This is because Post aimed to characterise *formal logical systems*; i.e. systems that generate *theorems* from *axioms* by the mechanical application of rules of logic. Thus a notion of effectiveness emerges from Post's work, initially in the guise of *effectively* (or *mechanically*) *generated sets*. We shall see how a notion of a Post-computable function can be derived from this.

In paragraph 5.17 below we explain the way in which Markov's approach is related to that of Post.

We must now define some notation to aid our discussion. Let $\Sigma = \{a_1, \ldots, a_k\}$ be a finite set of symbols, called an *alphabet*. A *string* from Σ is any sequence $a_{i_1} \ldots a_{i_n}$ of symbols from Σ. Strings are sometimes called *words*, by analogy with ordinary language. For any alphabet Σ, we write Σ^* to denote the set of all strings from Σ. Included in Σ^* is the *empty string*, denoted Λ, that has no symbols. If $\sigma = b_1 b_2 \ldots b_m$ and $\tau = c_1 \ldots c_n$ are strings then $\sigma\tau$ denotes the string $b_1 \ldots b_m c_1 \ldots c_n$. The empty string Λ has the property that for any string σ, $\sigma\Lambda = \sigma = \Lambda\sigma$.

5.1. *Post-systems*

In elementary algebra a common operation is to replace the string $(x-y)(x+y)$ whenever it occurs by the string (x^2-y^2). This string manipulation may be denoted by writing

$$S_1(x-y)(x+y)S_2 \rightarrow S_1(x^2-y^2)S_2$$

where S_1 and S_2 are arbitrary strings.

A more general manipulation of a string, yet still regarded by Post as elementary, takes the form

$$(5.2) \qquad g_0 S_1 g_1 S_2 \ldots g_{m-1} S_m g_m \rightarrow h_0 S_{i_1} h_1 S_{i_2} h_2 \ldots S_{i_n} h_n$$

where

(i) $g_0, \ldots, g_m, h_0, \ldots, h_n$ are fixed strings (and may be null),
(ii) the subscripts $i_1, \ldots, i_n$ are all from $1, 2, \ldots, m$, and need not be distinct.

Post called an operation of the form (5.2) a *production*; it may be applied to any string σ that can be analysed as

$$\sigma = g_0\sigma_1 g_1\sigma_2 \ldots \sigma_m g_m \qquad (\sigma_1, \ldots, \sigma_m \text{ are strings}),$$

to produce the string $h_0\sigma_{i_1}h_1\sigma_{i_2}h_2 \ldots \sigma_{i_n}h_n$.

5.3. *Example*

Let $\Sigma = \{a, b\}$; consider the production

(π) $aS_1bS_2 \to S_2aS_2a$.

Then the effect of (π) on some strings is given in the table

σ	Strings produced by (π)
aba	*aaaa*
abba	*aaaa* and *baabaa*
ba	(π) does not apply.

(The entries in the second line correspond to the two possible analyses of *abba*: as $a\underbrace{b}_{S_1}b\underbrace{a}_{S_2}$ and $a\underbrace{\Lambda}_{S_1}b\underbrace{ba}_{S_2}$.)

5.4. *Exercise*

Examine the ways in which the production

$S_1bS_2aaS_3b \to S_3abS_1$

applies to the string *babaabbaab*.

Productions form the main ingredient of Post's *canonical systems*:

5.5. *Definition*

A *Post-(canonical) system* $\mathscr{G}$ consists of

(*a*) a finite alphabet Σ,

(*b*) a finite subset A of Σ^*, the *axioms* of $\mathscr{G}$,

(*c*) a finite set Q of productions of the form (5.2), whose fixed strings are in Σ^*.

We say that $\mathscr{G}$ is a *Post-system over* Σ.

We write $\sigma \overset{Q}{\Rightarrow} \tau$ if the string τ can be obtained from the string σ by a finite succession of applications of productions in Q; then we write $\vdash_{\mathscr{G}} \tau$ if there is an axiom $\sigma \in A$ such that $\sigma \overset{Q}{\Rightarrow} \tau$. In this case we say that τ is *generated* by the Post-system; the set of all strings in Σ^* generated by $\mathscr{G}$ is denoted $T_{\mathscr{G}}$, i.e.

$$T_{\mathscr{G}} = \{\sigma \in \Sigma^* : \vdash_{\mathscr{G}} \sigma\}.$$

The set $T_{\mathcal{G}}$ is also called the set of *theorems* of $\mathcal{G}$, reflecting the original motivation of Post.

5.6. *Example*

Let $\mathcal{G}$ be the Post-system with alphabet $\Sigma = \{a, b\}$, axioms Λ, a, b and productions $S \to aSa$ and $S \to bSb$. Then $T_{\mathcal{G}}$ is the set of *palindromes* – the strings reading the same in either direction, such as *aba, bbabb, abba.*

Sometimes, in order to generate a particular set of strings in Σ^* it is necessary to use auxiliary symbols in the generation process. This leads to the following definition:

5.7. *Definition*

Let Σ be an alphabet and let $X \subseteq \Sigma^*$. Then X is *Post-generable* if there is an alphabet $\Sigma_1 \supseteq \Sigma$ and a Post-system $\mathcal{G}$ over Σ_1 such that X is the set of strings in Σ^* that are generated by $\mathcal{G}$, i.e. $X = T_{\mathcal{G}} \cap \Sigma^*$.

Post proved a remarkable theorem showing that really only very simple productions are needed to generate Post-generable sets. A set of productions Q (and any system in which they occur) is said to be *normal* if all the productions have the form $gS \to Sh$.

Post proved

5.8. *Theorem* (Post's normal form theorem)

Any Post-generable set can be generated by a normal system.

For an excellent proof consult Minsky [1967].

Post-systems having only productions of the kind

$$S_1 g S_2 \to S_1 h S_2$$

give models of grammars and languages. They reflect the way in which complex sentences of a language are built up from certain basic units according to the rules of grammar. Restrictions on the nature of g and h provide the *context-sensitive* and *context-free* languages of Chomsky, which provide useful models of languages used in computer programming. We cannot pursue this interesting topic here: the reader may consult the books of Arbib [1969] and Manna [1974] for further information.

5.9. *Post-systems and other approaches to computability*

As we have seen, Post-systems give a characterisation of the notion of an *effectively generated set.* We may compare this with the corresponding notion that emerges from the other approaches to computability. For URM-computability (or Turing-computability, etc.) effectively generated sets of numbers are called *recursively enumerable* (r.e.); these are the sets that are the range of some URM-computable function. (We shall study r.e. sets in chapter 7.)

To compare sets of *strings* with sets of numbers, we choose an (intuitively) effective coding function $\hat{}: \Sigma^* \to \mathbb{N}$ under which the string $\sigma \in \Sigma^*$ is coded by the number $\hat{\sigma}$. A convenient method for an alphabet $\Sigma = \{a_1, \ldots, a_k\}$ is by the *k-adic coding* where $\hat{}: \Sigma^* \to \mathbb{N}$ is defined by $\hat{\Lambda} = 0$; $\widehat{a_{r_0} \ldots a_{r_m}} = r_0 + r_1 k + \ldots + r_m k^m$. It is easily seen that $\hat{}$ is actually a bijection, so if the inverse of $\hat{}$ is denoted by $\tilde{}: \mathbb{N} \to \Sigma^*$ we also have a *representation* of each number n by a string $\tilde{n}$.

Suppose now that X is a set of strings: let $\hat{X} = \{\hat{\sigma}: \sigma \in X\}$, the set of numbers coding X. We have the equivalence result:

5.10. *Theorem*

X is Post-generable iff $\hat{X}$ is r.e.

Proof. We sketch one proof of this result. Let $X \subseteq \Sigma^*$ and suppose first that $\hat{X}$ is r.e. Let $\hat{X} = \text{Ran}(f)$, where f is URM-computable. Using earlier equivalences we can design a Turing machine M whose symbols include the alphabet Σ, so that when in state q_1 and given initial tape

(*) 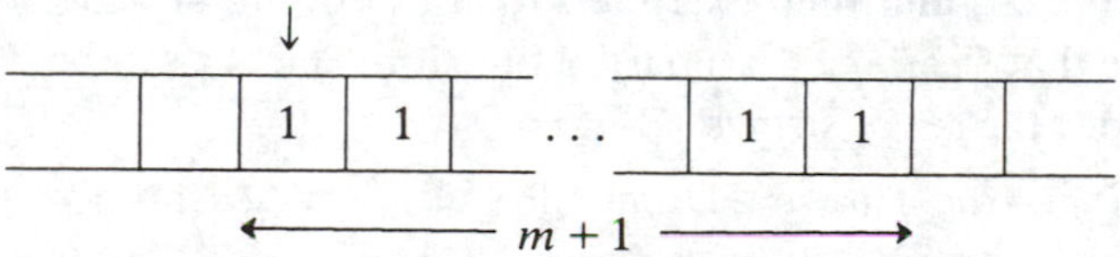

M halts if and only if $m \in \text{Dom}(f)$, and does so in the following configuration

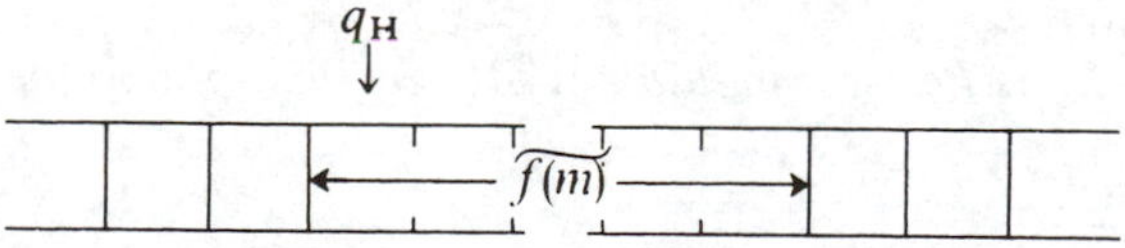

i.e. the symbols on the non-blank part of the tape indicated constitute the string $\widetilde{f(m)}$ from Σ, and M is in a special halting state q_H scanning the square marked ↓. Now devise a Post-system $\mathcal{G}$ to simulate the behaviour of M on its tape; the alphabet of $\mathcal{G}$ will include Σ and the symbols and states of M; $\mathscr{G}$ will generate strings of the form

$$s_{i_1}s_{i_2}\ldots q_k s_{i_j}\ldots s_{i_m}$$

to represent any situation

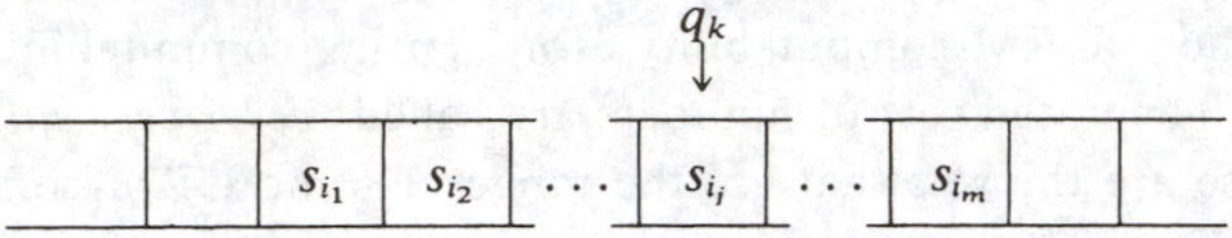

that occurs during the computation by M from an initial tape of the form (*). To get things going, $\mathscr{G}$ will generate all strings of the form $q_1\overset{\longleftarrow m+1 \longrightarrow}{111\ldots11}$, which represent such initial tapes. If we include in $\mathscr{G}$ the production $q_H S \to S$, then the strings from Σ^* generated by $\mathscr{G}$ will be the set

$$\{\widetilde{f(m)}: m \in \mathrm{Dom}(f)\} = \{\tilde{n}: n \in \mathrm{Ran}(f)\} = \{\tilde{n}: n \in \hat{X}\} = X.$$

Thus $X = T_{\mathscr{G}} \cap \Sigma^*$, so X is Post generable.

Conversely, if X is Post-generable by a Post-system $\mathscr{G}$, show that the relation

'$\tilde{n}$ is generated by $\mathscr{G}$ using at most m productions'

is decidable; from the theory of r.e. sets (chapter 7) it follows easily that $\hat{X}$ is r.e. □

5.11. *Post-computability*

We now explain two ways to derive a concept of computable function from Post-systems.In both cases the concept is defined first for functions on Σ^*, and then extended to $\mathbb{N}$ by coding or representation.

Suppose that $f: \Sigma^* \to \Sigma^*$ is a partial function. Select a symbol $\cdot$ not in Σ and consider the set of strings

$$G(f) = \{\sigma \cdot f(\sigma): \sigma \in \mathrm{Dom}(f)\}$$

from the alphabet $\Sigma \cup \{\cdot\}$. The set $G(f)$ contains all information about f, and we define:

5.12. *Definition*

$f: \Sigma^* \to \Sigma^*$ is *Post-computable* if $G(f)$ is Post-generable.

5.13. *Example*

Let $\Sigma = \{1\}$ and consider the function $f: \Sigma^* \to \Sigma^*$ given by

$f(\Lambda) = \Lambda$,

$f(\underset{\longleftarrow n \longrightarrow}{11\ldots11}) = \underset{\longleftarrow n^2 \longrightarrow}{1111\ldots1111}$.

The set $G(f)$ is generated by the following Post-system:

Alphabet $\{1, \cdot\}$

Axiom $\cdot\ (=\Lambda \cdot f(\Lambda))$

Production $S_1 \cdot S_2 \to S_1 1 \cdot S_2 S_1 S_1 1$.

The single production of this system applies to a string of the form

$$\underbrace{11\ldots11}_{n}\cdot\underbrace{111\ldots111}_{n^2}$$

to produce the string

$$\underbrace{11\ldots111}_{n+1}\cdot\underbrace{111\ldots111}_{n^2}\underbrace{11\ldots1111}_{n}\underbrace{\ldots111}_{n}1.$$

Hence f is Post-computable.

Suppose that $G(f)$ is generated by a Post-system $\mathcal{G}$. To see that f is computable in the informal sense, consider the following algorithm for finding $f(\sigma)$ (where $\sigma \in \Sigma^*$).

'Generate the strings $T_{\mathcal{G}}$ in some systematic fashion; examine these as they appear, looking for a string of the form $\sigma \cdot \tau$ with $\tau \in \Sigma^*$. Such a string will eventually be produced if, and only if, $\sigma \in \mathrm{Dom}(f)$, and then $\tau = f(\sigma)$.'

The definition (5.12) extends in an obvious way to partial functions $(\Sigma^*)^n \to \Sigma^*$. Post-computability on $\mathbb{N}$ is then defined using any effective representation $\tilde{}: \mathbb{N} \to \Sigma^*$ in the natural way:

5.14. *Definition*

Let $g: \mathbb{N}^n \to \mathbb{N}$ be a partial function, and let

$\tilde{g}: (\Sigma^*)^n \to \Sigma^*$ be the function defined by

$\tilde{g}(\tilde{m}_1, \tilde{m}_2, \ldots, \tilde{m}_n) = \widetilde{g(m_1, \ldots, m_n)}\quad (m_1, \ldots, m_n \in \mathbb{N})$.

Then g is *Post-computable* if $\tilde{g}$ is Post-computable.

If we let $\mathcal{PC}$ denote the class of Post-computable functions of natural numbers, we have the equivalence:

5.15. *Theorem*

$\mathcal{PC} = \mathcal{C} = \mathcal{TC} = \mathcal{R}$. (We omit a proof. When the reader has studied chapters 6 and 7 he should be able to see that this follows from theorem 5.10 and the results of chapters 6 and 7 linking r.e. sets with URM-computable functions.)

An alternative way to derive a notion of computability from Post-systems is to simulate computations by a machine directly. This can be done by using sets of productions Q such that *at most* one production in Q can apply to any given string. Such sets, and the systems in which they occur, are called *monogenic*. A monogenic system operates sequentially like a machine. It is convenient for the following to write $\sigma \overset{Q}{\Rightarrow}| \tau$ to mean that $\sigma \overset{Q}{\Rightarrow} \tau$ but no production in Q applies to τ.

We have the following characterisation of Post-computability.

5.16 *Theorem*

Let $f: \Sigma^* \to \Sigma^*$ be a partial function, and let X, Y be symbols not in Σ. Then the following are equivalent.

(*a*) *f is Post-computable;*

(*b*) *there is a monogenic set of productions Q over an alphabet $\Sigma_1 \supseteq \Sigma \cup \{X, Y\}$ such that for $\sigma \in \Sigma^*$ and $\tau \in \Sigma_1^*$*

$X\sigma \overset{Q}{\Rightarrow}| \tau$ iff $\sigma \in \mathrm{Dom}(f)$ and τ is the string $Yf(\sigma)$.

(*Note.* The symbols X and Y are needed to distinguish 'input' strings from 'output' strings. Otherwise a desired output string $f(\sigma)$ would be regarded as a new input string to which further productions might apply.)

Proof. The implication $(a)\Rightarrow(b)$ may be obtained by first showing that f is computable by a Turing machine M, and then devising a monogenic set of productions to simulate M. In fact it is possible to obtain a *normal* monogenic set of productions for this task.

For $(b) \Rightarrow (a)$ it is quite straightforward to show that the function $\hat{f}: \mathbb{N} \to \mathbb{N}$ coding f is partial recursive, then apply theorem 5.15. □

This equivalence extends to functions $f: (\Sigma^*)^n \to \Sigma^*$ by considering 'inputs' of the form $X\sigma_1 \cdot \sigma_2 \cdot \ldots \cdot \sigma_n$.

For a fuller discussion of Post systems the reader is referred to the excellent chapters in Minsky [1967].

5.17. *Markov-computability*

Markov's notion of computability is very similar to that derived from Post-systems by the second method above. Rather than restrict attention to monogenic systems, however, Markov gave rules to determine uniquely which of the available productions to apply next. Details are, briefly, as follows:

A *Markov normal algorithm* over an alphabet Σ is essentially a list Q of productions over Σ with the following features:

(i) every production in Q has the form $S_1gS_2 \to S_1hS_2$,

(ii) certain productions in Q are singled out as being *terminal.*

Given an input string σ, a Markov algorithm applies productions in Q sequentially, according to the following rules.

(*a*) if more than one production in Q applies to a string σ, use the first one in the list Q,

(*b*) if a production $S_1gS_2 \to S_1hS_2$ applies to σ in more than one way, apply it to the leftmost occurrence of g in σ,

(*c*) the process halts having produced a string τ *either* when a terminal production is used *or* if no production in Q applies to τ.

With these rules, the definition of *Markov-computable function* $f: \Sigma^* \to \Sigma^*$ is given in the obvious way. A Markov normal algorithm to compute f may use an alphabet extending Σ. It is quite straightforward to establish:

5.18. *Theorem*

Let $f: \Sigma^* \to \Sigma^*$. Then f is Markov-computable iff f is Post-computable.

Markov-computability on $\mathbb{N}$ is defined by using some system of representing numbers in the usual way, and thus coincides with the other approaches to computability.

6. Computability on domains other than $\mathbb{N}$

In chapter 1 § 5 we showed how any notion of computability on $\mathbb{N}$ can be extended to other domains by the device of coding. By contrast, in the previous section the definition of Post-computability on the domain of strings on a finite alphabet was given directly in terms of the objects (strings) and their intrinsic structure. A variety of such direct approaches to computability on other domains is possible: we give two examples.

6.1. *Example*

$D = \mathbb{Z}$. The URM idea may be extended to handle integers by making the following modifications:

(*a*) each register contains an integer,

(*b*) there is an additional instruction $S^-(n)$ for each $n = 1, 2, 3, \ldots$ that has the effect of *subtracting* 1 from the contents of register R_n.

6.2. *Example*

$D=\Sigma^*$, where $\Sigma=\{a, b\}$. The class $\mathscr{R}^D$ of *partial recursive functions* on Σ^* is the smallest class of partial functions such that

(*a*) the basic functions

(i) $f(\sigma)=\Lambda$

(ii) $f(\sigma)=\sigma a$

(iii) $f(\sigma)=\sigma b$

(iv) the projection functions $U_i^n(\sigma_1, \ldots, \sigma_n)=\sigma_i$,

are in $\mathscr{R}^D$,

(*b*) $\mathscr{R}^D$ is closed under substitution,

(*c*) $\mathscr{R}^D$ is closed under primitive recursive definitions of the following form:

$$\begin{cases} h(\boldsymbol{\sigma}, \Lambda)\simeq f(\boldsymbol{\sigma}) \\ h(\boldsymbol{\sigma}, \tau a)\simeq g_1(\boldsymbol{\sigma}, \tau, h(\boldsymbol{\sigma}, \tau)) \\ h(\boldsymbol{\sigma}, \tau b)\simeq g_2(\boldsymbol{\sigma}, \tau, h(\boldsymbol{\sigma}, \tau)) \end{cases}$$

where $f, g_1, g_2 \in \mathscr{R}^D$,

(*d*) $\mathscr{R}^D$ is closed under *minimalisation*: if $f(\boldsymbol{\sigma}, \tau)$ is in $\mathscr{R}^D$, so is the function h given by

$$h(\boldsymbol{\sigma})\simeq \mu\tau(f(\boldsymbol{\sigma}, \tau)=\Lambda)$$

where $\mu\tau$ means the first τ in the natural ordering Λ, a, b, aa, ab, ba, bb, aaa, aab, aba, ...

For each of these, and other approaches to computability on a domain D that utilise the intrinsic structure of D, we find as expected that they are equivalent to the approach that transfers the notion of computability from $\mathbb{N}$ by using coding. And, vice versa, any natural notion of computability on a domain D induces an alternative (but equivalent) notion of computability on $\mathbb{N}$ via coding, as with Post-computability in § 5.

6.3. *Exercises*

1. Prove that URM-computability on $\mathbb{Z}$ as outlined in example 6.1 is equivalent to URM-computability via coding (example 1-5.1).
2. Prove that the class $\mathscr{R}^D$ of partial recursive functions on Σ^*, as defined in example 6.2, is identical to the Post-computable functions on Σ^*.
3. Suggest natural definitions of computability on the domains (*a*) 3×3 matrices, (*b*) $\mathbb{Q}$ (rational numbers).
4. Give a natural definition of Turing-computability on Σ^*, where Σ is any finite alphabet.

7. Church's thesis

We now turn our attention to the second question of the introduction to this chapter: how well is the informal and intuitive idea of effectively computable function captured by the various formal characterisations?

In the light of their investigations, Church, Turing and Markov each put forward the claim that the class of functions he had defined coincides with the informally defined class of effectively computable functions. In view of the Fundamental result (1.1), these claims are all mathematically equivalent. The name *Church's thesis* (sometimes the *Church–Turing thesis*) is now used to describe any of these other claims. Thus, in terms of the URM approach, we can state:

Church's thesis

The intuitively and informally defined class of effectively computable partial functions coincides exactly with the class $\mathscr{C}$ of URM-computable functions.

Note immediately that this thesis is not a *theorem* which is susceptible to mathematical proof; it has the status of a *claim* or *belief* which must be substantiated by evidence. The evidence for Church's thesis, which we summarise below, is impressive.

1. The Fundamental result: many independent proposals for a precise formulation of the intuitive idea have led to the same class of functions, which we have called $\mathscr{C}$.
2. A vast collection of effectively computable functions has been shown explicitly to belong to $\mathscr{C}$; the particular functions of chapter 2 constitute the beginning of such a collection, which can be enlarged *ad infinitum* by the techniques of that chapter, and other more sophisticated methods.
3. The implementation of a program P on the URM to compute a function is clearly an example of an algorithm; thus, directly from the definition of the class $\mathscr{C}$, we see that all functions in $\mathscr{C}$ are computable in the informal sense. Similarly with all the other equivalent classes, the very definitions are such as to demonstrate that the functions involved are effectively computable.
4. No one has ever found a function that would be accepted as computable in the informal sense, that does not belong to $\mathscr{C}$.

On the basis of this evidence, and that of their own experience, most mathematicians are led to accept Church's thesis. For our part, we propose to accept and use Church's thesis throughout the rest of this book, in a way that we now explain.

Suppose that we have an informally described algorithm for computing the values of a function f. Such an algorithm may be described in English, or by means of diagrams, or in semi-formal mathematical terms, or by any other means that communicate unambiguously how to effectively calculate the values of f, where defined, in a finite amount of time. In such a situation we may wish to prove that f is URM-computable. There are, broadly, two methods open to us.

Method 1. Write a program that URM-computes f (and prove that it does so), or prove by indirect means that such a program exists. This could be done, for instance, by the methods of chapter 2, or by showing that f belongs to one of the many classes shown by the Fundamental result to be equivalent to $\mathscr{C}$.

Such a full and formal proof that f is URM-computable may be a long and rather technical process. Essentially it would involve translation of the informally described algorithm into a program or into the language of one of the other formal characterisations. Probably there would be various flow diagrams as intermediate translations.

Method 2. Give an informal (though rigorous) proof that the given informal algorithm is indeed an algorithm that serves to compute f. Then appeal to Church's thesis and conclude immediately that f is URM-computable.

We propose to accept method 2 as a valid method of proof, which we call *proof by Church's thesis*.

7.1. *Examples*

1. Let P be a URM program; define a function f by

$$f(x, y, t) = \begin{cases} 1 & \text{if } P(x)\downarrow y \text{ after } t \text{ or fewer steps} \\ & \text{of the computation } P(x), \\ 0 & \text{otherwise.} \end{cases}$$

An informal algorithm for computing f is as follows.

'Given (x, y, t), simulate the computation $P(x)$ (on a piece of paper, for example, as in example 1-2.1), carrying out t steps of $P(x)$ unless this computation stops after fewer than t steps. If $P(x)$ stops after t or fewer steps, with y finally in R_1, then $f(x, y, t) = 1$. Otherwise (i.e. if $P(x)$ stops in t or fewer steps with some number other than y in R_1, or if $P(x)$ has not stopped after t steps) we have $f(x, y, t) = 0$.'

Simulation of $P(x)$ for at most t steps is clearly a mechanical procedure, which can be completed in a finite amount of time. Thus, f *is* effectively computable. Hence, by Church's thesis, f is URM-computable.

2. Suppose that f and g are unary effectively computable functions. Define a function h by

$$h(x) = \begin{cases} 1 & \text{if } x \in \mathrm{Dom}(f) \text{ or } x \in \mathrm{Dom}(g), \\ \text{undefined} & \text{otherwise.} \end{cases}$$

An algorithm for h can be described in terms of given algorithms for the effectively computable functions f and g as follows:

'Given x, start the algorithms for computing $f(x)$ and $g(x)$ simultaneously. (Envisage two agents or machines working simultaneously, or one agent who does one step of each algorithm alternately.) If and when one of these computations terminates, then stop altogether, and set $h(x) = 1$. Otherwise, continue indefinitely.'

This algorithm gives $h(x) = 1$ for any x such that either $f(x)$ or $g(x)$ is defined; and it goes on for ever if neither is defined. Thus we have an algorithm for computing h, so by Church's thesis h is URM-computable.

3. Let $f(n) =$ the nth digit in the decimal expansion of $\pi = 3.14159\ldots$ (so we have $f(0) = 3$, $f(1) = 1$, $f(2) = 4$, etc.). We can obtain an informal algorithm for computing $f(n)$ as follows. Consider Hutton's series for π

$$\begin{aligned} \pi &= \frac{12}{5}\left\{1 + \frac{2}{3}\left(\frac{1}{10}\right) + \frac{2\times 4}{3\times 5}\left(\frac{1}{10}\right)^2 + \ldots\right\} \\ &\quad + \frac{14}{25}\left\{1 + \frac{2}{3}\left(\frac{1}{50}\right) + \frac{2\times 4}{3\times 5}\left(\frac{1}{50}\right)^2 + \ldots\right\} \\ &= \sum_{n=0}^{\infty} \frac{(n!2^n)^2}{(2n+1)!}\left\{\frac{12}{5}\left(\frac{1}{10}\right)^n + \frac{14}{25}\left(\frac{1}{50}\right)^n\right\} = \sum_{n=0}^{\infty} h_n, \text{ say.} \end{aligned}$$

Let $s_k = \sum_{n=0}^{k} h_n$; by the elementary theory of infinite series

$$s_k < \pi < s_k + 1/10^k.$$

Now s_k is rational, so the decimal expansion of s_k can be effectively calculated to any desired number of places using long division. Thus the following is an effective method for calculating $f(n)$ (given a number n):

'Find the first $N \geq n+1$ such that the decimal expansion

$s_N = a_0 . a_1 a_2 \ldots a_n a_{n+1} \ldots a_N \ldots$

does *not* have all of $a_{n+1}, \ldots, a_N$ equal to 9. (Such an N exists, for otherwise the decimal expansion of π would end in recurring 9, making π rational.) Then put $f(n) = a_n$.'

To see that this gives the required value, suppose that $a_m \neq 9$ with $n < m \leq N$. Then by the above

$$s_N < \pi < s_N + 1/10^N \\ \leq s_N + 1/10^m.$$

Hence $a_0 . a_1 \ldots a_n \ldots a_m \ldots \leqslant \pi < a_0 . a_1 \ldots a_n \ldots (a_m + 1) \ldots$ so the nth decimal place of π is indeed a_n.

Hence by Church's thesis, f is computable.

The student should try to provide complete formal proofs (method 1) that the functions in these examples are URM-computable (assuming, for example 2, that f and g are URM-computable). For all of them it is a lengthy and tedious task.

Note that in using Church's thesis we are not proposing to abandon all thought of proof, as if Church's thesis is a magic wand which we can wave instead. A proof by Church's thesis will always involve proof that is careful, and sometimes complicated, although informal. Moreover, anyone using Church's thesis in the way we propose should be able to provide a formal proof if challenged. (As if to anticipate such a challenge, we provide in the appendix to chapter 5 an alternative formal proof of one fundamental theorem in that chapter (theorem 5-1.2) on which almost all later development depends. This then serves to substantiate further Church's thesis; incidentally, it is a simple formal corollary that the functions in the first two examples above are URM-computable also.)

Church's thesis not only keeps proofs shorter, but also prevents the main idea of a proof or construction from being obscured by a mass of technical details. It remains, however, an expression of faith or confidence. The validity of faith depends on the evidence that can be mustered. In the case of Church's thesis, there is the mathematical evidence already outlined. For the practised student there is the additional evidence of his own experience in translating informal algorithms into formal counterparts. For the beginner, our use of Church's thesis in subsequent chapters may call on his willingness to place confidence in the ability of others until self confidence is developed.

To conclude: *for the remainder of this book, we accept Church's thesis and use it in the manner described above, often without explicit reference.*

7.2. *Exercises*

1. Suppose that $f(x)$ and $g(x)$ are effectively computable functions. Prove, using Church's thesis, that the function h given by

$$h(x)=\begin{cases} x & \text{if } x \in \mathrm{Dom}(f) \cap \mathrm{Dom}(g), \\ \text{undefined} & \text{otherwise} \end{cases}$$

is URM-computable.

2. Suppose that f is a total unary computable function. Prove, by Church's thesis, that the following function h is URM-computable

$$h(x)=\begin{cases} 1 & \text{if } x \in \mathrm{Ran}(f), \\ \text{undefined} & \text{otherwise.} \end{cases}$$

3. Give a detailed proof by Church's thesis that the Ackermann function (example 2-5.5) is computable.

4. Prove by Church's thesis that the function g given by

$g(n) = n$th digit in the decimal expansion of e

is computable (where the number e is the basis for natural logarithms).

4
Numbering computable functions

We return now to the study of URM-computable functions. Henceforth the term *computable* standing alone means URM-computable, and *program* means URM program.

The key fact established in this chapter is that the set of all programs is *effectively denumerable*: in other words there is an effective coding of programs by the set of all natural numbers. Among other things, it follows that the class $\mathscr{C}$ is denumerable, which implies that there are many functions that are not computable. In § 3 we discuss Cantor's diagonal method, whereby this is established.

The numbering or coding of programs, and particularly its effectiveness, is absolutely fundamental to the development of the theory of computability. We cannot overemphasise its importance. From it we obtain codes or indices for computable functions, and this means that we are able to pursue the idea of effective operations involving such codes.

In § 4 we prove the first of two important theorems involving codes of functions: the so-called *s–m–n* theorem of Kleene. (The second theorem is the main result of chapter 5.)

1. Numbering programs

We first explain the terminology that we shall use.

1.1. *Definitions*

(*a*) A set X is *denumerable* if there is a bijection $f: X \to \mathbb{N}$.

(*Note.* The term *countable* is normally used to mean finite or denumerable; thus, for infinite sets, countable means the same as denumerable. The term *countably infinite* is used by some authors instead of denumerable.)

(*b*) An *enumeration* of a set X is a surjection $g: \mathbb{N} \to X$; this is often represented by writing

$X = \{x_0, x_1, x_2, \ldots\}$

where $x_n = g(n)$. This is an enumeration *without repetitions* if g is injective.

(c) Let X be a set of finite objects (for example a set of integers, or a set of instructions, or a set of programs); then X is *effectively denumerable* if there is a bijection $f: X \to \mathbb{N}$ such that both f and f^{-1} are effectively computable functions.

(*Note.* We mean here the *informal* notion of effectively computable. This is compelled on us since, in general, there is no available formal notion of computability of functions from X to $\mathbb{N}$.[1] In cases where some formal notion does apply, we take this to be the meaning, as for example in theorem 1.2(a).)

Clearly, a set is denumerable if and only if it can be enumerated without repetitions.

For the main result of this section we need the following (recall that $\mathbb{N}^+$ denotes the set of all positive natural numbers):

1.2. *Theorem*

The following sets are effectively denumerable.

(a) $\mathbb{N} \times \mathbb{N}$,

(b) $\mathbb{N}^+ \times \mathbb{N}^+ \times \mathbb{N}^+$,

(c) $\bigcup_{k>0} \mathbb{N}^k$, *the set of all finite sequences of natural numbers.*

Proof

(a) A bijection $\pi: \mathbb{N} \times \mathbb{N} \to \mathbb{N}$ is defined by

$$\pi(m, n) = 2^m(2n+1) - 1.$$

It is clear from the definition that π is in fact a computable function; to see that the inverse is effectively computable observe that π^{-1} is given by

$$\pi^{-1}(x) = (\pi_1(x), \pi_2(x)),$$

where π_1, π_2 are the computable functions defined by $\pi_1(x) = (x+1)_1$, $\pi_2(x) = \frac{1}{2}((x+1)/2^{\pi_1(x)} - 1)$. (Cf. exercise 2-4.16(2).)

(b) An explicit bijection $\zeta: \mathbb{N}^+ \times \mathbb{N}^+ \times \mathbb{N}^+ \to \mathbb{N}$ is given, using the function π of (a), by

$$\zeta(m, n, q) = \pi(\pi(m-1, n-1), q-1).$$

Then we have

$$\zeta^{-1}(x) = (\pi_1(\pi_1(x)) + 1, \pi_2(\pi_1(x)) + 1, \pi_2(x) + 1).$$

[1] To say that we should use a notion of computability based on some coding begs the whole question, since a coding is an effective (in the informal sense) function.

Since the functions π, π_1, π_2 are effectively computable, then so are ζ and ζ^{-1}.

(*c*) A bijection $\tau: \bigcup_{k>0} \mathbb{N}^k \to \mathbb{N}$ is defined by

$$\tau(a_1, \ldots, a_k) = 2^{a_1} + 2^{a_1+a_2+1} + 2^{a_1+a_2+a_3+2} + \ldots$$
$$+ 2^{a_1+a_2+\ldots a_k+k-1} - 1.$$

Clearly τ is an effectively computable function. To see that τ is a bijection, and to calculate $\tau^{-1}(x)$, we use the fact that each natural number has a unique expression as a binary decimal. Thus, given x, we can effectively find unique numbers $k \geq 1$ and $0 \leq b_1 < b_2 \ldots < b_k$ such that

$$x + 1 = 2^{b_1} + 2^{b_2} + \ldots + 2^{b_k}$$

from which we obtain

$$\tau^{-1}(x) = (a_1, \ldots, a_k),$$

where $a_1 = b_1$ and $a_{i+1} = b_{i+1} - b_i - 1$ $(1 \leq i < k)$. (Cf. exercise 2-4.16(5), where functions closely connected with the calculation of τ^{-1} are to be proved computable.) □

Let us now denote the set of all URM instructions by $\mathscr{I}$, and the set of all programs by $\mathscr{P}$. A program consists of a finite list of instructions, so we next consider the set $\mathscr{I}$.

1.3. *Theorem*

$\mathscr{I}$ is effectively denumerable.

Proof. We define an explicit bijection $\beta: \mathscr{I} \to \mathbb{N}$ that maps the four kinds of instruction onto natural numbers of the forms $4u$, $4u+1$, $4u+2$, $4u+3$ respectively; we use the functions π and ζ defined in the proof of theorem 1.2.

$$\beta(\mathrm{Z}(n)) = 4(n-1),$$
$$\beta(\mathrm{S}(n)) = 4(n-1)+1,$$
$$\beta(\mathrm{T}(m, n) = 4\pi(m-1, n-1)+2,$$
$$\beta(\mathrm{J}(m, n, q)) = 4\zeta(m, n, q)+3.$$

This explicit definition shows that β is effectively computable. To find $\beta^{-1}(x)$, first find u, r such that $x = 4u + r$ with $0 \leq r < 4$. The value of r indicates which kind of instruction $\beta^{-1}(x)$ is, and from u we can effectively find the particular instruction of that kind. Specifically:

if $r = 0$, then $\beta^{-1}(x) = \mathrm{Z}(u+1)$;
if $r = 1$, then $\beta^{-1}(x) = \mathrm{S}(u+1)$;

if $r=2$, then $\beta^{-1}(x)=\mathrm{T}(\pi_1(u)+1, \pi_2(u)+1)$;

if $r=3$, then $\beta^{-1}(x)=\mathrm{J}(m, n, q)$, where $(m, n, q)=\zeta^{-1}(u)$.

Hence β^{-1} is also effectively computable. □

Now we can prove:

1.4. *Theorem*

$\mathcal{P}$ is effectively denumerable.

Proof. Define an explicit bijection $\gamma: \mathcal{P}\to\mathbb{N}$ as follows, using the bijections τ and β of theorems 1.2 and 1.3: if $P=I_1, I_2, \ldots, I_s$ then

$$\gamma(P)=\tau(\beta(I_1), \ldots, \beta(I_s)).$$

Since τ and β are bijections, so is γ; the fact that τ, β and their inverses are effectively computable ensures that γ and γ^{-1} are also effectively computable. □

The bijection γ will play an important role in subsequent development. For a program P, the number $\gamma(P)$ is called the *code number* of P, or the *Gödel*[2] *number* of P, or just the *number* of P. We define

$$P_n = \text{the program with (code) number } n$$
$$= \gamma^{-1}(n),$$

and say that P_n is the nth program. By construction of γ, if $m\neq n$, then P_m differs from P_n, although these programs may compute the same functions.

It is of the utmost importance for later results that the functions γ and γ^{-1} are effectively computable; i.e.

(*a*) Given a particular program P, we can effectively find the code number $\gamma(P)$;

(*b*) given a number n, we can effectively find the program $P_n=\gamma^{-1}(n)$.

In order to emphasise this we give two simple illustrations.

1.5. *Examples*

(*a*) Let P be the program T(1, 3), S(4), Z(6). We will calculate $\gamma(P)$.

$$\beta(\mathrm{T}(1,3))=4\pi(0,2)+2=4(2^0(2\times 2+1)-1)+2=18,$$
$$\beta(\mathrm{S}(4))=4\times 3+1=13,$$
$$\beta(\mathrm{Z}(6))=4\times 5=20.$$

[2] The term *Gödel number* is used after K. Gödel who first exploited the idea of coding non-numerical objects by numbers in his famous paper (Gödel [1931]).

Hence $\gamma(P) = 2^{18} + 2^{32} + 2^{53} - 1$

$= 9007203549970431.$

(*b*) Let $n = 4127$; we will find P_{4127}.

$4127 = 2^5 + 2^{12} - 1$; thus P_{4127} is a program with two instructions I_1, I_2 where

$\beta(I_1) = 5 = 4 \times 1 + 1,$

$\beta(I_2) = 12 - 5 - 1 = 6 = 4 \times 1 + 2 = 4\pi(1, 0) + 2.$

Hence from the definition of β, $I_1 = \mathrm{S}(2)$ and $I_2 = \mathrm{T}(2, 1)$, so P_{4127} is

S(2)

T(2, 1)

There are, of course, many other possible effective bijections from $\mathscr{P}$ to $\mathbb{N}$; our choice in defining the details of γ was somewhat arbitrary. What is vital, we again emphasise, is that γ and γ^{-1} are effectively computable. The particular details of γ are not so important. For subsequent theory, any other bijection γ' would suffice, provided that γ' and its inverse are effectively computable. However, we have to fix on one particular numbering of programs, and we have chosen that given by γ. ***For the rest of this book, γ remains fixed, so that for each particular number n, the meaning of P_n does not change.*** Thus, for instance, P_{4127} always means the program S(2), T(2, 1).

1.6. *Exercise*

Find

(*a*) $\beta(\mathrm{J}(3, 4, 2))$,

(*b*) $\beta^{-1}(503)$,

(*c*) the code number of the following program:

T(3, 4), S(3), Z(1),

(*d*) P_{100}.

2. Numbering computable functions

Using our fixed numbering of programs, we can now number computable functions and their domains and ranges. We introduce some important notation which is basic to the rest of the book.

2.1. *Definition*

For each $a \in \mathbb{N}$, and $n \geq 1$:

(a) $\phi_a^{(n)}$ = the n-ary function computed by P_a

$= f_{P_a}^{(n)}$ in the notation of chapter 1 § 3,

(b) $W_a^{(n)}$ = domain of $\phi_a^{(n)} = \{(x_1, \ldots, x_n): P_a(x_1, \ldots, x_n)\downarrow\}$,

$E_a^{(n)}$ = range of $\phi_a^{(n)}$.

We shall be mainly concerned with unary computable functions in later chapters, so for convenience we omit the superscript (1) when it occurs; thus we write ϕ_a for $\phi_a^{(1)}$, W_a for $W_a^{(1)}$, and E_a for $E_a^{(1)}$.

2.2. *Example*

Let $a = 4127$; from the previous section we know that P_{4127} is S(2), T(2, 1). Hence

$$\phi_{4127}(x) = 1 \qquad \text{(all } x\text{)}$$

and

$$\phi_{4127}^{(n)}(x_1, \ldots, x_n) = x_2 + 1 \qquad \text{if} \quad n > 1.$$

Thus

$$W_{4127} = \mathbb{N}, \qquad E_{4127} = \{1\};$$
$$W_{4127}^{(n)} = \mathbb{N}^n, \qquad E_{4127}^{(n)} = \mathbb{N}^+ \quad \text{if } n > 1.$$

Suppose that f is a unary computable function. Then there is a program P, say, that computes f, so $f = \phi_a$, where $a = \gamma(P)$. We say then that a is an *index* for f. Since there are many different programs that compute a given function, we cannot say that a is *the* index for f; in fact, each computable function has infinitely many indices.

We conclude that every unary computable function appears in the enumeration

$$\phi_0, \phi_1, \phi_2, \ldots.$$

and that this is an enumeration *with* repetitions.

Similar remarks apply to n-ary functions and their enumeration.

2.3. *Exercise*

Prove that every computable function has infinitely many indices.

Recall that we denoted the set of all n-ary computable function by $\mathscr{C}_n$.

2.4. *Theorem*

$\mathscr{C}_n$ is denumerable.

Proof. We use the enumeration $\phi_0^{(n)}, \phi_1^{(n)}, \phi_2^{(n)}, \ldots$ (which has repetitions) to construct one without repetitions.

$$\text{Let } \begin{cases} f(0) = 0, \\ f(m+1) = \mu z(\phi_z^{(n)} \neq \phi_{f(0)}^{(n)}, \ldots, \phi_{f(m)}^{(n)}). \end{cases}$$

Then

$$\phi_{f(0)}^{(n)}, \phi_{f(1)}^{(n)}, \phi_{f(2)}^{(n)}, \ldots$$

is an enumeration of $\mathscr{C}_n$ without repetitions. □

Note. We are not claiming that f as defined in this proof is computable; in fact, we will be able to show later that this is not the case. It is possible, nevertheless, to give a complicated construction of a total computable function h such that $\phi_{h(0)}^{(n)}, \phi_{h(1)}^{(n)}, \ldots$ is an enumeration of $\mathscr{C}_n$ without repetitions. This was proved by Friedberg [1958].

2.5. *Corollary*

$\mathscr{C}$ is denumerable.

Proof. Since $\mathscr{C} = \bigcup_{n \geq 1} \mathscr{C}_n$, this follows from the fact that a denumerable union of denumerable sets is denumerable.

Explicitly, for each n let f_n be the function used in theorem 2.4 to give an enumeration of $\mathscr{C}_n$ without repetitions. Let π be the bijection $\mathbb{N} \times \mathbb{N} \to \mathbb{N}$ of theorem 1.2. Define $\theta: \mathscr{C} \to \mathbb{N}$ by

$$\theta(\phi_{f_n(m)}^{(n)}) = \pi(m, n-1).$$

Clearly θ is a bijection. □

The next theorem shows that there are functions that are not computable. The idea of the proof is as important as the result itself.

2.6. *Theorem*

There is a total unary function that is not computable.

Proof. We shall construct a total function f that is simultaneously different from every function in the enumeration $\phi_0, \phi_1, \phi_2, \ldots$ of $\mathscr{C}_1$. Explicitly, define

$$f(n) = \begin{cases} \phi_n(n) + 1 & \text{if } \phi_n(n) \text{ is defined,} \\ 0 & \text{if } \phi_n(n) \text{ is undefined.} \end{cases}$$

Notice that we have constructed f so that for each n, f differs from ϕ_n at n:

if $\phi_n(n)$ is defined, then f differs from ϕ_n in that $f(n) \neq \phi_n(n)$;

if $\phi_n(n)$ is undefined, then f differs from ϕ_n in that $f(n)$ is defined.

Since f differs from every unary computable function ϕ_n, f does not appear in the enumeration of $\mathscr{C}_1$ and is thus not itself computable. Clearly f is total. □

3. Discussion: the diagonal method

The method of constructing the function f in theorem 2.6 is an example of the *diagonal method* of construction, due to Cantor. Many readers will be familiar with this method as used in proofs of the uncountability of the set of real numbers. The underlying idea is applicable in a wide variety of situations, and is central in the proofs of many results concerning computability and decidability.

To see why the term *diagonal* is used, consider again the construction of f in theorem 2.6. Complete details of the functions $\phi_0, \phi_1, \ldots$ can be represented by the following infinite table:

	0	1	2	3	4
ϕ_0	($\phi_0(0)$)	$\phi_0(1)$	$\phi_0(2)$	$\phi_0(3)$	...
ϕ_1	$\phi_1(0)$	($\phi_1(1)$)	$\phi_1(2)$	$\phi_1(3)$	...
ϕ_2	$\phi_2(0)$	$\phi_2(1)$	($\phi_2(2)$)	$\phi_2(3)$	...
ϕ_3	$\phi_3(0)$	$\phi_3(1)$	$\phi_3(2)$	($\phi_3(3)$)	...
⋮	⋮	⋮	⋮	⋮	

We suppose that in this table the word 'undefined' is written whenever $\phi_n(m)$ is not defined.

The function f was constructed by taking the diagonal entries on this table (circled)

$$\phi_0(0), \phi_1(1), \phi_2(2), \ldots$$

and systematically changing them, obtaining

$$f(0), f(1), f(2), \ldots$$

such that $f(n)$ differs from $\phi_n(n)$, for each n. Note that there was considerable freedom in choosing the value of $f(n)$; we only had to ensure that it differed from $\phi_n(n)$. Thus

$$g(n) = \begin{cases} \phi_n(n) + 27^n & \text{if } \phi_n(n) \text{ is defined,} \\ n^2 & \text{if } \phi_n(n) \text{ is undefined,} \end{cases}$$

is another non-computable total function.

We can summarise the diagonal method as we shall be using it, in the following way. Suppose that $\chi_0, \chi_1, \chi_2, \ldots$ is an enumeration of objects of a certain kind (functions or sets of natural numbers). Then we can construct an object χ of the same kind that is different from every χ_n, using the following motto:

'*Make* χ *and* χ_n *differ at* n.'

The interpretation of the phrase *differ at n* depends on the kind of object involved. Functions may differ at n over whether they are defined, or in their values at n if defined there; with functions, there is usually freedom to construct χ so as to meet specific extra requirements; for instance, that χ be computable, or that its domain (or range) should differ from that of each χ_n.

In the case of sets, the question at n is whether or not n is a member. We illustrate the diagonal construction when sets are involved.

3.1. *Example*

Suppose that $A_0, A_1, A_2, \ldots$ is an enumeration of subsets of $\mathbb{N}$. We can define a new set B, using the diagonal motto, by

$n \in B$ if and only if $n \notin A_n$.

Clearly, for each n, $B \neq A_n$.

There are important applications of the diagonal method in the next two chapters.

3.2. *Exercises*

1. Suppose that $f(x, y)$ is a total computable function. For each m, let g_m be the computable function given by

   $g_m(y) = f(m, y)$.

   Construct a total computable function h such that for each m, $h \neq g_m$.
2. Let $f_0, f_1, \ldots$ be an enumeration of partial functions from $\mathbb{N}$ to $\mathbb{N}$. Construct a function g from $\mathbb{N}$ to $\mathbb{N}$ such that $\mathrm{Dom}(g) \neq \mathrm{Dom}(f_i)$ for each i.
3. Let f be a partial function from $\mathbb{N}$ to $\mathbb{N}$, and let $m \in \mathbb{N}$. Construct a non-computable function g such that

   $g(x) \simeq f(x)$ for $x \leq m$.
4. (*a*) (Cantor) Show that the set of all functions from $\mathbb{N}$ to $\mathbb{N}$ is not denumerable.

(*b*) Show that the set of all non-computable total functions from $\mathbb{N}$ to $\mathbb{N}$ is not denumerable.

4. The *s–m–n* theorem

In the final section of this chapter we prove a theorem that has many important uses, especially in conjunction with the main theorem of the next chapter.

Suppose that $f(x, y)$ is a computable function (not necessarily total). Then for each fixed value a of x, f gives rise to a unary computable function g_a, where

$$g_a(y) \simeq f(a, y).$$

Since g_a is computable, it has an index e, say, so that

$$f(a, y) \simeq \phi_e(y).$$

The next theorem shows that such an index e can be obtained *effectively* from a. This is a particular case of a more general theorem, known as the *s–m–n* theorem, which we prove below. (The reason for this name will be explained after theorem 4.3.) For most purposes in this book, the following suffices.

4.1. *Theorem* (The *s–m–n* theorem, simple form)

Suppose that $f(x, y)$ is a computable function. There is a total computable function $k(x)$ such that

$$f(x, y) \simeq \phi_{k(x)}(y).$$

Proof. For each fixed a, $k(a)$ will be the code number of a program Q_a which, given initial configuration

(*)

R_1				
y	0	0	0	...

computes $f(a, y)$.

Let F be a program that computes f. Then for Q_a we write down F prefaced by instructions that transform the configuration (*) to

R_1	R_2			
a	y	0	0	...

Thus, define Q_a to be the following program

$$\begin{array}{l} \mathrm{T}(1,2) \\ \mathrm{Z}(1) \\ a \text{ times} \begin{cases} \mathrm{S}(1) \\ \vdots \\ \mathrm{S}(1) \end{cases} \\ F \end{array}$$

Now define

$$k(a) = \text{the code number of the program } Q_a.$$

Since F is fixed, and from the fact that our numbering γ of programs is effective, we see that k is an effectively computable function. Hence, by Church's thesis, k is computable. By construction

$$\phi_{k(a)}(y) \simeq f(a, y)$$

for each a. □

The *s–m–n* theorem is sometimes called the *Parametrisation theorem* because it shows that an index for a computable function (such as g_a in the discussion above) can be found effectively from a parameter (such as a) on which it effectively depends.

Before giving the full *s–m–n* theorem we give some simple illustrations of the use of theorem 4.1 in effectively indexing certain sequences of computable functions or their domains or ranges.

4.2. *Examples*

1. Let $f(x, y) = y^x$. By theorem 4.1 there is a total computable k such that $\phi_{k(x)}(y) = y^x$. Hence, for each fixed n, $k(n)$ is an index for the function y^n.
2. Let $f(x, y) = \begin{cases} y & \text{if } y \text{ is a multiple of } x \\ \text{undefined} & \text{otherwise.} \end{cases}$

   Then f is computable, so let k be a computable function such that $\phi_{k(x)}(y) \simeq f(x, y)$. Then, for each fixed n

   $$\begin{aligned} \phi_{k(n)}(y) \text{ is defined} &\text{ iff } y \text{ is a multiple of } n \\ &\text{ iff } y \text{ is in the range of } \phi_{k(n)}. \end{aligned}$$

   i.e.

   $$\begin{aligned} W_{k(n)} &= n\mathbb{N}\ (= \text{the set of all multiples of } n) \\ &= E_{k(n)}. \end{aligned}$$

   So we have an effective indexing of the sequence of sets $(n\mathbb{N})$ as (i) the domains of computable functions, (ii) the ranges of computable functions.

One obvious way to generalise theorem 4.1 is to replace the single variables x, y by m- and n-tuples $\mathbf{x}$ and $\mathbf{y}$ respectively. We can also reflect the fact that the function k defined in the proof of theorem 4.1 depended effectively on a particular program for the original function f. Thus, instead of considering a fixed computable function $f(x, y)$ we consider a general computable function $\phi_e^{(m+n)}(\mathbf{x}, \mathbf{y})$, and the question of effectively finding, for each e and $\mathbf{x}$, a number z such that

$$\phi_e^{(m+n)}(\mathbf{x}, \mathbf{y}) \simeq \phi_z^{(n)}(\mathbf{y}).$$

4.3. *Theorem* (The s–m–n theorem)

For each $m, n \geq 1$ there is a total computable $(m+1)$-ary function $s_n^m(e, \mathbf{x})$ such that

$$\phi_e^{(m+n)}(\mathbf{x}, \mathbf{y}) \simeq \phi_{s_n^m(e,\mathbf{x})}^{(n)}(\mathbf{y}).$$

Proof. We generalise the proof of theorem 4.1.

For any $i \geq 1$ let $Q(i, x)$ be the subroutine

$$\begin{array}{l} Z(i) \\ \left.\begin{array}{l} S(i) \\ \vdots \\ S(i) \end{array}\right\} x \text{ times} \end{array}$$

that replaces the current contents of R_i by x. Then for fixed m, n define $s_n^m(e, \mathbf{x})$ to be the code number of the following program:

$$\left.\begin{array}{l} T(n, m+n) \\ \vdots \\ T(2, m+2) \\ T(1, m+1) \\ Q(1, x_1) \\ Q(2, x_2) \\ \vdots \\ Q(m, x_m) \end{array}\right\}$$

P_e

This part of the program transforms any configuration

R_1		R_n			
y_1	...	y_n	0	0	...

into

R_1		R_m	R_{m+1}		R_{m+n}		
x_1	...	x_m	y_1	...	y_n	0	...

From this explicit definition, and the effectiveness of γ and γ^{-1}, we get that s_n^m is effectively computable, hence computable, by Church's thesis. □

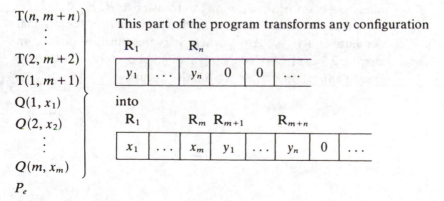

The notation s_n^m for the function given by theorem 4.3 has given rise to the standard description of this result as the *s–m–n* theorem. We will also use this name to describe the simpler version given in theorem 4.1.

It is not hard to see that the function s_n^m as defined above is in fact primitive recursive. With a little thought it is also possible to see that for each m there is a function s^m (also primitive recursive) that suffices in theorem 4.3 for all n. See the exercises 4.4(5) below.

4.4. *Exercises*

1. Show that there is a total computable function k such that for each n, $k(n)$ is an index of the function $[\sqrt[n]{x}]$.
2. Show that there is a total computable function k such that for each n, $W_{k(n)}=$ the set of perfect nth powers.
3. Let $n\geq 1$. Show that there is a total computable function s such that
   $W_{s(x)}^{(n)}=\{(y_1,\ldots,y_n): y_1+y_2+\ldots+y_n=x\}$
4. Show that the functions s_n^m defined in theorem 4.3 are all primitive recursive.
5. Show that for each m there is a total $(m+1)$-ary computable function s^m such that for all n
   $\phi_e^{(m+n)}(\boldsymbol{x},\boldsymbol{y})\simeq\phi_{s^m(e,\boldsymbol{x})}^{(n)}(\boldsymbol{y})$
   where $\boldsymbol{x}$, $\boldsymbol{y}$ are m- and n-tuples respectively.
   (*Hint.* Consider the definition of $s_n^m(e,\boldsymbol{x})$ given in the proof of theorem 4.3. The only way in which n was used was in determining how many of the $r_1, r_2, \ldots$ to transfer to $R_{m+1}, R_{m+2}, \ldots$. Now recall that the effect of P_e depends only on the original contents of $R_1, \ldots, R_{\rho(P_e)}$, where ρ is the function defined in chapter 2 § 2; $\rho(P_e)$ is independent of n.) Show further that there is such a function s^m that is primitive recursive.

5
Universal programs

In this chapter we establish the somewhat surprising result that there are *universal programs*; i.e. programs that in a sense embody all other programs. This result is one of the twin pillars that support computability theory (the other is the *s–m–n* theorem); both rest on the numbering of programs given in chapter 4.

Important among the applications of universal programs is the construction of specific non-computable functions and undecidable predicates, a topic pursued in chapter 6. We give a foretaste of such applications in § 2 of this chapter; we also use a universal program to construct a total computable function that is not primitive recursive, as promised in chapter 3.

The final section of this chapter is devoted to some illustrations of the use of the *s–m–n* theorem in conjunction with universal programs to show that certain operations on the indices of computable functions are effective (a foretaste of the topic of chapter 10).

1. Universal functions and universal programs

Consider the function $\psi(x, y)$ defined by

$$\psi(x, y) \simeq \phi_x(y).$$

There is an obvious sense in which the single function ψ embodies all the unary computable functions $\phi_0, \phi_1, \phi_2, \ldots$, since for any particular m, the function g given by

$$g(y) \simeq \psi(m, y)$$

is just the computable function ϕ_m. Thus we describe ψ as the *universal function* for unary computable functions. Generally, we make the following definition.

1.1. *Definition*

The *universal function for n-ary computable functions* is the $(n+1)$-ary function $\psi_U^{(n)}$ defined by

$$\psi_U^{(n)}(e, x_1, \ldots, x_n) \simeq \phi_e^{(n)}(x_1, \ldots, x_n).$$

We write ψ_U for $\psi_U^{(1)}$.

The question arises, is ψ_U (or, generally, $\psi_U^{(n)}$) a computable function? If so, then any program P that computes ψ_U would appear to embody all other programs, and P would be aptly called a *universal program*. At first, perhaps, the existence of a universal program seems unlikely. Nevertheless, it is not hard to see that ψ_U is indeed computable. The point is that a universal program P does *not* need to contain all other programs P_e in itself; P only needs the ability to *decode* any number e and hence mimic P_e.

1.2. *Theorem*

For each n, the universal function $\psi_U^{(n)}$ is computable.

Proof. Fix n, and suppose that we are given an index e and an n-tuple $\boldsymbol{x}$. An informal procedure for computing $\psi_U^{(n)}(e, \boldsymbol{x})$ is as follows:

'Decode the number e and write out the program P_e. Now mimic the computation $P_e(\boldsymbol{x})$ step by step, at each step writing down the configuration of the registers and the next instruction to be obeyed (as was done in example 1-2.1). If and when this computation stops, then the required value $\psi_U^{(n)}(e, \boldsymbol{x})$ is the number currently in R_1.'

We could conclude immediately (using Church's thesis) that $\psi_U^{(n)}(e, \boldsymbol{x})$ is computable. Because of the importance of this theorem, however, we prefer to outline the beginnings of a formal proof and then make a rather less sweeping appeal to Church's thesis. (For the sake of completeness of our exposition we shall provide the rest of the formal proof in an appendix to this chapter.)

The plan for a formal proof is to show first how to use a single number σ to code the current situation during a computation; then we show that there is a *computable* function expressing the dependence of σ on (a) the program number e, (b) the input $\boldsymbol{x}$, (c) the number of steps of the computation that have been completed. We will see that this suffices to prove the theorem.

Let us return, then, to the computation $P_e(\boldsymbol{x})$ considered above. As we have seen in examples, the current situation during a computation is completely specified by (i) the current configuration of the registers

$r_1, r_2, r_3, \ldots$ and (ii) the number j of the next instruction in the computation. Since only finitely many of the numbers r_i are not zero, the current configuration can be specified by the single number

$$c = 2^{r_1}3^{r_2}\ldots = \prod_{i\geq 1} p_i^{r_i}.$$

(Recall that p_i is the ith prime number.) We call this number the *configuration code* or just the *configuration* if there is no ambiguity. Note that the contents r_i of R_i can be easily recovered from c; in fact $r_i = (c)_i$ (using the function of theorem 2-4.15(d)).

The complete description of the current situation can now be coded by the single number $\sigma = \pi(c, j)$, which we call the current *state* of the computation $P_e(\boldsymbol{x})$. (Here π is the pairing function used in the proof of theorem 4-1.2.) We will make the convention that if the computation has stopped, then $j = 0$ and c is the final configuration. Note that $c = \pi_1(\sigma)$ and $j = \pi_2(\sigma)$ where π_1, π_2 are the computable functions defined in theorem 4-1.2.

Now c, j, σ change during the computation; their dependence on the program number e, the input $\boldsymbol{x}$ and the number t of steps completed is expressed by defining the following $(n+2)$-ary functions:

(1) $c_n(e, \boldsymbol{x}, t) =$ the configuration after t steps of $P_e(\boldsymbol{x})$ have been completed (= the final configuration if $P_e(\boldsymbol{x})\downarrow$ in t or fewer steps).

(2) $$j_n(e, \boldsymbol{x}, t) = \begin{cases} \text{the number}^1 \text{ of the next instruction for } P_e(\boldsymbol{x}) \text{ when } t \text{ steps have been completed,} & \text{if } P_e(\boldsymbol{x}) \text{ has not stopped after } t \text{ or fewer steps,} \\ 0 & \text{if } P_e(\boldsymbol{x})\downarrow \text{ in } t \text{ or fewer steps.} \end{cases}$$

(3) $\sigma_n(e, \boldsymbol{x}, t) =$ the state of the computation $P_e(\boldsymbol{x})$ after t steps $= \pi(c_n(e, \boldsymbol{x}, t), j_n(e, \boldsymbol{x}, t))$.

The aim now is to show that σ_n (and hence c_n and j_n) are computable functions. To see why this is sufficient, suppose that this has been done. Clearly, if the computation $P_e(\boldsymbol{x})$ stops it does so in $\mu t(j_n(e, \boldsymbol{x}, t) = 0)$ steps; then the final configuration is $c_n(e, \boldsymbol{x}, \mu t(j_n(e, \boldsymbol{x}, t) = 0))$, and so we

[1] We mean here the number j such that the next instruction I is the jth instruction of P_e; we do *not* mean the code number $\beta(I)$.

have

$$\psi_U^{(n)}(e, \mathbf{x}) \simeq (c_n(e, \mathbf{x}, \mu t(j_n(e, \mathbf{x}, t) = 0)))_1.$$

Thus, if c_n and j_n are computable, so is $\psi_U^{(n)}$ (using substitution and minimalisation) and our proof is complete.

We now use Church's thesis to show that σ_n (and hence c_n and j_n) are computable. We have the following informal algorithm for obtaining $\sigma_n(e, \mathbf{x}, t+1)$ effectively from $\sigma_n(e, \mathbf{x}, t)$ and e:

'Decode $\sigma_n(e, \mathbf{x}, t)$ to find the numbers $c = c_n(e, \mathbf{x}, t)$ and $j = j_n(e, \mathbf{x}, t)$. If $j = 0$, then $\sigma_n(e, \mathbf{x}, t+1) = \sigma_n(e, \mathbf{x}, t)$. Otherwise, write out the configuration coded by c,

(*)

$(c)_1$	$(c)_2$	$(c)_3$	...	$(c)_m$	0	0	...

say, and by decoding e write out the program P_e. Now find the jth instruction in P_e and operate with it on the configuration (*), producing a new configuration with code c' say. Find also the number j' of the new next instruction (with $j' = 0$ if the computation has now terminated). Then we have

$$\sigma_n(e, \mathbf{x}, t+1) = \pi(c', j').$$

This shows informally that $\sigma_n(e, \mathbf{x}, t)$ is computable by recursion in t, since for $t = 0$ we have

$$\sigma_n(e, \mathbf{x}, 0) = \pi(2^{x_1}3^{x_2} \dots p_n^{x_n}, 1)$$

to start the recursion off. Hence, by Church's thesis, σ_n is computable, and our theorem is now proved. □

Note. Since this theorem is so basic to further development, we provide in the appendix a complete formal proof that σ_n (and hence $\psi_U^{(n)}$) is computable. This then provides further evidence for Church's thesis. (Our formal proof also gives us the extra information that σ_n is actually *primitive* recursive.)

From the proof of this theorem we obtain:

1.3. *Corollary*

For each $n \geq 1$, *the following predicates are decidable.*

(*a*) $S_n(e, \mathbf{x}, y, t) \equiv$ '$P_e(\mathbf{x})\downarrow y$ *in* t *or fewer steps*',

(*b*) $H_n(e, \mathbf{x}, t) \equiv$ '$P_e(\mathbf{x})\downarrow$ *in* t *or fewer steps*'.

Proof. (*a*) $S_n(e, \mathbf{x}, y, t) \equiv$ '$j_n(e, \mathbf{x}, t) = 0$ and $(c_n(e, \mathbf{x}, t))_1 = y$'.

(*b*) $H_n(e, \mathbf{x}, t) \equiv$ '$j_n(e, \mathbf{x}, t) = 0$'. □

The significance of the next corollary is discussed in the first note below.

1.4. *Corollary* (Kleene's normal form theorem)
There is a total computable function $U(x)$ and for each $n \geq 1$ a decidable predicate $T_n(e, \mathbf{x}, z)$ such that
(*a*) $\phi_e^{(n)}(\mathbf{x})$ *is defined if and only if* $\exists z\, T_n(e, \mathbf{x}, z)$,
(*b*) $\phi_e^{(n)}(\mathbf{x}) \simeq U(\mu z\, T_n(e, \mathbf{x}, z))$.

Proof. To discover whether $\phi_e^{(n)}(\mathbf{x})$ is defined, and the value if it is, we need to search for a pair of numbers y, t such that $S_n(e, \mathbf{x}, y, t)$. We have the μ-operator that enables us to search effectively for a single number having a given property. To use this in searching for a pair of numbers, we can think of a single number z as coding the pair of numbers $(z)_1$ and $(z)_2$. Then, as z runs through $\mathbb{N}$, the pair $((z)_1, (z)_2)$ runs through $\mathbb{N}\times\mathbb{N}$. So we define

$$T_n(e, \mathbf{x}, z) \equiv S_n(e, \mathbf{x}, (z)_1, (z)_2).$$

For (*a*), suppose that $\phi_e^{(n)}(\mathbf{x})$ is defined; then there are y, t such that $S_n(e, \mathbf{x}, y, t)$, so putting $z = 2^y 3^t$ we have $T_n(e, \mathbf{x}, z)$.

Conversely, if there is z such that $T_n(e, \mathbf{x}, z)$, then from the definition of T_n, $P_e(\mathbf{x})\downarrow$; i.e. $\phi_e^{(n)}(\mathbf{x})$ is defined.

For (*b*), it is clear from the definition of T_n that if $\phi_e^{(n)}(\mathbf{x})$ is defined, then for any z such that $T_n(e, \mathbf{x}, z)$, we have $\phi_e^{(n)}(\mathbf{x}) = (z)_1$. So if we put $U(z) = (z)_1$ then

$$\phi_e^{(n)}(\mathbf{x}) \simeq U(\mu z\, T_n(e, \mathbf{x}, z)). \quad \square$$

Notes

1. From the appendix to this chapter it follows that the functions c_n and j_n are primitive recursive. Hence, the predicates S_n, H_n, T_n in corollaries 1.3 and 1.4 are also primitive recursive. Thus, in particular, the Kleene normal form theorem shows that every computable function (or partial recursive function) can be obtained from primitive recursive functions by using at most one application of the μ-operator. The theorem gives, moreover, a standard way of doing this.

2. The technique of searching for pairs of numbers by thinking of a single number z as coding the pair $(z)_1$, $(z)_2$ (as used in the proof of corollary 1.4) is often used in computability theory. We give an exercise needing this technique below (exercise 1.5(1)).

The technique can also be used in searching for sequences $(x_1, x_2, \ldots, x_n)$ for any $n > 1$.

1.5. *Exercises*

1. (i) Show that there is a decidable predicate $Q(x, y, z)$ such that
(*a*) $y \in E_x$ if and only if $\exists z\, Q(x, y, z)$,
(*b*) if $y \in E_x$, and $Q(x, y, z)$, then $\phi_x((z)_1) = y$.
(ii) Deduce that there is a computable function $g(x, y)$ such that
(*a*) $g(x, y)$ is defined if and only if $y \in E_x$.
(*b*) if $y \in E_x$, then $g(x, y) \in W_x$ and $\phi_x(g(x, y)) = y$; i.e. $g(x, y) \in \phi_x^{-1}(\{y\})$.
(iii) Deduce that if f is a computable injective function (not necessarily total or surjective) then f^{-1} is computable. (cf. exercise 2-5.4 (1)).
2. (cf. example 3-7.1(2)) Suppose that f and g are unary computable functions; assuming that T_1 has been formally proved to be decidable, prove formally that the function $h(x)$ defined by
$$h(x) = \begin{cases} 1 \text{ if } x \in \mathrm{Dom}(f) \text{ or } x \in \mathrm{Dom}(g), \\ \text{undefined otherwise,} \end{cases}$$
is computable.

2. Two applications of the universal program

We illustrate now the use of the computability of universal functions in diagonal constructions. This kind of application will be explored more thoroughly in the next chapter.

2.1. *Theorem*

The problem 'ϕ_x is total' is undecidable.

Proof. Let g be the characteristic function of this problem; i.e.
$$g(x) = \begin{cases} 1 & \text{if } \phi_x \text{ is total,} \\ 0 & \text{if } \phi_x \text{ is not total.} \end{cases}$$
We must show that g is not computable. To achieve this, we use the diagonal method to construct a total function f that is different from every computable function, yet such that if g is computable, then so is f. Explicitly, define f by
$$f(x) = \begin{cases} \phi_x(x) + 1 & \text{if } \phi_x \text{ is total,} \\ 0 & \text{if } \phi_x \text{ is not total.} \end{cases}$$
Clearly, f is total and differs from every computable function ϕ_x. Now, using g and ψ_U we can write f as follows:
$$f(x) = \begin{cases} \psi_U(x, x) + 1 & \text{if } g(x) = 1, \\ 0 & \text{if } g(x) = 0. \end{cases}$$

Now suppose that g is computable; since ψ_U is computable, then, by Church's thesis, so is f, which is a contradiction. Hence g is not computable. □

Our second application here fulfils the promise made in chapter 3 § 3.

2.2. *Theorem*

There is a total computable function that is not primitive recursive.

Proof. We give an informal proof. Recall that the primitive recursive functions are those functions that can be built up from the basic functions by a sequence of applications of the operations of substitution and recursion. Thus each primitive recursive function can be specified by a *plan* that indicates the basic functions used and the exact sequence of operations performed in its construction. To describe such a plan it is convenient to adopt some notation such as the following:

$\mathrm{Sub}(f; g_1, g_2, \ldots, g_m)$ denotes the function obtained by substituting $g_1, \ldots, g_m$ into f (assuming that f is m-ary, and $g_1, \ldots, g_m$ are n-ary for some n);

$\mathrm{Rec}(f, g)$ denotes the function obtained from f and g by recursion (assuming that f is n-ary and g is $(n+2)$-ary for some n).

If we write S for the function $x+1$, then we have, for example, the following plan for the function $f(x)=x^2$. We use letters $g_1, \ldots, g_4$ to denote intermediate functions.

Plan	Explanation of the steps
Step 1. $g_1 = \mathrm{Sub}(\mathrm{S}; \mathrm{U}_3^3)$.	$g_1(x, y, z) = \mathrm{U}_3^3(x, y, z)+1 = z+1$.
Step 2. $g_2 = \mathrm{Rec}(\mathrm{U}_1^1, g_1)$.	$\begin{cases} g_2(x, 0) = \mathrm{U}_1^1(x) = x, \\ g_2(x, y+1) = g_1(x, y, g_2(x, y)) \end{cases}$ $= g_2(x, y)+1$. So $g_2(x, y) = x+y$.
Step 3. $g_3 = \mathrm{Sub}(g_2; \mathrm{U}_1^3, \mathrm{U}_3^3)$.	$g_3(x, y, z) = g_2(x, z) = x+z$.
Step 4. $g_4 = \mathrm{Rec}(\mathbf{0}, g_3)$.	$\begin{cases} g_4(x, 0) = 0, \\ g_4(x, y+1) = g_3(x, y, g_4(x, y)) \end{cases}$ $= x + g_4(x, y)$. So $g_4(x, y) = xy$.
Step 5. $f = \mathrm{Sub}(g_4; \mathrm{U}_1^1, \mathrm{U}_1^1)$.	$f(x) = g_4(x, x) = x^2$.

Thus a plan is somewhat akin to a program, in that it is a finite and explicit specification of a function.

We now restrict our attention to plans for unary primitive recursive functions. As with programs, we can number these plans in an effective way, so that we may then define

$$\theta_n = \text{the unary primitive recursive function defined by plan number } n.$$

Then $\theta_0, \theta_1, \theta_2, \ldots$ is an effective enumeration of all unary primitive recursive functions.

From chapter 2 we know that every primitive recursive function is computable. Hence there is a total function p such that for each n, $p(n)$ is the number of a program that computes θ_n; i.e.

$$\theta_n = \phi_{p(n)}.$$

Now the crucial point is that we can find such a function p that is *computable*. We argue informally using Church's thesis.

Recall the proofs of theorems 2-3.1 and 2-4.4. There we showed explicitly how to obtain a program for the function

$$\mathrm{Sub}(f; g_1, \ldots, g_m)$$

given programs for $f, g_1, \ldots, g_m$; and also, how to obtain a program for the function

$$\mathrm{Rec}(f, g)$$

given programs for f and g. (In the next section (example 3.1(5)) we use the s–m–n theorem to show in detail that for each n there is a computable function r such that for any e_1, e_2 an index for $\mathrm{Rec}(\phi^{(n)}_{e_1}, \phi^{(n+2)}_{e_2})$ is given by $r(e_1, e_2)$; we can do a similar thing for substitution (see exercise 3.2(5a)).) We also have explicit programs for the basic functions. Hence, given a plan for a primitive recursive function f involving intermediate functions $g_1, \ldots, g_k$, say, we can effectively find programs for $g_1, g_2, \ldots, g_k$, and finally f. Thus there is an effectively computable function p such that

$$\theta_n = \phi_{p(n)}.$$

By Church's thesis, p is computable.

Now for the payoff! From p and the universal function ψ_U we can define a total computable function g that differs from every primitive recursive function θ_n. We use a diagonal construction as follows:

$$\begin{aligned} g(x) &= \theta_x(x) + 1 \\ &= \phi_{p(x)}(x) + 1 \\ &= \psi_U(p(x), x) + 1. \end{aligned}$$

From this we see immediately that g is a total function that is not primitive recursive; but g *is* computable, by the computability of ψ_U and p. □

3. Effective operations on computable functions

In this section we illustrate another important application of the computability of the universal functions, this time in conjunction with the *s–m–n* theorem.

Consider the following operations on computable functions or their domains:

(*a*) combining ϕ_x and ϕ_y to form the product $\phi_x\phi_y$;

(*b*) forming the union $W_x \cup W_y$ from W_x and W_y.

We are all familiar with a wide variety of operations of a similar kind, usually defined explicitly like these. Is there any sense in which these operations can be thought of as *effective* operations? Inasmuch as these are operations involving infinite objects (functions or sets), they seem to lie outside the scope of even our informal notion of computability, which implicitly applies only to finite objects. Nevertheless, we will see, for instance, that an *index* for the function $\phi_x\phi_y$ can be obtained effectively from the indices x, y. In the following examples and exercises we see that many other operations are effective when viewed thus as operations on indices of the objects involved. (We will return to the topic of effective operations on functions in chapter 10.)

3.1. *Examples*

1. There is a total computable function $s(x, y)$ such that for all x, y $\phi_{s(x,y)} = \phi_x\phi_y$.

   Proof. Let $f(x, y, z) \simeq \phi_x(z)\phi_y(z)$
   $$\simeq \psi_U(x, z)\psi_U(y, z).$$
   Thus f is computable, so by the *s–m–n* theorem there is a total computable function $s(x, y)$ such that $f(x, y, z) \simeq \phi_{s(x,y)}(z)$; hence $\phi_{s(x,y)} = \phi_x\phi_y$.

2. Taking $g(x) = s(x, x)$, with s as an example 1, we have $(\phi_x)^2 = \phi_{g(x)}$.

3. There is a total computable function $s(x, y)$ such that $W_{s(x,y)} = W_x \cup W_y$.

   Proof. Let $f(x, y, z) = \begin{cases} 1 & \text{if } z \in W_x \text{ or } z \in W_y, \\ \text{undefined} & \text{otherwise.} \end{cases}$

   By Church's thesis and the computability of ψ_U, f is computable; so there is a total computable function $s(x, y)$ such that $f(x, y, z) \simeq \phi_{s(x,y)}(z)$. Then clearly $W_{s(x,y)} = W_x \cup W_y$.

4. *Effectiveness of taking inverses.* Let $g(x,y)$ be a computable function as described in exercise 1.5; i.e. such that
   (*a*) $g(x, y)$ is defined if and only if $y \in E_x$,
   (*b*) if $y \in E_x$, then $g(x, y) \in W_x$ and $\phi_x(g(x, y)) = y$.
   By the *s–m–n* theorem there is a total computable function k such that $g(x, y) \simeq \phi_{k(x)}(y)$. Then from (*a*) and (*b*) we have
   (*a'*) $W_{k(x)} = E_x$,
   (*b'*) (i) $E_{k(x)} \subseteq W_x$,
   (ii) if $y \in E_x$, then $\phi_x(\phi_{k(x)}(y)) = y$.
   Hence, if ϕ_x is injective, then $\phi_{k(x)} = \phi_x^{-1}$ and $E_{k(x)} = W_x$.
5. *Effectiveness of recursion.* Let $\boldsymbol{x} = (x_1, \ldots, x_n)$ and consider the $(n+3)$-ary function f defined by
   $f(e_1, e_2, \boldsymbol{x}, 0) \simeq \phi_{e_1}^{(n)}(\boldsymbol{x})$,
   $f(e_1, e_2, \boldsymbol{x}, y+1) \simeq \phi_{e_2}^{(n+2)}(\boldsymbol{x}, y, f(e_1, e_2, \boldsymbol{x}, y))$.
   Then using the universal functions $\psi_U^{(n)}$ and $\psi_U^{(n+2)}$ to rewrite the expressions on the right, this is a definition by recursion from computable functions, so f is computable. Moreover, for fixed e_1, e_2 the function $g(\boldsymbol{x}, y) \simeq f(e_1, e_2, \boldsymbol{x}, y)$ is the function obtained from $\phi_{e_1}^{(n)}$ and $\phi_{e_2}^{(n+2)}$ by recursion.

   By the *s–m–n* theorem there is a total computable function $r(e_1, e_2)$ such that
   $\phi_{r(e_1,e_2)}^{(n+1)}(\boldsymbol{x}, y) \simeq f(e_1, e_2, \boldsymbol{x}, y)$.
   Hence $r(e_1, e_2)$ is an index for the $(n+1)$-ary function obtained from $\phi_{e_1}^{(n)}$ and $\phi_{e_2}^{(n+2)}$ by recursion. In the notation of theorem 2.2
   $\phi_{r(e_1,e_2)}^{(n+1)} = \mathrm{Rec}(\phi_{e_1}^{(n)}, \phi_{e_2}^{(n+2)})$
   for all e_1, e_2.

The following exercises give more examples of the use of the *s–m–n* theorem in showing that operations are effective on indices.

3.2. *Exercises*

1. Show that there is a total computable function $k(e)$ such that for any e, if ϕ_e is the characteristic function for a decidable predicate $M(x)$, then $\phi_{k(e)}$ is the characteristic function for 'not $M(x)$'.
2. Show that there is a total computable function $k(x)$ such that for every x, $E_{k(x)} = W_x$.
3. Show that there is a total computable function $s(x, y)$ such that for all x, y, $E_{s(x,y)} = E_x \cup E_y$.
4. Suppose that $f(x)$ is computable; show that there is a total computable function $k(x)$ such that for all x, $W_{k(x)} = f^{-1}(W_x)$.

5. Prove the equivalent of example 5 above for the operations of substitution and minimalisation, namely:
(*a*) Fix $m, n \geq 1$; there is a total computable function $s(e, e_1, \ldots, e_m)$ such that (in the notation of theorem 2.2)
$\phi^{(n)}_{s(e,e_1,\ldots,e_m)} = \mathrm{Sub}(\phi^{(m)}_e; \phi^{(n)}_{e_1}, \phi^{(n)}_{e_2}, \ldots, \phi^{(n)}_{e_m})$.
(*b*) Fix $n \geq 1$; there is a total computable function $k(e)$ such that for all e,
$\phi^{(n)}_{k(e)}(\mathbf{x}) \simeq \mu y(\phi^{(n+1)}_e(\mathbf{x}, y) = 0)$.
(We could extend the notation of theorem 2.2 in the obvious way and write $\phi^{(n)}_{k(e)} = \mathrm{Min}(\phi^{(n+1)}_e)$.)

Appendix
Computability of the function σ_n

In this appendix we give a formal proof that the function σ_n defined in the proof of theorem 1.2 is computable (in fact, primitive recursive) thus completing a formal proof of the computability of the universal function $\psi^{(n)}_U$.

Theorem.
The function σ_n *is primitive recursive.*

Proof. For the definition of σ_n and the functions c_n and j_n coded by σ_n, refer to the proof of theorem 1.2.

We define two functions 'config' and 'nxt' that describe the changes in c_n and j_n during computations. Suppose that at some stage during computation under P_e the current state is $\sigma = \pi(c, j)$, and suppose that P_e has s instructions. We can describe the effect of the jth instruction of P_e on the state σ by defining

$$\mathrm{config}(e, \sigma) = \begin{cases} \text{the new configuration after the } j\text{th instruction of } P_e \text{ has been obeyed,} & \text{if } 1 \leq j \leq s, \\ c & \text{otherwise.} \end{cases}$$

$$\mathrm{nxt}(e, \sigma) = \begin{cases} \text{the number of the next instruction for the computation, after the } j\text{th instruction of } P_e \text{ has been executed on the configuration } c, & \text{if } 1 \leq j \leq s \text{ and this next instruction exists in } P_e, \\ 0 & \text{otherwise.} \end{cases}$$

Now σ_n can be obtained from config and nxt by the following recursion equations:

$$\sigma_n(e, \boldsymbol{x}, 0) = \pi(2^{x_1}3^{x_2}\dots p_n^{x_n}, 1),$$
$$\sigma_n(e, \boldsymbol{x}, t+1) = \pi(\text{config}(e, \sigma_n(e, \boldsymbol{x}, t)), \text{nxt}(e, \sigma_n(e, \boldsymbol{x}, t))).$$

Thus, σ_n is primitive recursive if config and nxt are primitive recursive; we proceed to show that they are.

We must be careful now to distinguish between the code number $\beta(I)$ of an instruction I and its number in any program in which it occurs (i.e. the number j such that I is the jth instruction). We will always use the term code number when $\beta(I)$ is intended.

It is sufficient to establish that the following four functions are primitive recursive:

(1) $\text{ln}(e)$ = the number of instructions in program P_e;

(2) $$\text{gn}(e, j) = \begin{cases} \text{the code number of the } j\text{th instruction in } P_e, & \text{if } 1 \le j \le \text{ln}(e), \\ 0 & \text{otherwise;} \end{cases}$$

(3) $\text{ch}(c, z)$ = the configuration resulting when the configuration c is operated on by the instruction with code number z;

(4) $$\nu(c, j, z) = \begin{cases} \text{the number } j' \text{ of the `next instruction for the computation' when the configuration } c \text{ is operated on by the instruction with code } z\text{, and this occurs as the } j\text{th instruction in a program,} & \text{if } j > 0, \\ 0 & \text{otherwise} \end{cases}$$

(The 'next instruction for the computation' here is as defined in chapter 1 § 2, so $j' = j+1$ or, if I_j is a jump instruction $J(m_1, m_2, q)$ we may have $j' = q$.)

If these four functions are primitive recursive, then remembering that $\sigma = \pi(c, j)$ where $c = \pi_1(\sigma)$ and $j = \pi_2(\sigma)$ we have

$$\text{config}(e, \sigma) = \begin{cases} \text{ch}(\pi_1(\sigma), \text{gn}(e, \pi_2(\sigma))) & \text{if } 1 \le \pi_2(\sigma) \le \text{ln}(e), \\ \pi_1(\sigma) & \text{otherwise.} \end{cases}$$

$$\mathrm{nxt}(e,\sigma)=\begin{cases}\nu(\pi_1(\sigma),\pi_2(\sigma),\mathrm{gn}(e,\pi_2(\sigma))) & \text{if this number is} \leq \ln(e),\\ 0 & \text{otherwise.}\end{cases}$$

Thus config and nxt are primitive recursive, by the methods of chapter 2.

It remains to show that the functions (1)–(4) above are primitive recursive. A sequence of auxiliary functions is needed to decode the code numbers of programs and instructions. We use freely the standard functions and techniques of chapter 2 §§ 1–4, together with the functions defined in chapter 4 § 1 for coding instructions and programs.

(5) The functions $\alpha(i,x)$, $l(x)$, $b(i,x)$ and $a(i,x)$ of exercise 2-4.16(5) are primitive recursive.

Proof. (i) $x=\sum_{i=0}^{\infty}\alpha(i,x)2^i$; so we have $\mathrm{qt}(2^i,x)=\alpha(i,x)+\alpha(i+1,x)2+\ldots$ and hence $\alpha(i,x)=\mathrm{rm}(2,\mathrm{qt}(2^i,x))$.

(ii) $l(x)=$ number of *i*s such that $\alpha(i,x)=1$; hence

$$l(x)=\sum_{i<x}\alpha(i,x).$$

(iii) If $x>0$, $x=2^{b(1,x)}+2^{b(2,x)}+\ldots+2^{b(l(x),x)}$; thus, if $1\leq i\leq l(x)$, then $b(i,x)$ is the *i*th index k such that $\alpha(k,x)=1$. Hence

$$b(i,x)=\begin{cases}\mu y<x\left(\sum_{k\leq y}\alpha(k,x)=i\right) & \text{if } 1\leq i\leq l(x) \text{ and } x>0,\\ 0 & \text{otherwise.}\end{cases}$$

(iv) From the definition:

$$a(i,x)=b(i,x) \qquad (i=0,1)$$

$$a(i+1,x)=(b(i+1,x)\dot{-}b(i,x))\dot{-}1 \qquad (i\geq 1)$$

From the above explicit formulae, using the techniques of chapter 2, these functions are all primitive recursive.

(6) The functions $\ln(e)$ and $\mathrm{gn}(e,j)$ are primitive recursive.

Proof. From the definitions of the coding function γ:

$\ln(e)=l(e+1)$,

$\mathrm{gn}(e,j)=a(j,e+1)$,

where l and a are the functions in (5).

(7) There are primitive recursive functions u, u_1, u_2, v_1, v_2, v_3 such that:

if $z=\beta(\mathrm{Z}(m))$, then $u(z)=m$,

if $z=\beta(\mathrm{S}(m))$, then $u(z)=m$,

if $z=\beta(\mathrm{T}(m_1,m_2))$, then $u_1(z)=m_1$ and $u_2(z)=m_2$,

if $z=\beta(\mathrm{J}(m_1,m_2,q))$, then $v_1(z)=m_1$, $v_2(z)=m_2$, and $v_3(z)=q$.

Proof. From the definition of β, and writing $(z/4)$ for $\mathrm{qt}(4, z)$, take

$$u(z) = (z/4) + 1,$$

$$u_1(z) = \pi_1(z/4) + 1,$$

$$u_2(z) = \pi_2(z/4) + 1,$$

$$v_1(z) = \pi_1(\pi_1(z/4)) + 1,$$

$$v_2(z) = \pi_2(\pi_1(z/4)) + 1,$$

$$v_3(z) = \pi_2(z/4) + 1.$$

(8) The following functions are primitive recursive:

(i) $\mathrm{zero}(c, m)$ = the change in the configuration c effected by instruction $Z(m)$,
$= \mathrm{qt}(\mathrm{p}_m^{(c)_m}, c)$.

(ii) $\mathrm{suc}(c, m)$ = the change in the configuration c effected by instruction $S(m)$,
$= c\mathrm{p}_m$.

(iii) $\mathrm{transfer}(c, m, n)$ = the change in the configuration c effected by instruction $T(m, n)$,
$= \mathrm{qt}(\mathrm{p}_n^{(c)_n}, c\mathrm{p}_n^{(c)_m})$.

(9) The function $\mathrm{ch}(c, z)$ (defined in (3) above) is primitive recursive.
Proof.

$$\mathrm{ch}(c, z) = \begin{cases} \mathrm{zero}(c, u(z)) & \text{if } \mathrm{rm}(4, z) = 0 \text{ (i.e. } z \text{ is the code of a zero instruction),} \\ \mathrm{suc}(c, u(z)) & \text{if } \mathrm{rm}(4, z) = 1 \text{ (i.e. } z \text{ is the code of a successor instruction),} \\ \mathrm{transfer}(c, u_1(z), u_2(z)) & \text{if } \mathrm{rm}(4, z) = 2 \text{ (i.e. } z \text{ is the code of a transfer instruction),} \\ c & \text{otherwise.} \end{cases}$$

(10) The function $\nu(c, j, z)$ (defined in (4) above) is primitive recursive.

Proof. We have

$$\nu(c,j,z)=\begin{cases} j+1 & \text{if } \mathrm{rm}(4,z)\neq 3 \text{ (i.e. } z \text{ is the code of an arithmetic instruction),} \\ \left.\begin{array}{ll} j+1 & \text{if } (c)_{v_1(z)}\neq (c)_{v_2(z)} \\ v_3(z) & \text{if } (c)_{v_1(z)}=(c)_{v_2(z)} \end{array}\right\} & \text{if } \mathrm{rm}(4,z)=3 \text{ (i.e. } z \text{ is the code of a jump instruction).} \end{cases}$$

From this definition by cases, we see that ν is primitive recursive.

We have now shown that the functions (1)–(4) above are primitive recursive, so the proof of the theorem is complete. □

6

Decidability, undecidability and partial decidability

In previous chapters we have noted several decidable problems, but so far we have encountered only one explicit example of undecidability: the problem 'ϕ_x is total' (theorem 5-2.1). It is of considerable interest to identify decidable and undecidable problems; the latter, particularly, indicate the limitations of computability, and hence demonstrate the theoretical limits to the power of real world computers.

In this chapter the emphasis is largely on undecidability. In § 1 we give a survey of undecidable problems arising in the theory of computability itself, and discuss some methods for establishing undecidability. Sections 2–5 are devoted to a sample of decidable and undecidable problems from other areas of mathematics: these sections will not be needed in later chapters and may be omitted. In the final section we discuss *partial decidability*, a notion closely related to decidability.

Let us recall from chapter 1 that a predicate $M(\mathbf{x})$ is said to be *decidable* if its characteristic function c_M, given by

$$c_M(\mathbf{x}) = \begin{cases} 1 & \text{if } M(\mathbf{x}) \text{ holds,} \\ 0 & \text{if } M(\mathbf{x}) \text{ does not hold,} \end{cases}$$

is computable. This is the same as saying that $M(\mathbf{x})$ is recursive (see chapter 3 § 2). The predicate $M(\mathbf{x})$ is *undecidable* if it is not decidable. In the literature all of the following phrases are used to mean that $M(\mathbf{x})$ is decidable.

$M(\mathbf{x})$ is *recursively decidable*,

$M(\mathbf{x})$ has *recursive decision problem*,

$M(\mathbf{x})$ is *solvable*,

$M(\mathbf{x})$ is *recursively solvable*,

$M(\mathbf{x})$ is *computable.*

An algorithm for computing c_M is called a *decision procedure* for $M(\mathbf{x})$.

1. Undecidable problems in computability

Most proofs of undecidability rest on a diagonal construction, as in the following important example.

1.1. *Theorem*

'$x \in W_x$' (or, equivalently, '$\phi_x(x)$ is defined', or '$P_x(x)\downarrow$', or '$\psi_U(x, x)$ is defined') is undecidable.

Proof. The characteristic function f of this problem is given by

$$f(x) = \begin{cases} 1 & \text{if } x \in W_x, \\ 0 & \text{if } x \notin W_x. \end{cases}$$

Suppose that f is computable; we shall obtain a contradiction. Specifically, we make a diagonal construction of a *computable* function g such that $\mathrm{Dom}(g) \neq W_x (= \mathrm{Dom}(\phi_x))$ for every x; this is obviously contradictory.

The diagonal motto tells us to ensure that $\mathrm{Dom}(g)$ differs from W_x at x; so we aim to make

$$x \in \mathrm{Dom}(g) \Leftrightarrow x \notin W_x.$$

Let us define g, then, by

$$g(x) = \begin{cases} 0 & \text{if } x \notin W_x \text{ (i.e. if } f(x) = 0), \\ \text{undefined} & \text{if } x \in W_x \text{ (i.e. if } f(x) = 1). \end{cases}$$

Since f is computable, then so is g (by Church's thesis); so we have our contradiction. (To see this in detail: since g is computable take m such that $g = \phi_m$; then $m \in W_m \Leftrightarrow m \in \mathrm{Dom}(g) \Leftrightarrow m \notin W_m$, a contradiction).

We conclude that f is *not* computable, and so the problem '$x \in W_x$' is undecidable. □

Note that this theorem does *not* say that we cannot tell for any *particular* number a whether $\phi_a(a)$ is defined. For some numbers this is quite simple; for instance, if we have written a program P that computes a total function, and $P = P_a$, then we know immediately that $\phi_a(a)$ is defined. What the theorem says is that there is no single *general* method for deciding whether $\phi_x(x)$ is defined; i.e. there is no method that works for *every* x.

An easy corollary to the above result is

1.2. *Corollary*

There is a computable function h such that the problems '$x \in \mathrm{Dom}(h)$' and '$x \in \mathrm{Ran}(h)$' are both undecidable.

Proof. Let

$$h(x)=\begin{cases} x & \text{if } x\in W_x,\\ \text{undefined} & \text{if } x\notin W_x.\end{cases}$$

Then h is computable, by Church's thesis and the computability of the universal function ψ_U (or, formally, we have that $h(x)\simeq x\,\mathbf{1}(\psi_U(x,x))$ which is computable by substitution). Clearly we have $x\in \text{Dom}(h) \Leftrightarrow x\in W_x \Leftrightarrow x\in \text{Ran}(h)$, so the problems '$x\in\text{Dom}(h)$' and '$x\in\text{Ran}(h)$' are undecidable. □

Another important undecidable problem is derived easily from theorem 1.1:

1.3. *Theorem* (the Halting problem)

The problem '$\phi_x(y)$ is defined' (or, equivalently '$P_x(y)\downarrow$' or '$y\in W_x$') is undecidable.

Proof. Arguing informally, if the problem '$\phi_x(y)$ is defined' is decidable then so is the problem '$\phi_x(x)$ is defined', which is if anything easier. But this contradicts theorem 1.1.

Giving this argument in full detail, let g be the characteristic function for '$\phi_x(y)$ is defined'; i.e.

$$g(x,y)=\begin{cases}1 & \text{if } \phi_x(y) \text{ is defined},\\ 0 & \text{if } \phi_x(y) \text{ is not defined}.\end{cases}$$

If g is computable, then so is the function $f(x)=g(x,x)$; but f is the characteristic function of '$x\in W_x$', and is not computable by theorem 1.1. Hence g is not computable; so '$\phi_x(y)$ is defined' is undecidable. □

Theorem 1.3 is often described as the Unsolvability of the Halting problem (for URM programs): there is no effective general method for discovering whether a given program running on a given input eventually halts. The implication of this for the theory of computer programming is obvious: there can be no perfectly general method for checking programs to see if they are free from possible infinite loops.

The undecidable problem '$x\in W_x$' of theorem 1.1 is important for several reasons. Among these is the fact that many problems can be shown to be undecidable by showing that they are at least as difficult as this one. We have already done this in a simple way in showing that the Halting problem is undecidable (theorem 1.3): this process is known as *reducing* one problem to another.

Speaking generally, consider a problem $M(x)$. Often we can show that a solution to the general problem $M(x)$ would lead to a solution to the general problem '$x \in W_x$'. Then we say that the problem '$x \in W_x$' is *reduced* to the problem $M(x)$. In other words, we can give a decision procedure for '$x \in W_x$' if only we could find one for $M(x)$. In this case, the decidability of $M(x)$ implies the decidability of '$x \in W_x$', from which we conclude immediately that $M(x)$ is undecidable.

The *s–m–n* theorem is often useful in reducing '$x \in W_x$' to other problems, as illustrated in the proof of the next result.

1.4. *Theorem*

The problem '$\phi_x = \mathbf{0}$' is undecidable.

Proof. Consider the function f defined by

$$f(x, y) = \begin{cases} 0 & \text{if } x \in W_x, \\ \text{undefined} & \text{if } x \notin W_x. \end{cases}$$

We have defined f anticipating that we shall use the *s–m–n* theorem; thus we are thinking of x as a parameter, and are concerned about the functions g_x where $g_x(y) \simeq f(x, y)$. We have actually designed f so that $g_x = \mathbf{0} \Leftrightarrow x \in W_x$.

By Church's thesis (or by substitution using $\mathbf{0}$ and ψ_U) f is computable; so there is a total computable function $k(x)$ given by the *s–m–n* theorem such that $f(x, y) \simeq \phi_{k(x)}(y)$; i.e. $\phi_{k(x)} = g_x$. Thus from the definition of f we see that

(*) $\quad x \in W_x \Leftrightarrow \phi_{k(x)} = \mathbf{0}$.

Hence, a particular question Is $x \in W_x$? can be settled by answering the question Is $\phi_{k(x)} = \mathbf{0}$? We have thus reduced the general problem '$x \in W_x$' to the general problem '$\phi_x = \mathbf{0}$'; the former is undecidable, hence so is the latter, as was to be proved.

Let us present the final part of this argument in more detail as it is the first example of its kind. Let g be the characteristic function of '$\phi_x = \mathbf{0}$'; i.e.

$$g(x) = \begin{cases} 1 & \text{if } \phi_x = \mathbf{0}, \\ 0 & \text{if } \phi_x \neq \mathbf{0}. \end{cases}$$

Suppose that g is computable; then so is the function $h(x) = g(k(x))$. But from (*) above we have

$$h(x) = \begin{cases} 1 & \text{if } \phi_{k(x)} = \mathbf{0}; \text{ i.e. } x \in W_x, \\ 0 & \text{if } \phi_{k(x)} \neq \mathbf{0}; \text{ i.e. } x \notin W_x. \end{cases}$$

So by theorem 1.1 h is *not* computable. Hence g is not computable, and the problem '$\phi_x = \mathbf{0}$' is undecidable. □

From theorem 1.4 we can see that there are inherent limitations when it comes to checking the correctness of computer programs; this theorem shows that there can be no perfectly general effective method for checking whether a program will compute the zero function. By adapting the proof of theorem 1.4 we can see that the same is true for any particular computable function (see exercise 1.8(1*i*) below).

The following easy corollary to theorem 1.4 shows that the question of whether two programs compute the same unary function is undecidable. Again there are obvious implications for computer programming theory.

1.5. *Corollary*

The problem '$\phi_x = \phi_y$' is undecidable.

Proof. We can easily see that this is a harder problem than the problem '$\phi_x = \mathbf{0}$'.

Let c be a number such that $\phi_c = \mathbf{0}$; if $f(x, y)$ is the characteristic function of the problem $\phi_x = \phi_y$, then the function $g(x) = f(x, c)$ is the characteristic function of '$\phi_x = \mathbf{0}$'. By theorem 1.4, g is not computable, so neither is f. Thus '$\phi_x = \phi_y$' is undecidable. □

We use the *s–m–n* theorem again to reduce the problem '$x \in W_x$' in the following results.

1.6. *Theorem*

Let c be any number. The following problems are undecidable.

(*a*) (the Input or Acceptance problem) '$c \in W_x$' (*equivalently*, '$P_x(c)\downarrow$' *or* '$c \in \mathrm{Dom}(\phi_x)$'),

(*b*) (the Output or Printing problem) '$c \in E_x$' (*equivalently*, '$c \in \mathrm{Ran}(\phi_x)$').

Proof. We are able to reduce '$x \in W_x$' to these problems simultaneously. Consider the function $f(x, y)$ given by

$$f(x, y) = \begin{cases} y & \text{if } x \in W_x, \\ \text{undefined} & \text{otherwise.} \end{cases}$$

(With the *s–m–n* theorem in mind, we are concerned about the functions g_x where $g_x(y) \simeq f(x, y)$: we have designed f so that $c \in \mathrm{Dom}(g_x) \Leftrightarrow$

$x \in W_x \Leftrightarrow c \in \text{Ran}(g_x)$.) By Church's thesis f is computable, and so the s–m–n theorem provides a total computable function k such that $f(x, y) \simeq \phi_{k(x)}(y)$. From the definition of f we see that

$$x \in W_x \Rightarrow W_{k(x)} = E_{k(x)} = \mathbb{N}, \text{ so } c \in W_{k(x)} \text{ and } c \in E_{k(x)};$$

and

$$x \notin W_x \Rightarrow W_{k(x)} = E_{k(x)} = \varnothing, \text{ so } c \notin W_{k(x)} \text{ and } c \notin E_{k(x)}.$$

Thus we have reduced the problem '$x \in W_x$' to each of the problems '$c \in W_x$' and '$c \in E_x$'.

Completing the proof of (a) in detail, we see that if g is the characteristic function of '$c \in W_x$', then

$$g(k(x)) = \begin{cases} 1 & \text{if } x \in W_x, \\ 0 & \text{if } x \notin W_x. \end{cases}$$

This function is not computable (theorem 1.1), so g cannot be computable. Hence '$c \in W_x$' is undecidable.

A detailed proof of (b) is similar. □

We conclude this section with a very general undecidability result, from which theorems 1.4 and 1.6 follow immediately. It is another use of the s–m–n theorem to reduce '$x \in W_x$'.

1.7. *Theorem* (Rice's theorem)

Suppose that $\mathcal{B} \subseteq \mathcal{C}_1$, and $\mathcal{B} \neq \varnothing, \mathcal{C}_1$. Then the problem '$\phi_x \in \mathcal{B}$' is undecidable.

Proof. From the algebra of decidability (theorem 2-4.7) we know that '$\phi_x \in \mathcal{B}$' is decidable iff '$\phi_x \in \mathcal{C}_1 \backslash \mathcal{B}$' is decidable; so we may assume without any loss of generality that the function $f_\varnothing$ that is nowhere defined does not belong to $\mathcal{B}$ (if not, prove the result for $\mathcal{C}_1 \backslash \mathcal{B}$).

Choose a function $g \in \mathcal{B}$. Consider the function $f(x, y)$ defined by

$$f(x, y) \simeq \begin{cases} g(y) & \text{if } x \in W_x, \\ \text{undefined} & \text{if } x \notin W_x. \end{cases}$$

The s–m–n theorem provides a total computable function $k(x)$ such that $f(x, y) \simeq \phi_{k(x)}(y)$. Thus we see that

$$x \in W_x \Rightarrow \phi_{k(x)} = g, \text{ i.e. } \phi_{k(x)} \in \mathcal{B};$$

$$x \notin W_x \Rightarrow \phi_{k(x)} = f_\varnothing, \text{ i.e. } \phi_{k(x)} \notin \mathcal{B}.$$

So we have reduced the problem '$x \in W_x$' to the problem '$\phi_x \in \mathcal{B}$' using the computable function k. In the standard way we conclude that '$\phi_x \in \mathcal{B}$' is undecidable. □

Theorem 1.4, for example, is obtained immediately from Rice's theorem by taking $\mathscr{B}=\{\mathbf{0}\}$, and theorem 1.6($a$) by taking $\mathscr{B}=\{g\in\mathscr{C}_1 : c\in \mathrm{Dom}(g)\}$. Rice's theorem may be similarly applied in several of the exercises below.

1.8. *Exercises*

1. Show that the following problems are undecidable.
   (a) '$x\in E_x$' (*Hint.* Either use a direct diagonal construction, or reduce '$x\in W_x$' to this problem using the s–m–n theorem.),
   (b) '$W_x = W_y$' (*Hint.* Reduce 'ϕ_x is total' to this problem.),
   (c) '$\phi_x(x)=0$',
   (d) '$\phi_x(y)=0$',
   (e) '$x\in E_y$',
   (f) 'ϕ_x is total and constant',
   (g) '$W_x=\varnothing$',
   (h) 'E_x is infinite'.
   (i) '$\phi_x = g$', where g is any fixed computable function.
2. Show that there is no total computable function $f(x, y)$ with the following property: if $P_x(y)$ stops, then it does so in $f(x, y)$ or fewer steps. (*Hint.* Show that if such a function exists, then the Halting problem is decidable.)

Decidability and undecidability in other areas of mathematics In many areas of mathematics there arise general problems for which the informal idea of decidability is meaningful. Generally such problems involve finite objects from a particular field of study. The idea of decidability of some property involving these objects can always be made precise using a suitable coding by natural numbers.

Much research has been directed towards identifying both decidable and undecidable problems in a variety of mathematical situations: in the next sections we give a small sample of the results that have been obtained.

2. The word problem for groups[1]

Suppose that G is a group with identity element 1, and that G is generated by a set of elements $S=\{g_1, g_2, g_3, \ldots\}\subseteq G$. A *word* on S is

[1] The reader with no knowledge of group theory should omit this section.

any expression such as $g_2^{-1}g_3^6g_1g_2^5g_8$ involving the elements of S and the group operations. Each word represents an element of G, and to say that G is *generated* by S means that every element of G is represented by some word on S.

The *word problem* for G (relative to S) is the problem of deciding for which words w on S is it the case that $w = 1$.

There are many groups with decidable word problem: for example any finite group (with S finite, of course). For many years mathematicians searched for an example of a *finitely presented*[2] group with *un*decidable word problem. Eventually it was shown by Novikov in 1955 and Boone in 1957 that such groups do exist. Proofs of the Novikov–Boone Theorem are beyond the scope of this survey: the reader is referred to expositions in Rotman [1965] or Manin [1977].

Group theory, and modern algebra in general, abounds with interesting decidable and undecidable problems; a great many of them involve properties of words or generators akin to the basic word problem for groups.

3. Diophantine equations

Suppose that $p(x_1, x_2, \ldots, x_n)$ is a polynomial in the variables $x_1, \ldots, x_n$, with integer coefficients. Then the equation

$$p(x_1, x_2, \ldots, x_n) = 0$$

for which *integer* solutions are sought is called a *diophantine equation*. Diophantine equations do not always have solutions: for instance the equation $x^2 - 2 = 0$.

Hilbert's tenth problem, posed in 1900, asks whether there is an effective procedure that will determine whether any given diophantine equation has a solution. It was shown in 1970 by Y. Matiyasevich that there is no such procedure; his proof was the culmination of earlier work by M. Davis, J. Robinson and H. Putnam.

Actually Matiyasevich established rather more than the unsolvability of Hilbert's tenth problem; the full Matiyasevich theorem and its application to Hilbert's tenth problem are discussed in § 6. For complete details consult Davis [1973] or Manin [1977], or Bell & Machover [1977].

[2] A group G is *finitely presented* if there is a finite set of generators S and a finite set B of *relations* of the form $w = 1$ (where w is a word on S) such that (i) all relations in B are true in G, and (ii) all other relations holding in G can be deduced from those in B by using the group axioms alone.

4. Sturm's algorithm

To redress the emphasis on undecidability in the previous two sections, we now mention a theorem of Sturm that gives us positive results for computability and decidability in connection with the zeros of polynomials.

4.1. *Sturm's theorem*

Let $p(x)$ be a real polynomial, and let $p_0, p_1, \ldots, p_r$ be the sequence of real polynomials given by

(*a*) $p_0 = 0$,

(*b*) $p_1 = p'$ (*the derivative of* p),

(*c*) *for* $0 < i < r$, *there is a polynomial* q_i *such that* $p_{i-1} = p_i q_i - p_{i+1}$ *with* $p_{i+1} \neq 0$ *and* $\text{degree}(p_{i+1}) < \text{degree}(p_i)$ (*so that* q_i *and* $-p_{i+1}$ *are the quotient and remainder respectively when* p_{i-1} *is divided by* p_i),

(*d*) $p_{r-1} = p_r q_r$.

For any real number c denote by $\delta(c)$ *the number of sign changes in the sequence* $p_0(c), \ldots, p_r(c)$ (*ignoring zeros*).

Suppose that a, b are real numbers that are not zeros of $p(x)$, *and* $a < b$. *Then the number of zeros of* $p(x)$ *in the interval* $[a, b]$ *is* $\delta(a) - \delta(b)$, (*each zero being counted once only*).

This is not the place to give a proof of Sturm's theorem, which the reader may find clearly expounded in Cohn [1977] or Van der Waerden [1949]. From our point of view, Sturm's theorem is interesting because of the algorithm it embodies. It gives us positive results about the *computability* of the number of zeros of a polynomial, and the *decidability* of statements about zeros of polynomials.

To frame such results, we must restrict attention to polynomials over the rational numbers, denoted by $\mathbb{Q}$, so that the objects we are dealing with are finite. Thus we are thinking in terms of computability over the domain $\mathbb{Q}$ (which can be defined in terms of computability on $\mathbb{N}$ by the usual coding device); note that a polynomial $p(x)$ with coefficients in $\mathbb{Q}$ is essentially a sequence of rational numbers.

A sample of the results that follow from Sturm's theorem is the following.

4.2. *Theorem*

(*a*) *There is an effective procedure for calculating the number of real zeros of a polynomial over* $\mathbb{Q}$;

(*b*) *The predicate 'p has a zero in* $[a, b]$*' is decidable, where p denotes a polynomial over* $\mathbb{Q}$ *and* $a, b \in \mathbb{Q}$.

Proof. Given any polynomial p, the polynomials $p_0, p_1, \ldots, p_r$ defined in Sturm's theorem may be found effectively by using the standard rules for differentiation and the division algorithm for polynomials.

For (*a*), it is a routine matter to find for any polynomial $p(x)$ a rational number $M > 0$ such that all the zeros of p lie in the interval $]-M, M[$. In fact, if $p(x) = a_0 + a_1x + \ldots + a_nx^n$, the number

$$M = 1 + \frac{1}{|a_n|}(|a_0| + \ldots + |a_{n-1}|)$$

suffices. Then by Sturm's theorem the number of zeros of p is $\delta(-M) - \delta(M)$ which may be calculated effectively.

For (*b*), suppose that we are given a polynomial p and rationals a, b. To decide whether p has a zero in $[a, b]$, first calculate $p(a)$ and $p(b)$; if neither of these is zero, calculate $\delta(a) - \delta(b)$ and apply Sturm's theorem. □

Of course, Sturm's theorem can be used to show that many other questions about polynomials over $\mathbb{Q}$ are computable or decidable.

4.3. *Exercise*

Show that there is an effective procedure, given a polynomial p and rational numbers a, b, for finding the number of zeros of p in $[a, b]$. (Remember that a or b may be zeros of p.)

5. Mathematical logic

Early investigations into the idea of effective computability were very much linked with the development of mathematical logic, because decidability was regarded as a basic question about any formalisation of mathematics. We shall describe some of the results that have been obtained in this area, in general terms that do not assume any acquaintance with mathematical logic. (The reader interested to learn the basics of this subject may consult one of the many introductory texts, such as Margaris [1966].)

The simplest logical system reflecting something of mathematical reasoning is the *propositional calculus*. In this calculus compound statements are formed from basic propositions using symbols for the logical connectives 'not', 'and', 'or', and 'implies'. It is quite easy, once the propositional calculus has been carefully defined, to see that it is *decidable*. By this we mean that there is an effective procedure for deciding whether a statement σ of the calculus is (*universally*) *valid*; i.e. true in all possible situations. The method of truth tables gives an algorithm for this that will be familiar to many readers.

A logical system that has greater expressive power than the propositional calculus is the (*first-order*) *predicate calculus*: using the language of this calculus it is possible to formalise a great deal of mathematics. The basic statements are formed from symbols representing individual objects (or elements) and predicates and functions of them. The compound statements are formed using the logical symbols of the propositional calculus together with $\forall$ and $\exists$.

There is a precise notion of a *proof* of a statement of the predicate calculus, such that a statement is provable if and only if it is valid.[3] In 1936 Church showed that provability (and hence validity) in the predicate calculus is *undecidable*, unlike the simpler propositional calculus. (This result was regarded by Hilbert as the most fundamental undecidability result for the whole of mathematics.)

We can use the URM to give an easy proof of the undecidability of validity, although this calls upon a certain familiarity with the predicate calculus. We advise the reader who does not have a rudimentary knowledge of predicate logic to omit the proof that we now sketch.

5.1. *Theorem*

Validity in the first-order predicate calculus is undecidable.

Proof. (Not advised for strangers to the predicate calculus.)

Let P be a program in standard form having instructions $I_1, \ldots, I_s$ and let $u = \rho(P)$ (as defined in chapter 2 § 2). We use the following symbols of the predicate calculus.

$\mathsf{0}$ a symbol for an individual,

$'$ a symbol for a unary function (whose value at x is x'),

R a symbol for a $(u+1)$-ary relation,

$\mathsf{x}_1, \mathsf{x}_2, \ldots \mathsf{x}_u, \mathsf{y}$ symbols for variable individuals.

The interpretation we have in mind is that $\mathsf{0}$ represents the number 0, $'$ represents the function $x+1$, and R represents the possible states of a computation under P. Thus if we write $\mathsf{1}$ for $\mathsf{0}'$, $\mathsf{2}$ for $\mathsf{0}''$, etc. the statement

$$\mathsf{R}(\mathsf{r}_1, \ldots, \mathsf{r}_u, \mathsf{k})$$

[3] This is described by saying that the notion of provability is *complete*, and is the content of Gödel's completeness theorem.

where $r_1, \ldots r_u, k \in \mathbb{N}$ means that the state

r_1	r_2	$\ldots$	r_u	0	0	$\ldots$

; next instruction I_k

occurs in the computation.

Now for each instruction I_i we can write down a statement τ_i of the predicate calculus that describes the effect of I_i on states, using the symbol $\wedge$ for 'and' and $\rightarrow$ for 'implies':

(*a*) if $I_i = Z(n)$ let τ_i be the statement

$$\forall x_1 \ldots \forall x_u\colon \mathsf{R}(x_1, \ldots, x_n, \ldots, x_u, i) \rightarrow \mathsf{R}(x_1, \ldots, 0, \ldots, x_u, i').$$

(*b*) If $I_i = S(n)$ let τ_i be the statement

$$\forall x_1 \ldots \forall x_u\colon \mathsf{R}(x_1, \ldots, x_n, \ldots, x_u, i) \rightarrow \mathsf{R}(x_1, \ldots, x_n', \ldots, x_u, i').$$

(*c*) If $I_i = T(m, n)$ let τ_i be the statement

$$\forall x_1 \ldots \forall x_u\colon \mathsf{R}(x_1, \ldots, x_n, \ldots, x_u, i) \rightarrow \mathsf{R}(x_1, \ldots, x_m, \ldots, x_u, i').$$

(*d*) If $I_i = J(m, n, q)$ let τ_i be the statement

$$\forall x_1 \ldots \forall x_u\colon \mathsf{R}(x_1, \ldots, x_u, i) \rightarrow ((x_m = x_n \rightarrow \mathsf{R}(x_1, \ldots, x_u, q)) \wedge (x_m \neq x_n \rightarrow \mathsf{R}(x_1, \ldots, x_u, i'))).$$

Now for any $a \in \mathbb{N}$ let σ_a be the statement

$$(\tau_0 \wedge \tau_1 \wedge \ldots \wedge \tau_s \wedge \mathsf{R}(a, 0, \ldots, 0, 1)) \rightarrow \exists x_1 \ldots \exists x_u\, \mathsf{R}(x_1, \ldots, x_u, s+1),$$

where τ_0 is the statement $\forall x \forall y((x' = y' \rightarrow x = y) \wedge x' \neq 0)$. (This ensures that in any interpretation, if $m, n \in \mathbb{N}$ and $\mathsf{m} = \mathsf{n}$ then $m = n$.)

The statement $\mathsf{R}(a, 0, \ldots, 0, 1)$ corresponds to a starting state

a	0	0	$\ldots$

; next instruction I_1,

and any statement $\mathsf{R}(x_1, \ldots, x_u, s+1)$ corresponds to a halting state (since there is no instruction I_{s+1}). Thus we shall see that

(*) $\quad P(a){\downarrow} \Leftrightarrow \sigma_a$ is valid.

Suppose first that $P(a){\downarrow}$, and that we have a structure in which $\tau_0, \ldots, \tau_s$ and $\mathsf{R}(a, 0, \ldots, 0, 1)$ hold. Using the statements $\tau_0, \ldots, \tau_s$ we find that each of the statements $\mathsf{R}(r_1, \ldots, r_u, k)$ corresponding to the successive states in the computation also holds. Eventually we find that a halting statement $\mathsf{R}(b_1, \ldots, b_u, s+1)$ holds, for some $b_1, \ldots, b_u \in \mathbb{N}$, and hence $\exists x_1 \ldots \exists x_u\, \mathsf{R}(x_1, \ldots, x_u, s+1)$ holds. Thus σ_a is valid.

Conversely, if σ_a is valid, it holds in particular in the structure $\mathbb{N}$ with the predicate symbol R interpreted by the predicate R_a where

$$R_a(a_1, \ldots, a_u, k) \equiv \text{At some stage in the computation } P(a) \text{ the registers contain } a_1, a_2, \ldots, a_u, 0, 0, \ldots \text{ and the next instruction is } I_k.$$

Then $\tau_0, \ldots, \tau_s$ and $\mathsf{R}(\mathsf{a}, 0, \ldots, 0, 1)$ all hold in this structure, hence so does $\exists \mathsf{x}_1 \ldots \exists \mathsf{x}_u\, \mathsf{R}(\mathsf{x}_1, \ldots, \mathsf{x}_u, \mathsf{s}+1)$. Therefore $P(a)\downarrow$.

If we take P to be a program that computes the function $\psi_U(x, x)$, the equivalence (*) gives a reduction of the problem '$x \in W_x$' to the problem 'σ is valid'. Hence the latter is undecidable. □

The field of mathematical logic abounds with decidability and undecidability results. A common type of problem that arises is whether a statement is true in all mathematical structures of a certain kind. It has been shown, for example, that the problem

'σ is a statement that is true in all groups'

is undecidable (here σ is a statement of the first-order predicate language appropriate to groups), whereas the problem

'σ is a statement that is true in all abelian groups'

is decidable. (We say that the first-order theory of groups is *undecidable* whereas the first-order theory of abelian groups is *decidable*.) It was shown by Tarski [1951] that the problem

'σ is true in the field of real numbers'

is decidable. On the other hand, many problems connected with the formalisation of ordinary arithmetic on the natural numbers are undecidable, as we shall see in chapter 8.

For further examples and proofs of decidability and undecidability results in logic the reader should consult books such as Tarski, Mostowski & Robinson [1953], or Boolos & Jeffrey [1974].

6. Partially decidable predicates

Although the predicate '$x \in W_x$' has non-computable characteristic function, the following function connected with this problem *is* computable:

$$f(x) = \begin{cases} 1 & \text{if } x \in W_x, \\ \text{undefined} & \text{if } x \notin W_x. \end{cases}$$

If we continue to think of 1 as a code for Yes, then any algorithm for f is a procedure that gives answer Yes when $x \in W_x$, but goes on for ever when $x \in W_x$ does not hold. Such a procedure is called a *partial decision procedure* for the problem '$x \in W_x$', and we say that this problem or predicate is *partially decidable.*

Many undecidable predicates turn out to be partially decidable: let us formulate the general definition.

6.1. *Definition*

A predicate $M(\mathbf{x})$ of natural numbers is *partially decidable* if the function f given by

$$f(\mathbf{x}) = \begin{cases} 1 & \text{if } M(\mathbf{x}) \text{ holds,} \\ \text{undefined} & \text{if } M(\mathbf{x}) \text{ does not hold,} \end{cases}$$

is computable. (This function is called the *partial characteristic function* for M.) If M is partially decidable, any algorithm for computing f is called a *partial decision procedure* for M.

Note. In the literature the terms *partially solvable*, *semi-computable*, and *recursively enumerable*[4] are used with the same meaning as partially decidable.

6.2. *Examples*

1. The Halting problem (theorem 1.3) is partially decidable, since its partial characteristic function

   $$f(x, y) = \begin{cases} 1 & \text{if } P_x(y)\downarrow, \\ \text{undefined} & \text{otherwise,} \end{cases}$$

   is computable, by Church's thesis (or by observing that $f(x, y) \simeq \mathbf{1}(\psi_U(x, y))$).
2. Any decidable predicate is partially decidable: simply arrange for the decision procedure to enter a loop whenever it gives output 0.
3. For any computable function $g(\mathbf{x})$ the problem '$\mathbf{x} \in \mathrm{Dom}(g)$' is partially decidable, since it has the computable partial characteristic function $\mathbf{1}(g(\mathbf{x}))$. (Cf. corollary 1.2.)
4. The problem '$x \notin W_x$' is *not* partially decidable: for if f is its partial characteristic function, then

   $$x \in \mathrm{Dom}(f) \Leftrightarrow x \notin W_x.$$

   Thus $\mathrm{Dom}(f)$ differs from the domain of every unary computable function: hence f is not computable.

[4] The reason for the use of this term will be explained in the next chapter.

We proceed to establish some of the important characteristics of partially decidable predicates. First we have the alternative characterisation that is given essentially in example 6.2(3) above.

6.3. *Theorem*

A predicate $M(\mathbf{x})$ is partially decidable if and only if there is a computable function $g(\mathbf{x})$ such that

$$M(\mathbf{x}) \quad \textit{iff} \ \mathbf{x} \in \mathrm{Dom}(g).$$

Proof. If $M(\mathbf{x})$ is partially decidable with computable partial characteristic function $f(\mathbf{x})$, then from the definition we have $M(\mathbf{x})$ iff $\mathbf{x} \in \mathrm{Dom}(f)$. The converse is given by example 6.2(3) above. □

The following characterisation of partially decidable predicates shows how they are related to decidable predicates.

6.4. *Theorem*

A predicate $M(\mathbf{x})$ is partially decidable if and only if there is a decidable predicate $R(\mathbf{x}, y)$ such that

$$M(\mathbf{x}) \quad \textit{iff} \ \exists y R(\mathbf{x}, y).$$

Proof. Suppose that $R(\mathbf{x}, y)$ is a decidable predicate and that $M(\mathbf{x})$ iff $\exists y R(\mathbf{x}, y)$. By corollary 2-5.3 the function $g(\mathbf{x}) \simeq \mu y R(\mathbf{x}, y)$ is computable; clearly

$$M(\mathbf{x}) \Leftrightarrow \mathbf{x} \in \mathrm{Dom}(g),$$

so $M(\mathbf{x})$ is partially decidable by theorem 6.3.

For the converse, suppose that $M(\mathbf{x})$ is partially decidable, with partial decision procedure given by a program P. Define a predicate $R(\mathbf{x}, y)$ by

$$R(\mathbf{x}, y) \equiv P(\mathbf{x})\downarrow \text{ in } y \text{ steps.}$$

By corollary 5-1.3, $R(\mathbf{x}, y)$ is decidable. Moreover,

$$\begin{aligned} M(\mathbf{x}) &\Leftrightarrow P(\mathbf{x})\downarrow \\ &\Leftrightarrow \exists y R(\mathbf{x}, y) \end{aligned}$$

as required. □

Note. From the appendix to chapter 5 it follows that the predicate R in this characterisation may be taken to be primitive recursive (see the note 1 following corollary 5-1.4).

The characterisation given by theorem 6.4 indicates an important way to think of partially decidable predicates. It shows that partial decision procedures can always be cast in the form of an unbounded search for a number y having some decidable property $R(\mathbf{x}, y)$. This search is most naturally carried out by examining successively $y = 0, 1, 2, \ldots$ to find such a y. The search halts if and when y is found such that $R(\mathbf{x}, y)$ holds; otherwise the search goes on for ever.

We can use theorem 6.4 to establish some further properties of partially decidable predicates, that aid us in their recognition.

6.5. *Theorem*

If $M(\mathbf{x}, y)$ is partially decidable, then so is the predicate $\exists y M(\mathbf{x}, y)$.

Proof. Take a decidable predicate $R(\mathbf{x}, y, z)$ such that $M(\mathbf{x}, y)$ iff $\exists z R(\mathbf{x}, y, z)$. Then we have

$$\exists y M(\mathbf{x}, y) \Leftrightarrow \exists y \exists z R(\mathbf{x}, y, z).$$

We can use the standard technique of coding the pair of numbers y, z by the single number $u = 2^y 3^z$; then the search for a pair y, z such that $R(\mathbf{x}, y, z)$ reduces to the search for a single number u such that $R(\mathbf{x}, (u)_1, (u)_2)$, i.e.

$$\exists y M(\mathbf{x}, y) \Leftrightarrow \exists u R(\mathbf{x}, (u)_1, (u)_2).$$

The predicate $S(\mathbf{x}, u) \equiv R(\mathbf{x}, (u)_1, (u)_2)$ is decidable (by substitution) and so by theorem 6.4 $\exists y M(\mathbf{x}, y)$ is partially decidable. □

Theorem 6.5 is described by saying that partially decidable predicates are *closed under existential quantification*. Its repeated application gives

6.6. *Corollary*

If $M(\mathbf{x}, \mathbf{y})$ is partially decidable, where $\mathbf{y} = (y_1, \ldots, y_m)$, then so is the predicate $\exists y_1 \ldots \exists y_m M(\mathbf{x}, y_1, \ldots, y_m)$.

Let us now consider some applications of the above results.

6.7. *Examples*

1. The following predicates are partially decidable.
   (*a*) $x \in E_y^{(n)}$ (n fixed). (The Printing problem: cf. theorem 1.6.)
   (*b*) $W_x \neq \varnothing$ (Cf. exercise 1.8(1*g*).)

   Proofs

   (*a*) $x \in E_y^{(n)} \Leftrightarrow \exists z_1 \ldots \exists z_n \exists t (P_y(z_1, \ldots, z_n)\downarrow x$ in t steps). The predicate in the brackets on the right is decidable; apply corollary 6.6.

   (*b*) $W_x \neq \varnothing \Leftrightarrow \exists y \exists t (P_x(y)\downarrow$ in t steps); again the predicate in brackets is decidable, so corollary 6.6 applies.

2. Provability in the predicate calculus is partially decidable (this is for those who have read § 5).

Proof. We proceed informally; in the predicate calculus a *proof* is defined as a finite object (usually a sequence of statements) in such a way that the predicate

$\Pr(d, \sigma) \equiv$ 'd is a proof of the statement σ'

is decidable. Then we have

σ is provable $\Leftrightarrow \exists d \Pr(d, \sigma)$,

hence 'σ is provable' is partially decidable.

6.8. *Diophantine predicates* (cf. § 3)

Suppose that $p(x_1, \ldots, x_n, y_1, \ldots, y_m)$ is a polynomial with integer coefficients. Then the predicate $M(\mathbf{x})$ given by

$$M(\mathbf{x}) \equiv \exists y_1 \ldots \exists y_m (p(\mathbf{x}, y_1, \ldots, y_m) = 0)$$

is called a *diophantine* predicate, because of its obvious connection with diophantine equations. (The quantifiers $\exists y_1, \ldots, \exists y_m$ are taken as ranging over $\mathbb{N}$.)

Example The predicate 'x is a perfect square' is diophantine, since it is equivalent to $\exists y(x - y^2 = 0)$.

From corollary 6.6 we have immediately

6.9. *Theorem*

Diophantine predicates are partially decidable.

Proof. The predicate $p(\mathbf{x}, \mathbf{y}) = 0$ is decidable; apply corollary 6.6. □

Clearly, diophantine predicates are partially decidable predicates that can be cast in a relatively simple form, and for a long time it was not known whether any undecidable diophantine predicates existed. This question is closely connected with Hilbert's tenth problem (§ 3), as we shall see. It was a most remarkable achievement, therefore, when Matiyasevich proved in 1970:

6.10. *Theorem*

Every partially decidable predicate is diophantine.

The proof of this result by Matiyasevich rested heavily on earlier work of Davis, Robinson and Putnam, and is far too long to present here. Full proofs are given in Davis [1973], Bell & Machover [1977] and Manin [1977]. The major part of the proof consists in showing that diophantine predicates are closed under bounded universal quantification; i.e. if $M(\mathbf{x}, y)$ is diophantine then so is the predicate $\forall z<yM(\mathbf{x}, z)$. (It is an easy exercise to show that partially decidable predicates are closed under bounded universal quantification; see exercise 6.14(5) below.)

We can see how a negative solution to Hilbert's tenth problem is easily derived from Matiyasevich's theorem. First note that if the problem posed by Hilbert is decidable, then so is the problem of deciding for a general polynomial equation $p(x_1, \ldots, x_n)=0$ (with integer coefficients) whether it has a solution in the natural numbers: this is because any natural number is expressible as the sum of four squares, so we simply look for integer solutions to

$$p(s_1^2+t_1^2+u_1^2+v_1^2, \ldots, s_n^2+t_n^2+u_n^2+v_n^2)=0.$$

Now take a polynomial $p(x, y_1, \ldots, y_m)$ such that

$$x \in W_x \Leftrightarrow \exists y_1 \ldots \exists y_m(p(x, y_1, \ldots, y_m)=0)$$

(this is possible by Matiyasevich's theorem). Then a decision procedure for Hilbert's problem would give the following decision procedure for '$x \in W_x$': to test whether $a \in W_a$ see whether the polynomial $q(y_1, \ldots, y_m)=p(a, y_1, \ldots, y_m)$ has a solution in $\mathbb{N}$. So '$x \in W_x$' has been reduced to Hilbert's problem; hence the latter is undecidable.

We shall mention another (surprising) consequence of Matiyasevich's theorem in the next chapter.

We conclude this chapter with two important results, linking partially decidable predicates with decidable predicates (theorem 6.11) and computable functions (theorem 6.13).

6.11. *Theorem*

A predicate $M(\mathbf{x})$ is decidable if and only if both $M(\mathbf{x})$ and 'not $M(\mathbf{x})$' are partially decidable.

Proof. If $M(\mathbf{x})$ is decidable, so is 'not $M(\mathbf{x})$', so both are partially decidable.

Conversely, suppose that partial decision procedures for $M(\mathbf{x})$ and 'not $M(\mathbf{x})$' are given by programs F, G. Then

$$F(\mathbf{x})\downarrow \Leftrightarrow M(\mathbf{x}) \text{ holds}$$

and

$$G(\mathbf{x})\downarrow \Leftrightarrow \text{'not } M(\mathbf{x})\text{' holds.}$$

Moreover, for any $\mathbf{x}$, *either* $F(\mathbf{x})\downarrow$ *or* $G(\mathbf{x})\downarrow$ but not *both*. Thus the following is an algorithm for deciding $M(\mathbf{x})$. Given $\mathbf{x}$, run the computations $F(\boldsymbol{x})$ and $G(\boldsymbol{x})$ simultaneously (or carry out alternately one step in each computation), and go on until one of them stops. If it is $F(\boldsymbol{x})$ that stops, then conclude that $M(\boldsymbol{x})$ holds; if it is $G(\boldsymbol{x})$ that stops, then $M(\boldsymbol{x})$ does not hold. □

This theorem gives an alternative proof that the predicate '$x \notin W_x$' is not partially decidable. Similarly we have

6.12. *Corollary*

The predicate '$P_x(y)\uparrow$' (the Divergence problem: *equivalently,* '$y \notin W_x$', *or* '$\phi_x(y)$ *is undefined*') *is not partially decidable.*

Proof. If this problem were partially decidable, then by theorem 6.11 and example 6.2(1) the Halting problem $P_x(y)\downarrow$ would be decidable. □

The final result of this chapter gives a useful way to show that a function is computable.

6.13. *Theorem*

Let $f(\boldsymbol{x})$ *be a partial function. Then* f *is computable if and only if the predicate*

'$f(\boldsymbol{x}) \simeq y$'

is partially decidable.

Proof. If f is computable by a program P, then we have

$$f(\boldsymbol{x}) \simeq y \Leftrightarrow \exists t(P(\boldsymbol{x})\downarrow y \text{ in } t \text{ steps}).$$

The predicate on the right is partially decidable by theorem 6.4 and corollary 5-1.3.

Conversely, suppose that the predicate '$f(\boldsymbol{x}) \simeq y$' is partially decidable. Let $R(\boldsymbol{x}, y, t)$ be a decidable predicate such that $f(\boldsymbol{x}) \simeq y \Leftrightarrow \exists t R(\boldsymbol{x}, y, t)$. Then we have the following algorithm for computing $f(\boldsymbol{x})$.

Search for a pair of numbers y, t such that $R(\boldsymbol{x}, y, t)$ holds; if and when such a pair is found, then $f(\boldsymbol{x}) \simeq y$.

Hence f is computable. (A formal proof of the computability of f could be given by the standard technique of coding a pair y, t by the single number $z = 2^y 3^t$. See exercise 6.14(8) below.) □

Further properties of partially decidable predicates are given in the exercises below (see in particular exercises 6.14(4, 5, 9)).

In the next chapter we will be studying unary partially decidable predicates in greater detail, in the guise of *recursively enumerable sets.* We shall see in particular why partially decidable predicates are often described as recursively enumerable predicates.

6.14. *Exercises*

1. Show that the following predicates are partially decidable:
(*a*) '$E_x^{(n)} \neq \emptyset$' (n fixed),
(*b*) '$\phi_x(y)$ is a perfect square',
(*c*) 'n is a Fermat number'. (We say that n is a *Fermat number* if there are numbers $x, y, z > 0$ such that $x^n + y^n = z^n$.)
(*d*) 'There is a run of exactly x consecutive 7s in the decimal expansion of π'.
2. (For those knowing some group theory) Show that the word problem for any finitely presented group is partially decidable.
3. A finite set S of 3×3 matrices is said to be *mortal* if there is a finite product of members of S that equals the zero matrix. Show that the predicate 'S is mortal' is partially decidable. (It has been shown that this problem is *not* decidable; see Paterson [1970].)
4. Suppose that $M(\mathbf{x})$ and $N(\mathbf{x})$ are partially decidable; prove that the predicates '$M(\mathbf{x})$ and $N(\mathbf{x})$', '$M(\mathbf{x})$ or $N(\mathbf{x})$' are partially decidable. Show that the predicate 'not $M(\mathbf{x})$' is not necessarily partially decidable.
5. Suppose that $M(\mathbf{x}, y)$ is partially decidable. Show that
(*a*) '$\exists y < z\, M(\mathbf{x}, y)$' is partially decidable,
(*b*) '$\forall y < z\, M(\mathbf{x}, y)$' is partially decidable.
(*Hint.* If $f(\mathbf{x}, y)$ is the partial characteristic function of M, consider the function $\prod_{y<z} f(\mathbf{x}, y)$.)
(*c*) '$\forall y M(\mathbf{x}, y)$' is not necessarily partially decidable.
6. Show that the following predicates are diophantine.
(*a*) 'x is even',
(*b*) 'x divides y'.
7. (This exercise shows how the technique of reducibility (§ 1) may be used to show that a predicate is not partially decidable.)
(a) Suppose that $M(x)$ is a predicate and k a total computable function such that $x \in W_x$ iff $M(k(x))$ does not hold. Prove that $M(x)$ is not partially decidable.
(*b*) Prove that 'ϕ_x is not total' is not partially decidable.
(*Hint.* Consider the function k in the proof of theorem 1.6.)
(*c*) By considering the function

$$f(x, y) = \begin{cases} 1 & \text{if } P_x(x) \text{ does not converge in } y \text{ or fewer steps,} \\ \text{undefined} & \text{otherwise,} \end{cases}$$

show that 'ϕ_x is total' is not partially decidable. (*Hint.* Use the *s–m–n* theorem and (a).)

8. Give a formal proof of the second half of Theorem 6.13; i.e. if '$f(\mathbf{x}) \simeq y$' is partially decidable, then f is computable.
9. Suppose that $M(x_1, \ldots, x_n)$ is partially decidable and $g_1, \ldots, g_n$ are computable partial functions. Show that the predicate $N(\mathbf{y})$ given by

   $N(\mathbf{y}) \equiv M(g_1(\mathbf{y}), \ldots, g_n(\mathbf{y}))$

   is partially decidable. (We take this to mean that $N(\mathbf{y})$ does not hold if any one of $g_1(\mathbf{y}), \ldots, g_n(\mathbf{y})$ is undefined.)

7

Recursive and recursively enumerable sets

The sets mentioned in the title to this chapter are subsets of $\mathbb{N}$ corresponding to decidable and partially decidable predicates. We discuss recursive sets briefly in § 1. The major part of this chapter is devoted to the study of recursively enumerable sets, beginning in § 2; many of the basic properties of these sets are derived directly from the results about partially decidable predicates in the previous chapter. The central new result in § 2 is the characterisation of recursively enumerable sets that gives them their name: they are sets that can be enumerated by a recursive (or computable) function.

In §§ 3 and 4 we introduce *creative* sets and *simple* sets: these are special kinds of recursively enumerable sets that are in marked contrast to each other; they give a hint of the great variety existing within this class of sets.

1. Recursive sets

There is a close connection between unary predicates of natural numbers and subsets of $\mathbb{N}$: corresponding to any predicate $M(x)$ we have the set $\{x : M(x) \text{ holds}\}$, called the *extent* of M (which could, of course, be $\varnothing$); while to a set $A \subseteq \mathbb{N}$ there corresponds the predicate '$x \in A$'.[1] The name *recursive* is given to sets corresponding in this way to predicates that are *decidable*.

1.1. *Definition*

Let A be a subset of $\mathbb{N}$. The *characteristic function* of A is the function c_A given by

$$c_A(x) = \begin{cases} 1 & \text{if } x \in A, \\ 0 & \text{if } x \notin A. \end{cases}$$

[1] As mentioned in a footnote to § 3 of the Prologue, predicates are often identified with their extent: that view would not be inconsistent with our exposition.

Then A is said to be *recursive* if c_A is computable, or equivalently, if '$x \in A$' is a decidable predicate.

Notes

1. For obvious reasons, recursive sets are also called *computable* sets.
2. If c_A is primitive recursive, the set A is said to be *primitive recursive.*
3. The idea of a recursive set can be extended in the obvious way to subsets of $\mathbb{N}^n$ $(n > 1)$, although in the text we shall (as is common practice) restrict the use of the term to subsets of $\mathbb{N}$. There is no loss of generality in doing this, because recursive subsets of $\mathbb{N}^n$ can easily be coded as recursive subsets of $\mathbb{N}$. See exercise 1.4(2) below for details.

1.2. *Examples*

1. The following sets are recursive.
   (*a*) $\mathbb{N}$,
   (*b*) $\mathbb{E}$ (the even numbers),
   (*c*) any finite set,
   (*d*) the set of prime numbers.
2. The following sets are *not* recursive.
   (*a*) $\{x : \phi_x \text{ is total}\}$ (theorem 5-2.1),
   (*b*) $\{x : x \in W_x\}$ (theorem 6-1.1),
   (*c*) $\{x : \phi_x = \mathbf{0}\}$ (theorem 6-1.4).

The algebra of decidability (corollary 2-4.7) gives us the following properties of recursive sets immediately.

1.3. *Theorem*

If A, B are recursive sets, then so are the sets $\bar{A}$, $A \cap B$, $A \cup B$, $A \backslash B$.

Proof. Direct translation of corollary 2-4.7. □

Further facts about recursive sets will emerge in § 2.

1.4. *Exercises*

1. Let A, B be subsets of $\mathbb{N}$. Define sets $A \oplus B$ and $A \otimes B$ by

   $A \oplus B = \{2x : x \in A\} \cup \{2x + 1 : x \in B\}$

   $A \otimes B = \{\pi(x, y) : x \in A \text{ and } y \in B\}$,

   where π is the pairing function $\pi(x, y) = 2^x(2y + 1) - 1$ of theorem 4-1.2. Prove that

   (*a*) $A \oplus B$ is recursive iff A and B are both recursive,

   (*b*) If $A, B \neq \varnothing$, then $A \otimes B$ is recursive iff A and B are both recursive.

2. (*a*) Let $B \subseteq \mathbb{N}$ and let $n > 1$; prove that if B is recursive then the predicate $M(x_1, \ldots, x_n)$ given by

$$M(x_1, \ldots, x_n) \equiv 2^{x_1}3^{x_2} \ldots \mathrm{p}_n^{x_n} \in B$$

is decidable.

(*b*) Let $A \subseteq \mathbb{N}^n$; define A to be *recursive* if the predicate '$\mathbf{x} \in A$' is decidable. Prove that A is recursive iff $\{2^{x_1}3^{x_2} \ldots \mathrm{p}_n^{x_n} : (x_1, \ldots, x_n) \in A\}$ is recursive.

2. Recursively enumerable sets

We turn now to the subsets of $\mathbb{N}$ that correspond to partially decidable predicates. These constitute an important class, if only because of the many situations in which they occur.

2.1. *Definition*

Let A be a subset of $\mathbb{N}$. Then A is *recursively enumerable* if the function f given by

$$f(x) = \begin{cases} 1 & \text{if } x \in A, \\ \text{undefined} & \text{if } x \notin A \end{cases}$$

is computable (or, equivalently, if the predicate '$x \in A$' is partially decidable). The phrase recursively enumerable is almost universally abbreviated r.e.

Notes

1. The terms *semi-recursive* sets and *semi-computable* sets are also used to describe r.e. sets; indeed, from the above definition these names would appear more appropriate than *recursively enumerable.* We will, nevertheless, adhere to the standard name recursively enumerable, which stems from the fact that these sets may also be defined as sets that can be enumerated by a recursive (or computable) function. This alternative characterisation is given in theorem 2.7 below.

2. As with recursive sets, the idea of r.e. sets can be extended in the obvious way to subsets of $\mathbb{N}^n$ $(n > 1)$, but there is no loss of generality in confining attention (as we do in the text) to r.e. subsets of $\mathbb{N}$. See exercise 2.18(9) below.

2.2. *Examples*

1. Let $K = \{x : x \in W_x\}$; then K is an r.e. set that is not recursive. (example 6-6.2(1)). Its complement $\bar{K}$ is not r.e. (example 6-6.2(4)).
2. Any recursive set is r.e. (example 6-6.2(2)).

3. The set $\{x: W_x \neq \emptyset\}$ is r.e. (example 6-6.7(1(*b*))).
4. If f is a computable function, then Ran(f) is r.e. (example 6-6.7(1*a*); cf. theorem 2.7 below).

Note. K is the standard notation for the set $\{x : x \in W_x\}$ (example 1 above), which plays a prominent role in the study of r.e. sets.

Most of the results for partially decidable predicates in chapter 6 § 6 translate immediately into the language of r.e. sets. We begin with

2.3. *Theorem*

A set is r.e. if and only if it is the domain of a unary computable function.

Proof. Theorem 6-6.3. □

We conclude from this theorem that the enumeration

$$W_0, W_1, W_2, \ldots$$

is an enumeration (with repetitions) of *all* r.e. sets. If $A = W_e$, then e is called an *index* for A.

From theorem 6-6.4 we obtain the next characterisation of r.e. sets.

2.4. *Theorem*

The set A is r.e. if and only if there is a decidable predicate $R(x, y)$ such that

$$x \in A \text{ iff } \exists y R(x, y).$$

(From the note following the proof of theorem 6-6.4 this predicate R may be taken to be primitive recursive.)

We also have the following immediately from theorem 6-6.5.

2.5. *Theorem*

Suppose that $M(x, y_1, \ldots, y_n)$ is partially decidable; then the set $\{x : \exists y_1 \ldots \exists y_n M(x, y_1, \ldots, y_n)\}$ is r.e.

The following link between r.e. sets and recursive sets is an immediate application of theorem 6-6.11.

2.6. *Theorem*

The set A is recursive if and only if A and $\bar{A}$ are r.e.

Proof. This is immediate from theorem 6-6.11, but it is instructive to give a formal proof of the non-trivial half of the proof. Suppose then that R and S are decidable predicates such that

$$x \in A \Leftrightarrow \exists y R(x, y)$$
$$x \in \bar{A} \Leftrightarrow \exists y S(x, y)$$

(we are using theorem 2.4). Now define a function $f(x)$ by

$$f(x) = \mu y(R(x, y) \text{ or } S(x, y)).$$

By the results of chapter 2, f is computable; further, since for every x, either $x \in A$ or $x \in \bar{A}$, $f(x)$ is always defined, and we have

$$x \in A \Leftrightarrow R(x, f(x)).$$

Thus '$x \in A$' is decidable, so A is recursive. □

We now turn to the characterisation of r.e. sets that gives them their name.

2.7. *Theorem*

Let $A \subseteq \mathbb{N}$. Then the following are equivalent:

(a) A is r.e.,

(b) $A = \emptyset$ or A is the range of a unary total computable function,

(c) A is the range of a (partial) computable function.

Proof. We shall prove the chain of implications $(a) \Rightarrow (b) \Rightarrow (c) \Rightarrow (a)$.

$(a) \Rightarrow (b)$ Suppose that $A \neq \emptyset$ and that $A = \text{Dom}(f)$, where f is computed by a program P. Choose an element $a \in A$. Then A is the range of the following total *binary* function:

$$g(x, t) = \begin{cases} x & \text{if } P(x)\downarrow \text{ in } t \text{ steps,} \\ a & \text{otherwise.} \end{cases}$$

Clearly g is computable. To complete the proof we construct a *unary* total computable function h having the same range as g. Let

$$h(z) = g((z)_1, (z)_2).$$

Clearly $\text{Ran}(h) = \text{Ran}(g) = A$.

$(b) \Rightarrow (c)$ is trivial.

$(c) \Rightarrow (a)$ Suppose that $A = \text{Ran}(h)$ where h is an n-ary computable function. Then

$$x \in A \Leftrightarrow \exists y_1 \ldots \exists y_n (h(y_1, \ldots, y_n) \simeq x).$$

The predicate in brackets on the right is partially decidable (theorem 6-6.13) so applying theorem 2.5 we see that A is r.e. □

(The reader may have noticed that various parts of this theorem have been given, more or less explicitly, in examples and exercises earlier in this and other chapters.)

Notice that it is from theorem 2.7(b) particularly that the name *recursively enumerable* comes: a non-empty r.e. set is a set that can be enumerated as $A = \{h(0), h(1), h(2), \dots\}$ where h is a *recursive* (i.e. total computable) function. In fact, by using the results of chapter 5 (and appendix) it is easily seen that the enumerating function h in the proof of $(a) \Rightarrow (b)$ is *primitive* recursive.

Note also that theorem 2.7 tells us that the enumeration $E_0, E_1, E_2, \dots$ of the ranges of unary computable functions is another enumeration (with repetitions) of all r.e. sets. In informal terms, theorem 2.7 shows that r.e. sets are the same as *effectively generated* sets. We would call a set A *effectively generated* if there is an informal effective procedure for compiling a list of the members of A. Such a procedure would from time to time (not necessarily at regular intervals) output a number to be added to the list. The procedure may go on *ad infinitum* (and certainly must if A is infinite). To see that a set A generated in this way is r.e., simply put

$$
\begin{aligned}
f(0) &= \text{1st number listed by the procedure,}\\
&\;\;\vdots \qquad\qquad\qquad\qquad \vdots\\
f(n) &= (n+1)\text{th number listed by the procedure,}
\end{aligned}
$$

where $f(n)$ is defined iff there is an $(n+1)$th number listed. Then clearly f is computable, and $A = \text{Ran}(f)$ is r.e.

We can illustrate this with an example.

2.8. *Example*

The set $\{x$: there is a run of exactly x consecutive 7s in the decimal expansion of $\pi\}$ is r.e. (cf. exercise 6-6.14(1d)). The following is an informal procedure that generates this set of numbers. 'Run an algorithm that computes successive digits in the decimal expansion of π. Each time a run of 7s appears, count the number of consecutive 7s in the run and add this number to the list.'

The characterisation of theorem 2.7 gives us a straightforward diagonal proof that total computable functions cannot be recursively enumerated.

2.9. *Theorem*

The set $\{x : \phi_x$ is total$\}$ is not r.e.

Proof. (Cf. the suggested proof of this result given in exercise 6-6.14(7c).)

Suppose to the contrary that f is a total unary computable function that enumerates this set; i.e. $\phi_{f(0)}, \phi_{f(1)}, \phi_{f(2)}, \ldots$ is a list of *all* unary computable functions. Then we can easily make a diagonal construction of a total computable function g that differs from every function in this list. The diagonal motto says 'make g differ from $\phi_{f(n)}$ at n', so we put

$$g(x) = \phi_{f(x)}(x) + 1.$$

Then g is computable and total, but $g \neq \phi_{f(m)}$ for every m. This is a contradiction. □

There is one important result about partially decidable predicates that we have so far omitted to transfer to the setting of r.e. sets, namely the connection with diophantine predicates. First we make a definition.

2.10. *Definition*

A set $A \subseteq \mathbb{N}$ is *diophantine* if there is a polynomial $p(x, y_1, \ldots, y_n)$ with integer coefficients such that

$$x \in A \quad \text{iff} \quad \exists y_1 \ldots \exists y_n (p(x, y_1, \ldots, y_n) = 0).$$

Of course, diophantine sets are r.e., and Matiyasevich's theorem (6-6.10) may be expressed (as it often is) as:

2.11. *Theorem* (Matiyasevich)

All r.e. sets are diophantine.

This is an appropriate place to mention a surprising (but easy) consequence of Matiyasevich's theorem.

2.12. *Theorem*

A set is r.e. if and only if it is the set of non-negative values taken by some polynomial $p(x_1, \ldots, x_n)$ with integer coefficients (for values of $x_1, \ldots, x_n$ from $\mathbb{N}$).

Proof. Suppose that A is the set of non-negative values taken by $p(x_1, \ldots, x_n)$: then $x \in A \Leftrightarrow \exists x_1 \ldots \exists x_n (p(x_1, \ldots, x_n) = x)$, so A is clearly r.e.

Conversely, if A is r.e. then by Matiyasevich's theorem there is a polynomial $q(x, y_1, \ldots, y_m)$ such that

$$x \in A \Leftrightarrow \exists y_1 \ldots \exists y_m (q(x, y_1, \ldots, y_m) = 0).$$

Then consider the polynomial $p(x, \mathbf{y})$ given by

$$p(x, \mathbf{y}) = x - (x+1)(q(x, \mathbf{y}))^2.$$

$p(x, \mathbf{y})$ is non-negative if, and only if, $q(x, \mathbf{y}) = 0$, and then it takes the value x. Thus A is the set of non-negative values taken by $p(x, \mathbf{y})$ as $x, y_1, \ldots, y_m$ run through $\mathbb{N}$. □

(The restriction of $x_1, \ldots, x_n$ to $\mathbb{N}$ in the statement of this theorem is somewhat arbitrary; it is an easy exercise to see that the theorem is valid when $x_1, \ldots, x_n$ are allowed to range over $\mathbb{Z}$.)

One application of this result that has aroused considerable interest among mathematicians is to the set of prime numbers: this set, being r.e., is the set of positive values taken by a polynomial with integer coefficients, a result thought to be most unlikely before Matiyasevich came on the scene.

A refinement of theorem 2.12 shows that there is a single *universal polynomial*, which generates all r.e. sets; i.e. a polynomial $p(z, x, y_1, \ldots, y_m)$ with the property that for any r.e. set A there is a number z such that

$$x \in A \Leftrightarrow \exists y_1 \ldots \exists y_m (p(z, x, y_1, \ldots, y_m) = 0).$$

To see this, simply note that the Halting problem '$x \in W_z$' is diophantine and take z to be an index for A.

At this stage we should summarise the various characterisations of r.e. sets that we now have available. The following are all equivalent conditions on a set A of natural numbers:

(1) '$x \in A$' is partially decidable (we have taken this as our basic definition),

(2) A is the domain of a unary computable function; i.e. $A = W_e$ for some e (theorem 2.3),

(3) For some decidable predicate $R(x, y)$, $x \in A \Leftrightarrow \exists y\, R(x, y)$ (theorem 2.4),

(4) For some partially decidable predicate $M(x, y_1, \ldots, y_n)$, $x \in A \Leftrightarrow \exists y_1 \ldots \exists y_n M(x, y_1, \ldots, y_n)$ (theorem 2.5),

(5) If $A \neq \emptyset$, A is the range of a total unary computable function (theorem 2.7),

(6) A is the range of a computable function (theorem 2.7),

(7) A is diophantine (theorem 2.11),

(8) A is the set of non-negative values taken by a polynomial with integer coefficients (theorem 2.12).

Naturally, when working with r.e. sets one chooses the characterisation that is most convenient for the purpose in hand. We illustrate this in the proof of the next theorem.

2.13. *Theorem*

If A and B are r.e., then so are $A \cap B$ and $A \cup B$.

Proof. For $A \cap B$ use characterisation (2). Suppose that $A = \mathrm{Dom}(f)$ and $B = \mathrm{Dom}(g)$ with f, g computable. Then $A \cap B = \mathrm{Dom}(fg)$, and fg is computable.

For $A \cup B$ use characterisation (5). If $A = \varnothing$ or $B = \varnothing$ there is nothing to prove. So suppose that $A = \mathrm{Ran}(f)$ and $B = \mathrm{Ran}(g)$ where f, g are total computable. Define h by

$$h(2x) = f(x),$$
$$h(2x+1) = g(x).$$

Then h is computable and clearly $\mathrm{Ran}(h) = A \cup B$. □

(It is instructive to find proofs for this theorem using each of the other characterisations of r.e. sets.)

Our next theorem gives another link between r.e. sets and recursive sets.

2.14. *Theorem*

An infinite set is recursive if and only if it is the range of a total increasing computable function, i.e. if it can be recursively enumerated in increasing order.

Proof. Suppose that A is recursive and infinite; then A is enumerated by the increasing function f given by

$$f(0) = \mu y(y \in A),$$
$$f(n+1) = \mu y(y \in A \text{ and } y > f(n)).$$

Moreover, f is computable by minimalisation, recursion and the recursiveness of A.

Conversely, suppose that A is the range of the computable total increasing function f; i.e. $f(0) < f(1) < f(2) < \ldots$ It is clear that if $y = f(n)$ then $n \leq y$. Hence we have

$$y \in A \Leftrightarrow y \in \mathrm{Ran}(f)$$
$$\Leftrightarrow \exists n \leq y (f(n) = y)$$

and the predicate on the right is decidable. Hence A is recursive. □

(An alternative proof could be given by showing that $\bar{A}$ is r.e.; we leave this as an exercise for the reader.)

The above theorem may be applied to prove

2.15. *Theorem*

Every infinite r.e. set has an infinite recursive subset.

Proof. Let $A = \mathrm{Ran}(f)$ where f is a total computable function. We can effectively enumerate a subset of A in increasing order by a function g as follows

$$g(0) = f(0),$$
$$g(n+1) = f(x), \text{ where } x = \mu y(f(y) > g(n)).$$

Since $A = \mathrm{Ran}(f)$ is infinite, g is totally defined. By construction, $\mathrm{Ran}(g) \subseteq \mathrm{Ran}(f)$ and g is increasing. It is clear that g is computable, by minimalisation and recursion. Hence by theorem 2.14, $\mathrm{Ran}(g)$ is an infinite recursive subset of A. □

We conclude this section with a theorem of Rice and Shapiro about r.e. sets of indices. We shall need this result in chapter 10, and there are other applications we can make immediately, but it is of significance in its own right. The theorem and its proof are generalisations of Rice's theorem (6-1.7). (In the statement of this theorem, by a *finite function* θ we mean a function whose domain is finite: note that all finite functions are computable.)

2.16. *Theorem* (Rice–Shapiro)

Suppose that $\mathscr{A}$ is a set of unary computable functions such that the set $\{x : \phi_x \in \mathscr{A}\}$ is r.e. Then for any unary computable function f,

$$f \in \mathscr{A} \text{ iff there is a finite function } \theta \subseteq f \text{ with } \theta \in \mathscr{A}.$$

Before we prove this result, let us illustrate how it can be used to give quick proofs of non-recursive enumerability. (Further applications of this kind are given in exercises 2.18 below.)

2.17. *Corollary*

The sets $\{x : \phi_x$ is total$\}$ and $\{x : \phi_x$ is not total$\}$ are not r.e.

Proof. For $A = \{x : \phi_x \text{ is total}\}$ we apply the Rice–Shapiro theorem to the set $\mathscr{A} = \{f : f \in \mathscr{C}_1 \text{ and } f \text{ is total}\}$. For no $f \in \mathscr{A}$ is there a finite $\theta \subseteq f$ with $\theta \in \mathscr{A}$. Hence A is not r.e.

For $B=\{x:\phi_x \text{ is not total}\}$, consider the set $\mathscr{B}=\{f: f\in\mathscr{C}_1 \text{ and } f \text{ is not total}\}$. Then if f is any total computable function, $f\notin\mathscr{B}$; but every finite function $\theta\subseteq f$ is in $\mathscr{B}$. So B cannot be r.e., by the Rice–Shapiro theorem. □

(*Note*. This is the third proof we have of the non-recursive enumerability of the indices of total functions: others are exercise 6-6.14(7c) and theorem 2.9 above. The reader will see that the proof suggested in the first of these is actually the specialisation of the following proof.)

We return to the proof of the Rice–Shapiro theorem.

Proof of theorem 2.16

Let $A=\{x:\phi_x\in\mathscr{A}\}$. We are given that A is r.e. We shall show that if either implication in the statement of the theorem is false, then the problem '$x\in\bar{K}$' can be reduced to '$x\in A$'. (Recall from example 2.2(1) that $K=\{x:x\in W_x\}$.) This would show that $\bar{K}$ is r.e., a contradiction.

Suppose first that $f\in\mathscr{A}$ but $\theta\notin\mathscr{A}$ for all finite $\theta\subseteq f$. Let P be a program such that $P(z)\downarrow$ iff $z\in K$. Define a computable function $g(z,t)$ by

$$g(z,t)\simeq\begin{cases} f(t) & \text{if } P(z)\not\downarrow \text{ in } t \text{ or fewer steps,}\\ \text{undefined} & \text{if } P(z)\downarrow \text{ in } t \text{ or fewer steps.}\end{cases}$$

The s–m–n theorem provides a total computable function $s(z)$ such that $g(z,t)\simeq\phi_{s(z)}(t)$. Note that by construction $\phi_{s(z)}\subseteq f$ for all z. We claim further that

$$(*)\qquad \begin{cases} z\in K \Rightarrow \phi_{s(z)} \text{ is finite (hence } \phi_{s(z)}\notin\mathscr{A}),\\ z\notin K \Rightarrow \phi_{s(z)}=f \text{ (hence } \phi_{s(z)}\in\mathscr{A}).\end{cases}$$

For if $z\in K$, there is t such that $P(z)\downarrow$ in t steps. Then $g(z,t')\simeq\phi_{s(z)}(t')$ is undefined for $t'\geq t$. Hence $\phi_{s(z)}$ is finite. On the other hand, if $z\notin K$, then $g(z,t)\simeq f(t)$ for all t, so $\phi_{s(z)}=f$.

Now (*) means that $z\in\bar{K}\Leftrightarrow s(z)\in A$, which implies that $\bar{K}$ is r.e., a contradiction. Hence there must be a finite $\theta\subseteq f$ with $\theta\in\mathscr{A}$.

For the reverse implication, suppose that f is a computable function, such that there is a finite function $\theta\in\mathscr{A}$ with $\theta\subseteq f$, but $f\notin\mathscr{A}$. Define a computable function $g(z,t)$ by

$$g(z,t)\simeq\begin{cases} f(t) & \text{if } t\in\text{Dom}(\theta) \text{ or } z\in K,\\ \text{undefined} & \text{otherwise.}\end{cases}$$

The s–m–n theorem provides a total computable $s(z)$ such that $g(z,t)\simeq\phi_{s(z)}(t)$. From the definition of g and the fact that $\theta\subseteq f$ we see that

$$z\in K \Rightarrow \phi_{s(z)}=f \text{ (hence } \phi_{s(z)}\notin\mathscr{A})$$

and

$$z \notin K \Rightarrow \phi_{s(z)} = f|\text{Dom}(\theta) = \theta \text{ (hence } \phi_{s(z)} \in \mathscr{A}).$$

But this means that $z \in \bar{K} \Leftrightarrow s(z) \in A$, again showing that $\bar{K}$ is r.e., a contradiction. Thus $f \in \mathscr{A}$ as required. □

We leave it as an exercise for the reader to see how the Rice–Shapiro theorem generalises Rice's theorem (exercise 2.18(12) below).

2.18. *Exercises*

1. For any $a \in \mathbb{N}$, let ${}^aW_e = \{x : \phi_e(x) = a\}$. Show that ${}^aW_e$ is r.e. (all a). Does the enumeration ${}^aW_0, {}^aW_1, {}^aW_2, \ldots$ include all r.e. sets?
2. Show that the set $\{x : \phi_x \text{ is not injective}\}$ is r.e.
3. Show that there are total computable functions k, l such that for every x, $W_x = E_{k(x)}$ and $E_x = W_{l(x)}$.
4. Suppose that A is an r.e. set. Show that the sets $\bigcup_{x \in A} W_x$ and $\bigcup_{x \in A} E_x$ are both r.e.

   Show that $\bigcap_{x \in A} W_x$ is not necessarily r.e. as follows. For any t let $K_t = \{x : P_x(x)\downarrow \text{ in } t \text{ steps}\}$. Show that for any t, K_t is recursive; moreover $K = \bigcup_{t \in \mathbb{N}} K_t$ and $\bar{K} = \bigcap_{t \in \mathbb{N}} \bar{K}_t$.
5. Let f be a unary computable function, and suppose that $A \subseteq \text{Dom}(f)$, and let $g = f|A$. Prove that g is computable iff A is r.e.
6. Let f be a unary function. Prove that f is computable iff the set $\{2^x 3^{f(x)} : x \in \text{Dom}(f)\}$ is r.e.
7. (Cf. theorem 2.14.) Let A be an infinite r.e. set. Show that A can be enumerated without repetitions by a total computable function.
8. Which of the following sets are recursive? Which are r.e.? Which have r.e. complement?

   (*a*) $\{x : x \in E_x\}$,

   (*b*) $\{x : x \text{ is a perfect square}\}$,

   (*c*) $\{x : \phi_x \text{ is injective}\}$,

   (*d*) $\{x$: there is a run of *at least* x consecutive 7s in the decimal expansion of $\pi\}$,

   (*e*) $\{x : P_m(x)\uparrow\}$ (m is fixed).
9. (Cf. Exercise 1.4(2).) (*a*) Let $B \subseteq \mathbb{N}$ and let $n > 1$; prove that if B is r.e. then the predicate $M(x_1, \ldots, x_n)$ given by

   $M(x_1, \ldots, x_n) \equiv 2^{x_1} 3^{x_2} \ldots p_n^{x_n} \in B$

   is partially decidable.

(*b*) Let $A \subseteq \mathbb{N}^n$; define A to be *r.e.* if the predicate '$\mathbf{x} \in A$' is partially decidable. Prove that A is r.e. iff

$$\{2^{x_1}3^{x_2}\dots p_n^{x_n}: (x_1, \dots, x_n) \in A\} \text{ is r.e.}$$

(*c*) Prove that $A \subseteq \mathbb{N}^n$ is r.e. iff $A = \emptyset$ or there is a total computable function $f: \mathbb{N} \to \mathbb{N}^n$ such that $A = \text{Ran}(f)$. (By a *computable function* f from $\mathbb{N}$ to $\mathbb{N}^n$ we mean an n-tuple $f = (f_1, \dots, f_n)$ where each f_i is a unary computable function and $f(x) = (f_1(x), \dots, f_n(x))$.)

10. Suppose that f is a total computable function, A a recursive set and B an r.e. set. Show that $f^{-1}(A)$ is recursive and that $f(A)$, $f(B)$ and $f^{-1}(B)$ are r.e. but not necessarily recursive. What extra information about these sets can be obtained if f is a bijection?
11. Use the Rice–Shapiro theorem to show that the following problems are not partially decidable: (*a*) '$W_x = \emptyset$', (*b*) 'W_x is finite', (*c*) 'W_x is infinite', (*d*) '$\phi_x = \mathbf{0}$', (*e*) '$\phi_x \neq \mathbf{0}$'.
12. Prove Rice's theorem (theorem 6-1.7) from the Rice–Shapiro theorem (theorem 2.16). (*Hint.* Suppose that '$\phi_x \in \mathscr{B}$' is decidable; then both $\mathscr{B}$ and $\mathscr{C}_1 \setminus \mathscr{B}$ satisfy the conditions of Rice–Shapiro: consider the cases $f_\emptyset \in \mathscr{B}$ and $f_\emptyset \notin \mathscr{B}$.)
13. (*a*) Let $K_0 = \{x : \phi_x(x) = 0\}$ and $K_1 = \{x : \phi_x(x) = 1\}$. Show that K_0 and K_1 are r.e., and that they are *recursively inseparable*, i.e. $K_0 \cap K_1 = \emptyset$ and there is no recursive set C such that $K_0 \subseteq C$ and $K_1 \subseteq \bar{C}$; in particular neither K_0 nor K_1 is recursive. (*Hint.* Suppose that there is such a set C and let m be an index for its characteristic function; consider whether or not $m \in C$.) (*b*) Show that two disjoint sets A, B are recursively inseparable (in the above sense) iff whenever $A \subseteq W_a$, $B \subseteq W_b$ and $W_a \cap W_b = \emptyset$, then there is a number $x \notin W_a \cup W_b$. (*Note.* Recursive inseparability for a pair of disjoint sets corresponds to non-recursiveness for a single set; pairs of recursively inseparable sets that are also r.e. correspond to r.e. sets that are not recursive.)

3. Productive and creative sets

Our chief concern in this section is to discuss a special class of r.e. sets called *creative* sets. These are r.e. sets whose complement fails to be r.e. in a rather strong way. Thus we begin by considering a class of non-r.e. sets, among whose complements creative sets are to be found.

Suppose that A is any set that is not r.e.; then if W_x is an r.e. set contained in A, there must be a number $y \in A \setminus W_x$. This number y is a witness to the fact that $A \neq W_x$. It turns out that for some non-r.e. sets it is possible to find such a witness in an effective way. Consider, for example, the non-r.e., set $\bar{K} = \{x : x \notin W_x\}$. If $W_x \subseteq \bar{K}$, we cannot have $x \in W_x$ (for then $x \in K$, so $W_x \not\subseteq \bar{K}$); hence $x \in \bar{K} \setminus W_x$. So x itself is a witness that $W_x \neq \bar{K}$.

The name *productive* is used to describe non-r.e. sets for which a witness can always be computed in this way.

3.1. *Definition*

A set A is *productive* if there is a total computable function g such that whenever $W_x \subseteq A$, then $g(x) \in A \setminus W_x$. The function g is called a *productive function* for A. This is illustrated by fig. 7*a*.

Example. The set $\bar{K}$ is productive, with productive function $g(x) = x$.

Many examples of productive sets are obtained from the following theorem, which incorporates the idea of reducibility that was discussed in the previous chapter.

3.2. *Theorem*

Suppose that A and B are sets such that A is productive, and there is a total computable function f such that $x \in A$ iff $f(x) \in B$. Then B is productive.

Proof. Let g be a productive function for A. Suppose that $W_x \subseteq B$. Then $f^{-1}(W_x) \subseteq f^{-1}(B) = A$; moreover, $f^{-1}(W_x)$ is r.e., so there is z such that $f^{-1}(W_x) = W_z$. Now $W_z \subseteq A$, and so $g(z) \in A \setminus W_z$, from which we see

Fig. 7*a*. A productive set.

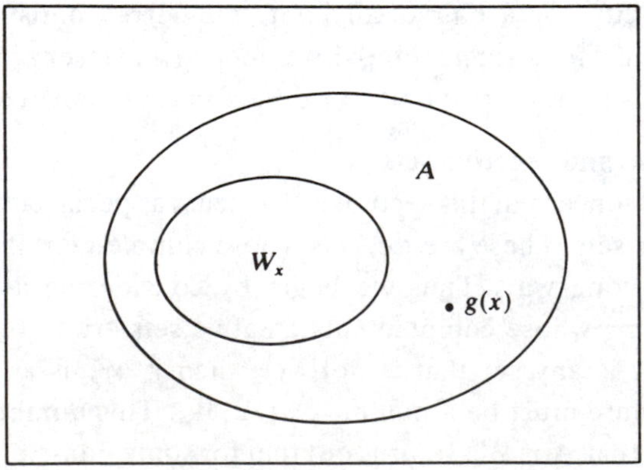

Fig. 7*b*. Theorem 3.2.

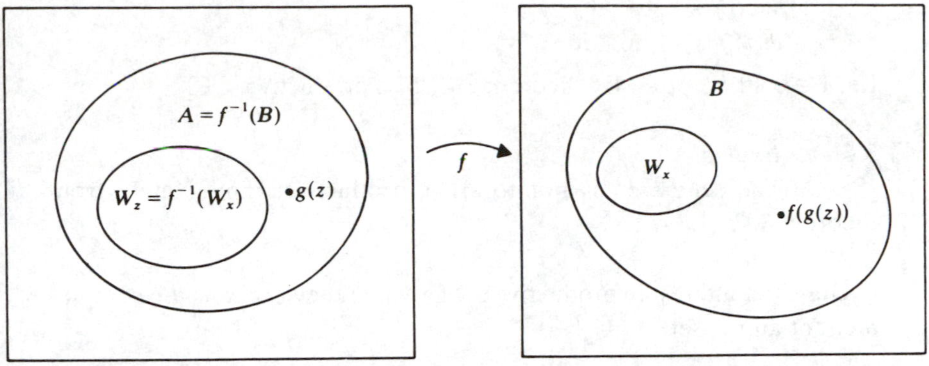

that $f(g(z)) \in B \setminus W_x$; i.e. $f(g(z))$ is a witness to the fact that $W_x \neq B$ (fig. 7*b*).

We now need to obtain the witness $f(g(z))$ *effectively* from x. A simple application of the *s–m–n* theorem provides a total computable function $k(x)$ such that $W_{k(x)} = f^{-1}(W_x)$ (apply the *s–m–n* theorem to the function $\phi_x(f(y))$). Then putting $z = k(x)$ we see from the above reasoning that if $W_x \subseteq B$ then $f(g(k(x))) \in B \setminus W_x$. Hence B is productive, with productive function $f(g(k(x)))$. □

3.3. *Examples*

The following sets are productive:

(*a*) $\{x : \phi_x \neq \mathbf{0}\}$,

(*b*) $\{x : c \notin W_x\}$ (c a fixed number),

(*c*) $\{x : c \notin E_x\}$ (c a fixed number).

(For each of these sets apply theorem 3.2 using $\bar{K}$ and the functions obtained in theorem 6-1.4 (for (*a*)) and theorem 6-1.6 (for (*b*) and (*c*)).)

The above examples of productive sets and many more may be obtained from the following general application of theorem 3.2, based on our proof of Rice's theorem.

3.4. *Theorem*

Suppose that $\mathscr{B}$ is a set of unary computable functions with $f_\varnothing \in \mathscr{B}$ and $\mathscr{B} \neq \mathscr{C}_1$. Then the set $B = \{x : \phi_x \in \mathscr{B}\}$ is productive.

Proof. Choose a computable function $g \notin \mathscr{B}$. Proceeding exactly as in the proof of Rice's theorem (6-1.7) obtain a total computable function

$k(x)$ such that

$$\phi_{k(x)} = g \quad \text{if } x \in K,$$

$$\phi_{k(x)} = f_{\varnothing} \quad \text{if } x \notin K.$$

I.e. $x \in \bar{K}$ iff $k(x) \in B$. By theorem 3.2, B is productive. □

3.5. *Example*

The set $\{x : \phi_x \text{ is not total}\}$ is productive, immediately from theorem 3.4.

Our chief interest in productive sets is when they occur as the complement of an r.e. set:

3.6. *Definition*

A set A is *creative* if it is r.e. and its complement $\bar{A}$ is productive.

The simplest example of a creative set is of course K. Using theorem 2.6 we can say that a creative set is an r.e. set that fails to be recursive in a very strong way. We will see in chapter 9 that there is a sense in which creative sets are the r.e. sets having the most difficult decision problem.

3.7. *Examples*

The following sets are creative

(*a*) $\{x : c \in W_x\}$ (the complements of these sets were
(*b*) $\{x : c \in E_x\}$ shown to be productive in examples 3.3).

(*c*) The set $A = \{x : \phi_x(x) = 0\}$. Clearly A is r.e.; to obtain a productive function for $\bar{A}$, use the *s–m–n* theorem to construct a total computable function g such that

$$\phi_{g(x)}(y) = 0 \Leftrightarrow \phi_x(y) \text{ is defined.}$$

Then $g(x) \in A \Leftrightarrow g(x) \in W_x$; so if $W_x \subseteq \bar{A}$ we must have $g(x) \in \bar{A} \setminus W_x$. Thus g is a productive function for $\bar{A}$.

Many examples of creative sets of indices are provided from the following application of theorem 3.4.

3.8. *Theorem*

Suppose that $\mathscr{A} \subseteq \mathscr{C}_1$ *and let* $A = \{x : \phi_x \in \mathscr{A}\}$. *If* A *is r.e. and* $A \neq \varnothing$ *or* $\mathbb{N}$, *then* A *is creative.*

Proof. Suppose that A is r.e. and $A \neq \varnothing, \mathbb{N}$. If $f_{\varnothing} \in \mathscr{A}$ then A is productive, by theorem 3.4; this is a contradiction. Thus $f_{\varnothing} \notin \mathscr{A}$, so $\bar{A}$ is productive (theorem 3.4), hence A is creative. □

The examples 3.7(a), (b) could be obtained by immediate application of this theorem; similarly we have:

3.9. *Example*

The set $A = \{x: W_x \neq \emptyset\}$ is creative; this set is obviously r.e. and corresponds to the set $\mathscr{A} = \{f \in \mathscr{C}_1 : f \neq f_\emptyset\}$.

Many of the exercises at the end of the section may be done with the aid of theorem 3.8.

All examples of non-recursive r.e. sets that we have encountered so far are creative. (The reader might care to prove this for the examples that we have not dealt with explicitly.) The question then arises as to whether *all* non-recursive r.e. sets are creative. The idea that this might be the case is reinforced by theorem 3.8, and further examples in the exercises below. It turns out, however, that this conjecture is false: by a special construction we can obtain r.e. sets that are neither recursive nor creative. Section 4 will be devoted to that task.

The construction to be made in the next section is inspired by theorem 3.11 below, which will show that a productive set (and hence the complement of a creative set), although not itself r.e., does contain an infinite r.e. subset. (The secret of constructing an r.e. set A that is neither recursive nor creative will be to ensure that $\bar{A}$ does *not* have this property.)

The proof of the theorem will be facilitated by first isolating the following technical result.

3.10. *Lemma*

Suppose that g is a total computable function. Then there is a total computable function k such that for all x, $W_{k(x)} = W_x \cup \{g(x)\}$.

Proof. Using the *s–m–n* theorem, take $k(x)$ to be a total computable function such that

$$\phi_{k(x)}(y) = \begin{cases} 1 & \text{if } y \in W_x \text{ or } y = g(x), \\ \text{undefined} & \text{otherwise.} \end{cases} \quad \square$$

3.11. *Theorem*

A productive set contains an infinite r.e. subset.

Proof. Let A be a productive set with productive function g. The idea is to enumerate without repetition an infinite set $B = \{y_0, y_1, \ldots\} \subseteq A$ in the following way.

(1) Take e_0 such that $W_{e_0} = \emptyset$; since $W_{e_0} \subseteq A$, then $g(e_0) \in A$. Put $y_0 = g(e_0)$.

(2) For $n \geq 0$, suppose that $y_0, \ldots, y_n$ have been given so that $\{y_0, \ldots, y_n\} \subseteq A$. Find an index e_{n+1} such that $\{y_0, \ldots, y_n\} = W_{e_{n+1}} \subseteq A$. Then $g(e_{n+1}) \in A \setminus W_{e_{n+1}}$; thus if we put $y_{n+1} = g(e_{n+1})$ we have $y_{n+1} \in A$ and $y_{n+1} \neq y_0, \ldots, y_n$ (see fig. 7*c*).

To see that this enumeration of $y_0, y_1, \ldots$ is an effective one, we use lemma 3.10. From the above discussion, when looking for the index e_{n+1} we require that

$$\begin{aligned} W_{e_{n+1}} &= W_{e_n} \cup \{y_n\} = W_{e_n} \cup \{g(e_n)\} \\ &= W_{k(e_n)} \end{aligned}$$

(where k is the function given by lemma 3.10). Thus we may *define* e_{n+1} to be $k(e_n)$; then the sequence $e_0, e_1, \ldots$ is given by the recursion equations

$$\begin{aligned} &e_0 = \text{some index for } \emptyset, \\ &e_{n+1} = k(e_n), \end{aligned}$$

and is hence computable. Now $y_n = g(e_n)$, so the sequence $y_0, y_1, \ldots$ is also computable. Thus $B = \{y_0, y_1, \ldots\}$, being the range of a computable function, is r.e. By construction, $B \subseteq A$ and B is infinite. □

For the record, we state the obvious

3.12. *Corollary*

If A is creative, then $\bar{A}$ contains an infinite r.e. subset.

3.13. *Exercises*

1. Show that the following sets are productive:
   (*a*) $\{x: W_x \text{ is finite}\}$,

Fig. 7*c*. Enumerating an infinite subset of A (theorem 3.11).

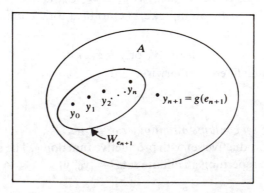

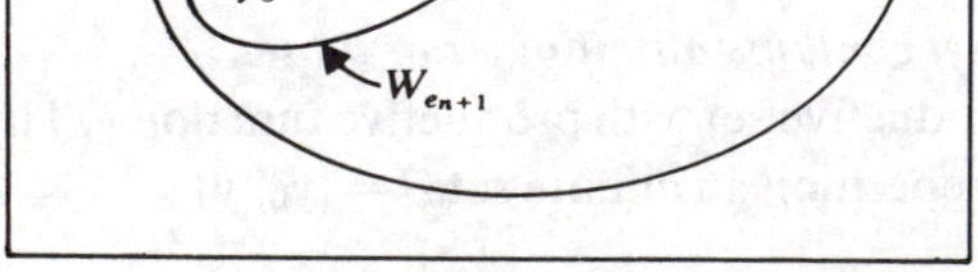

(*b*) $\{x : \phi_x$ is not surjective$\}$,
(*c*) $\{x : \phi_x$ is injective$\}$,
(*d*) $\{x : \phi_x$ is not a polynomial function$\}$.

2. Prove that the following sets are creative:
   (*a*) $\{x : x \in E_x\}$,
   (*b*) $\{x : E_x^{(n)} \neq \emptyset\}$ (n fixed),
   (*c*) $\{x : \phi_x$ is not injective$\}$,
   (*d*) $\{x : \phi_x(x) \in A\}$, where A is any non-empty r.e. set.
   (*e*) $\{x : \phi_x(x) = f(x)\}$, where f is any total computable function.
3. Prove that if B is r.e. and $A \cap B$ is productive, then A is productive.
4. Prove that if C is creative and A is an r.e. set such that $A \cap C = \emptyset$, then $C \cup A$ is creative.
5. Prove that every productive set contains an infinite recursive subset.
6. For any sets A, B define the sets $A \oplus B$ and $A \otimes B$ as in exercise 1.4(1). Suppose that B is r.e. Show that (*a*) if A is creative, then so are $A \oplus B$ and $A \otimes B$ (provided $B \neq \emptyset$),
   (*b*) if B is recursive, then the implications in (*a*) reverse.
7. Let $\mathscr{B}$ be a set of unary computable functions, and suppose that $g \in \mathscr{B}$ is such that for all finite $\theta \subseteq g$, $\theta \notin \mathscr{B}$. Prove that the set $\{x : \phi_x \in \mathscr{B}\}$ is productive.
   (*Hint*. Follow the first part of the proof of the Rice–Shapiro theorem.)
8. Use the result of question 7 to show that the following sets are productive:
   (*a*) $\{x : \phi_x$ is total$\}$,
   (*b*) $\{x : \phi_x$ is a polynomial function$\}$.
9. (Cf. exercise 2.18(13).) Disjoint sets A, B are said to be *effectively recursively inseparable* if there is a total computable function f such that whenever $A \subseteq W_a$, $B \subseteq W_b$ and $W_a \cap W_b = \emptyset$, then $f(a, b) \notin W_a \cup W_b$ (see fig. 7*d*).
   (*a*) Prove that the sets $K_0 = \{x : \phi_x(x) = 0\}$ and $K_1 = \{x : \phi_x(x) = 1\}$ are effectively recursively inseparable.
   (*Hint*. Find a total computable function f such that if $W_a \cap W_b = \emptyset$, then

$$\phi_{f(a,b)}(x) = \begin{cases} 1 & \text{if } x \in W_a, \\ 0 & \text{if } x \in W_b, \\ \text{undefined} & \text{otherwise.)} \end{cases}$$

Fig. 7*d*. Effectively recursively inseparable sets (exercise 3.13(9)).

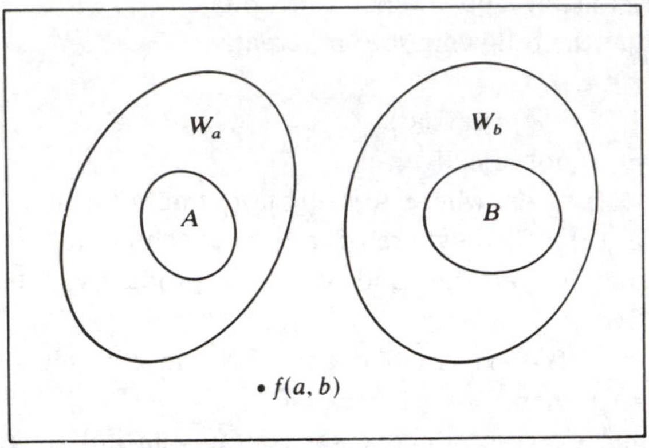

(*b*) Suppose that A, B are effectively recursively inseparable. Prove that if A, B are both r.e. then they are both creative. (*Note.* Extending the idea of effectiveness to a pair of recursively inseparable sets in this way parallels the step from a non-recursive set to a set having productive complement; the counterpart to a single creative set is then a pair of effectively recursively inseparable sets that are both r.e.)

4. Simple sets

Our task in this section is to show that there are sets satisfying the following definition and hence (in view of theorem 4.2 below) to establish that not all non-recursive r.e. sets are creative.

4.1. *Definition*

A set A is *simple* if

(*a*) A is r.e.,

(*b*) $\bar{A}$ is infinite,

(*c*) $\bar{A}$ contains no infinite r.e. subset.

The idea in (*b*), (*c*) of this definition is to pinpoint some features of a set that are *not* possessed by any recursive or creative set. Thus, although as yet we have no examples of simple sets, we can easily see that

4.2. *Theorem*

A simple set is neither recursive nor creative.

Proof. Suppose that A is a simple set. From (b) and (c) of the definition, $\bar{A}$ is not r.e., so A is not recursive. By theorem 3.11 and (c) of the definition, A is not creative. □

The following construction of a simple set is due to Post.

4.3. *Theorem*

There is a simple set.

Proof. We shall define a computable partial function f such that the range of f contains at least one member from every infinite r.e. set. This is done by arranging that if ϕ_x is total and E_x is infinite, then $f(x) \in E_x$. To make Ran(f) simple we must at the same time ensure that $\overline{\text{Ran}(f)}$ is infinite. We shall see that both conditions are met by the function f defined informally as follows:

To compute $f(x)$: compute $\phi_x(0), \phi_x(1), \ldots$ in succession (do not proceed to the computation of $\phi_x(y+1)$ unless and until $\phi_x(y)$ has been computed); stop if and only if a number z is found such that $\phi_x(z) > 2x$; in that case put $f(x) = \phi_x(z)$. (Formally we have $f(x) \simeq \phi_x(\mu z(\phi_x(z) > 2x))$, demonstrating clearly that f is computable.)

Put $A = \text{Ran}(f)$; then A is r.e. We now verify that A is simple.

Suppose that B is any infinite r.e. set. Then there is a *total* computable function ϕ_b such that $B = E_b$. Since B is infinite, the construction ensures that $f(b)$ is defined and $f(b) \in E_b = B$. Hence $B \not\subseteq \bar{A}$.

To see that $\bar{A}$ is infinite, note that if $f(x)$ is defined, then $f(x) > 2x$. Thus, for any n, the members of A that are in the set $\{0, 1, 2, \ldots, 2n\}$ are among $f(0), \ldots, f(n-1)$. This means that $\bar{A}$ contains more than n elements, for any n. Hence $\bar{A}$ is infinite. □

The construction of a simple set is but the first and one of the easiest of a wide variety of constructions that yield r.e. sets with all kinds of special properties. These are beyond the scope of this book; the interested reader should consult a text such as Rogers [1967], where he will find r.e. sets rejoicing in names such a hypersimple, hyperhypersimple, pseudocreative, and maximal. (See also exercise 4.4(3) below for an example of an r.e. set that is neither recursive, creative nor simple.)

4.4. *Exercises*

1. Suppose that A and B are simple sets. Show that the set $A \oplus B$ is simple. (For the definition of $\oplus$ see exercise 1.4(1).)

2. Suppose that f is a total injective computable function such that Ran(f) is not recursive. (Exercise 2.18(7) showed that such functions abound.) Show that the set

   $A = \{x : \exists y (y > x \text{ and } f(y) < f(x))\}$

   is simple. (*Hint.* To see that $\bar{A}$ is infinite, assume the contrary and show that there would then be a sequence of numbers $y_0 < y_1 < y_2 < \ldots$ such that $f(y_0) > f(y_1) > f(y_2) > \ldots$ To see that $\bar{A}$ does not contain an infinite r.e. set B, suppose to the contrary that $B \subseteq \bar{A}$. Then show that the problem $z \in \text{Ran}(f)$ is decidable as follows. Given z, find $n \in B$ such that $f(n) > z$; now use the fact that $n \notin A$ to devise a finite procedure for testing whether $z \in \text{Ran}(f)$.)
3. Show that if A is simple, then $A \otimes \mathbb{N}$ is r.e., but neither recursive, creative nor simple (see exercise 3.13(6)).
4. Let A, B be simple sets. Prove that $A \otimes B$ is not simple but that $\overline{\bar{A} \otimes \bar{B}}$ is simple.

8

Arithmetic and Gödel's incompleteness theorem

The celebrated incompleteness theorem of Gödel [1931] is one of many results about formal arithmetic that involve an interplay between computability and logic. Although full proofs in this area are beyond the scope of this book, we are able to outline some of the arguments discovered by Gödel and others. We shall highlight particularly the part played by computability theory, which in many cases can be viewed as an application of the phenomenon of creative and productive sets.

In §§ 1 and 2 we present some results about formal arithmetic that lead up to the full Gödel incompleteness theorem in § 3. In the final section the question of undecidability in formal arithmetic, already touched upon in § 1, is taken up again. Our presentation in this chapter does not assume any knowledge of formal logic.

1. Formal arithmetic

The formalisation of arithmetic begins by specifying a formal logical language L that is adequate for making statements of ordinary arithmetic of the natural numbers. The language L has its own *alphabet*, which includes the symbols $\mathsf{0}, \mathsf{1}, +, \times, =$ (having the obvious meanings), and also symbols for logical notions as follows: $\neg$ ('not'), $\wedge$ ('and'), $\vee$ ('or'), $\rightarrow$ ('implies'), $\forall$ ('for all'), $\exists$ ('there exists'). (In this chapter we will reserve the symbols $\forall$, $\exists$ for use in L, and write the phrase 'for all' and 'there exists' when needed in informal contexts.) In addition, L has symbols $\mathsf{x}, \mathsf{y}, \mathsf{z}, \ldots$ for variables, and brackets (and), and there may be other symbols besides.

The *statements* (or *formulas*) of L are defined to be the meaningful finite sequences of symbols from the alphabet of L. For instance, the statement

$$\exists \mathsf{y}(\mathsf{y} \times (\mathsf{1}+\mathsf{1}) = \mathsf{x})$$

is the formal counterpart of the informal statement 'x is even'. It is helpful to abbreviate the expression $1+1$ by 2, $(1+1)+1$ by 3, and so on for all natural numbers. Then the false informal statement '5 is even' would be expressed formally in L by the statement

$$\exists y(y \times 2 = 5).$$

We can similarly express in L formal counterparts of many informal statements of ordinary arithmetic: for '$x > y$' we would write

$$\exists z(\neg(z = 0) \wedge (y + z = x)).$$

(The statement $\neg(z = 0)$ is often abbreviated by $z \neq 0$.) For 'x is prime' we would write

$$(x \neq 0) \wedge (x \neq 1) \wedge \forall y \forall z(x = y \times z \rightarrow (y = 1 \vee z = 1)).$$

Let us denote by $\mathcal{S}$ the set of all possible meaningful statements of the language L. Then $\mathcal{S}$ divides into two important sets, namely

$\mathcal{T}$ = the set of all statements that are true in the ordinary arithmetic of $\mathbb{N}$,

$\mathcal{F}$ = the set of all statements that are false in the ordinary arithmetic of $\mathbb{N}$.

Mathematicians would like to discover as much as possible about the set $\mathcal{T}$. A natural question from the point of view of computability is

(1.1)(*a*) Is $\mathcal{T}$ recursive, or even recursively enumerable?

Another question, important for the mathematician and philosopher alike is

(1.1)(*b*) Is there a simple-minded subset of $\mathcal{T}$ (a set of *axioms*) from which all other statements in $\mathcal{T}$ can be proved?

We shall discover that the answer to both of these questions is *no*.

Question 1.1(*a*) above can be made precise by means of a standard coding procedure. It is quite routine to specify an effective enumeration of the set $\mathcal{S}$, without repetitions, using a procedure similar to that used to enumerate programs in chapter 4. Let us assume that this has been done, and let us denote by θ_n the $(n+1)$th statement of $\mathcal{S}$ in this enumeration, so that

$$\mathcal{S} = \{\theta_0, \theta_1, \theta_2, \ldots\}.$$

The effectiveness of this enumeration means that given n we can effectively find and write down the statement θ_n, and conversely, given any statement σ in $\mathcal{S}$ we can effectively compute the code number n such that $\sigma = \theta_n$.

This coding of statements is now used to code any set of statements $\mathscr{X}$ by the set of numbers

$$X = \{n : \theta_n \in \mathscr{X}\}.$$

$$\text{We say that } \mathscr{X} \text{ is} \begin{Bmatrix} \textit{recursive} \\ \textit{r.e.} \\ \textit{productive} \\ \textit{creative} \\ \text{etc.} \end{Bmatrix} \text{ if } X \text{ is} \begin{cases} \text{recursive} \\ \text{r.e.} \\ \text{productive} \\ \text{creative} \\ \text{etc.} \end{cases}$$

This gives the question 1.1(a) above a precise meaning.

One of the key results that makes computability an extremely useful tool when investigating formal arithmetic is the following, due to Gödel; we present it without any proof.

1.2. *Lemma*

Suppose that $M(x_1, \ldots, x_n)$ is a decidable predicate. Then it is possible to construct a statement $\sigma(\mathsf{x}_1, \ldots, \mathsf{x}_n)$ of L that is a formal counterpart of $M(x_1, \ldots, x_n)$ in the following sense: for any $a_1, \ldots, a_n \in \mathbb{N}$

$$M(a_1, \ldots, a_n) \textit{ holds} \quad \textit{iff} \quad \sigma(\mathsf{a}_1, \ldots, \mathsf{a}_n) \in \mathscr{T}.$$

Consider now the creative set K. By theorem 7-2.4 there is a decidable predicate $R(x, y)$ such that

$$x \in K \Leftrightarrow \text{there is } y \text{ such that } R(x, y).$$

Applying lemma 1.2 to the predicate $R(x, y)$ let us fix on one particular formal counterpart of this predicate, which we denote by $\sigma_R(\mathsf{x}, \mathsf{y})$. Then for any $n \in \mathbb{N}$ the statement $\exists \mathsf{y}\sigma_R(\mathsf{n}, \mathsf{y})$ is a formal counterpart for '$n \in K$', and $\neg\exists \mathsf{y}\sigma_R(\mathsf{n}, \mathsf{y})$ is a formal counterpart of '$n \notin K$'. Let us therefore write

$$\mathsf{n} \in \mathsf{K} \quad \text{for} \quad \exists \mathsf{y}\sigma_R(\mathsf{n}, \mathsf{y})$$

and

$$\mathsf{n} \notin \mathsf{K} \quad \text{for} \quad \neg\exists \mathsf{y}\sigma_R(\mathsf{n}, \mathsf{y}).$$

Then using lemma 1.2 we have immediately

1.3. *Lemma*

For any $n \in \mathbb{N}$

(a) *$n \in K$ iff $\mathsf{n} \in \mathsf{K} \in \mathscr{T}$*

(b) *$n \notin K$ iff $\mathsf{n} \notin \mathsf{K} \in \mathscr{T}$*

We are almost ready to answer the question 1.1(a) above; we shall need the following lemma.

1.4. *Lemma*

There is a total computable function g such that for all n, $\theta_{g(n)}$ is $n \notin K$

Proof. This is immediate from the effectiveness of the coding of statements, since given n we can effectively write down the statement $n \notin K$ $(= \neg \exists y \sigma_R(n, y))$. □

Now we have, in answer to question 1.1(*a*):

1.5. *Theorem*

$\mathcal{T}$ is not r.e.; in fact $\mathcal{T}$ is productive.

Proof. Let $\mathbb{T} = \{n : \theta_n \in \mathcal{T}\}$; taking g as in lemma 1.4 we have

$$n \in \bar{K} \Leftrightarrow n \notin K$$
$$\Leftrightarrow n \notin K \in \mathcal{T} \text{ (by lemma 1.3).}$$
$$\Leftrightarrow g(n) \in \mathbb{T} \text{ (by lemma 1.4).}$$

So, since $\bar{K}$ is not r.e., neither is $\mathbb{T}$. In fact, by theorem 7-3.2 we see that $\mathbb{T}$ is productive. □

1.6. *Exercise*

Show that $\mathcal{F}$ is productive.

2. Incompleteness

A simple version of Gödel's incompleteness theorem follows easily from theorem 1.5. We must first describe the setting of this famous result.

Consider the second question (1.1(*b*)) posed in § 1. This question is made precise by using the idea of a *formal system*. A *formal system* $(\mathcal{A}, \mathcal{D})$ (for the language L) consists of a set $\mathcal{A} \subseteq \mathcal{S}$ (the *axioms*) and an explicit definition $\mathcal{D}$ of the notion of a *formal proof* of a statement in $\mathcal{S}$ from these axioms, satisfying the conditions:

(2.1) (*a*) Proofs are finite objects (hence capable of being coded),

(*b*) The explicit definition $\mathcal{D}$ of proof is such that if $\mathcal{A}$ is recursive then the relation

'*p* is a proof of the statement σ from the axioms $\mathcal{A}$'

is decidable.

We can now interpret the question 1.1(*b*) as asking whether there is a formal system for L such that

(2.2) (*a*) $\mathcal{A}$ is recursive (so we are taking simple-minded in a fairly wide sense),

(*b*) The provable statements are precisely those in $\mathcal{T}$.

The condition (b) poses a problem for the philosopher who may be trying to *define* the very notion of arithmetic truth by means of a formal system. For him, this condition is meaningless, and must be replaced by conditions reflecting some of the properties to be expected of truth, such as

(2.2)(b')*Consistency*: there is no statement σ such that both σ and $\neg\sigma$ are provable,

(2.2)(b'')*Completeness*: for any statement σ, either σ is provable or $\neg\sigma$ is provable.

A simplified version of Gödel's theorem shows that there is no formal system of arithmetic satisfying the conditions 2.2(a) and (b). This is easily derived from theorem 1.5, and is given below. The full theorem of Gödel [1931] together with its improvement by Rosser shows that there is no formal system of arithmetic (of a certain minimal strength) satisfying conditions 2.2(a) and (b'), (b''). In other words, any consistent formal system of arithmetic having a recursive set of axioms is incomplete. This will be proved in § 3.

We shall need the following lemma to establish the simplified Gödel theorem.

2.3. *Lemma*

In any recursively axiomatised formal system the set of provable statements is r.e.

Proof. Let $\mathscr{P}\imath$ be the set of statements in $\mathscr{S}$ that are provable. Since proofs are finite, they can be effectively numbered; then if $\mathscr{A}$ is a recursive set of axioms the predicate

$$M(x, y) \equiv \text{‘}y \text{ is the number of a proof of } \theta_x \text{ from the axioms } \mathscr{A}\text{’}$$

is decidable, by (2.1)(b). Then

$$\theta_x \text{ is provable} \Leftrightarrow \text{there is } y \text{ such that } M(x, y) \text{ holds.}$$

Hence, by theorem 7-2.4, $\mathscr{P}\imath$ is r.e. $\square$

Now we have

2.4. *Theorem.* (The simplified Gödel incompleteness theorem)

Suppose that $(\mathscr{A}, \mathscr{D})$ *is a recursively axiomatised formal system in which all provable statements are true. Then there is a statement* σ *that is true but not provable (and consequently* $\neg\sigma$ *is not provable either).*

Proof. By lemma 2.3, the set $\mathscr{P}\imath$ of provable statements is r.e., and we are given that $\mathscr{P}\imath \subseteq \mathscr{T}$. Now $\mathscr{T}$ is not r.e. (theorem 1.5) so we immediately have a statement $\sigma \in \mathscr{T} \backslash \mathscr{P}\imath$; i.e. σ is true but not provable. Clearly $\neg\sigma$ is not provable either (otherwise $\neg\sigma$ would be true). □

(Using the productiveness of $\mathscr{T}$ (theorem 1.5) we could strengthen this theorem to say that the statement σ can be obtained effectively from a specification of the formal system (which would yield an index for $\mathscr{P}\imath$).)

To aid an understanding of the proof of the full Gödel theorem in § 3 it is useful to examine the inner workings that were hidden when we applied theorem 1.5 in the above proof to obtain the statement σ.

Let us say that a statement is *refutable* if its negation is provable. Consider the sets of numbers Pr* and Ref* given by

$$\begin{aligned}\text{Pr}^* &= \{n : \mathsf{n} \in \mathsf{K} \text{ is provable}\},\\ \text{Ref}^* &= \{n : \mathsf{n} \in \mathsf{K} \text{ is refutable}\}\\ &= \{n : \mathsf{n} \notin \mathsf{K} \text{ is provable}\}\\ &= \{n : \theta_{g(n)} \in \mathscr{P}\imath\},\end{aligned}$$

(where g is the computable function given by lemma 1.4 and used in the proof of theorem 1.5). The assumption that provable statements are true means in particular that $\text{Pr}^* \subseteq K$ and $\text{Ref}^* \subseteq \bar{K}$. Now Ref* is r.e. (from the fact that $n \in \text{Ref}^* \Leftrightarrow \theta_{g(n)} \in \mathscr{P}\imath$, and $\mathscr{P}\imath$ is r.e.), so there is a number m such that $\text{Ref}^* = W_m$.

By the productiveness of $\bar{K}$ we have immediately that $m \in \bar{K} \backslash \text{Ref}^*$, i.e. $m \notin K$, and $\mathsf{m} \notin \mathsf{K}$ is not provable. Taking σ to be the statement $\mathsf{m} \notin \mathsf{K}$ we thus see that σ is true but not provable (and $\neg\sigma$ is not provable, as before). The argument is illustrated by fig. 8*a*. (For comparison with the

Fig. 8*a*. Simplified Gödel incompleteness (theorem 2.4).

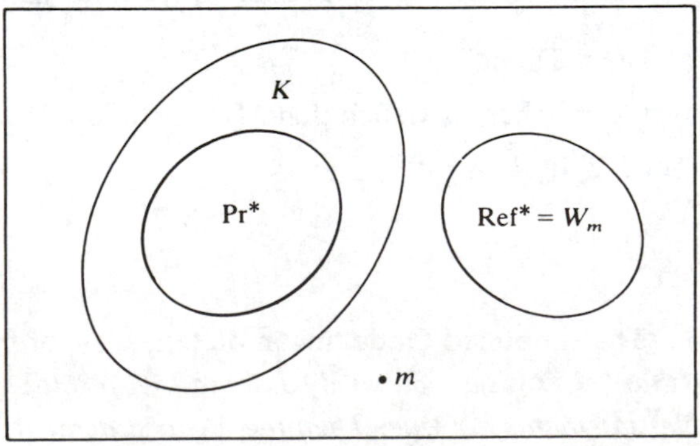

proof of the full Gödel theorem in the next section, note that the non-provability of $\neg\sigma$ can be seen as a consequence of the fact that $\mathrm{Pr}^* \subseteq K$: for $m \notin K$ (as above), so $m \notin \mathrm{Pr}^*$, i.e. $\mathsf{m} \in \mathsf{K}$ is not provable. Then, by the rules of formal proof $\neg \mathsf{m} \notin \mathsf{K}$ (i.e. $\neg\sigma$) is not provable.)

Notice now the intended meaning of the statement σ thus obtained: σ is the formal counterpart of the statement $m \notin K$, i.e. $m \notin W_m$. But we have

$$\begin{aligned} m \notin W_m &\Leftrightarrow m \notin \mathrm{Ref}^* \\ &\Leftrightarrow \mathsf{m} \notin \mathsf{K} \text{ is not provable} \\ &\Leftrightarrow \sigma \notin \mathcal{P}r \end{aligned}$$

Thus σ is a formal counterpart of the statement 'σ is not provable'; i.e. speaking rather loosely, σ says 'I am not provable'. This is reminiscent of the paradox of the liar, involving the informal statement

$$\Lambda \equiv \text{'I am lying'}.$$

Informal reasoning about Λ results in the paradox

$$\Lambda \text{ is true} \quad \text{iff} \quad \Lambda \text{ is not true}.$$

If the same informal reasoning is applied to the informal statement 'I am not provable' the paradox is avoided by the conclusion that *provable is not the same as true*. This informal conclusion is rigorously justified by the proof of theorem 2.4.

3. Gödel's incompleteness theorem

We proceed in this section to show how the idea behind the proof of theorem 2.4 can be refined so as to avoid any reference to truth.

For the moment we fix on a particular formal system of arithmetic known as *Peano arithmetic*. The axioms for this system consist of a recursive subset of $\mathcal{S}$ known as *Peano's axioms*; these reflect the simple properties of the successor operation on $\mathbb{N}$, and the recursive definition of addition and multiplication in terms of it, together with an axiom scheme reflecting the principle of induction on $\mathbb{N}$. The notion of a formal proof is taken as that defined for the first-order predicate calculus. Full details of Peano arithmetic (sometimes called *formal number theory*) may be found in any textbook on mathematical logic. For our purposes, the important fact we need to know about Peano arithmetic is given by the following lemma, to which a substantial part of Gödel's proof is devoted.

3.1. *Lemma*

Let $M(x_1, \ldots, x_n)$ be a decidable predicate, and let $\sigma(\mathsf{x}_1, \ldots, \mathsf{x}_n)$ be the statement of L that is the formal counterpart of $M(x_1, \ldots, x_n)$ as *given by lemma 1.2. Then M is represented in Peano arithmetic in the following sense: for any $a_1, \ldots, a_n \in \mathbb{N}$*

(*a*) *if $M(a_1, \ldots, a_n)$ holds, then $\sigma(\mathsf{a}_1, \ldots, \mathsf{a}_n)$ is provable,*
(*b*) *if $M(a_1, \ldots, a_n)$ does not hold, then $\neg\sigma(\mathsf{a}_1, \ldots, \mathsf{a}_n)$ is provable.*

(For a proof refer to a textbook such as Mendelson [1964].) □

Consider now the statement $\mathsf{n} \in \mathsf{K}$ (i.e. $\exists \mathsf{y} \sigma_R(\mathsf{x}, \mathsf{y})$) that we took in § 1 as a formal counterpart of the statement $n \in K$. Then from lemma 3.1 we can obtain

3.2. *Corollary*

For any natural number n, if $n \in K$ then $\mathsf{n} \in \mathsf{K}$ is provable in Peano arithmetic.

Proof. Suppose that $n \in K$. Then there is a natural number m such that $R(n, m)$ holds, so by lemma 3.1 we have that $\sigma_R(\mathsf{n}, \mathsf{m})$ is provable. The rules of the predicate calculus are such that we can immediately find a proof of $\exists \mathsf{y} \sigma_R(\mathsf{n}, \mathsf{y})$; i.e. $\mathsf{n} \in \mathsf{K}$ is provable.

For part of his proof, Gödel needed an extra technical condition called *ω-consistency*: a formal system is said to be *ω-consistent* if there is no statement $\tau(\mathsf{y})$ such that all of the following are provable:

$$\exists \mathsf{y} \tau(\mathsf{y}), \neg\tau(0), \neg\tau(1), \neg\tau(2), \ldots$$

(ω-consistency is a stronger condition than consistency (2.2)(*b'*)).

We can easily derive the converse of corollary 3.2 from lemma 3.1, with the assumption of ω-consistency.

3.3. *Lemma*

Suppose that Peano arithmetic is ω-consistent; then for any natural number n, if $\mathsf{n} \in \mathsf{K}$ is provable then $n \in K$.

Proof. Suppose that $n \notin K$; then for every $m \in \mathbb{N}$ we have that $R(n, m)$ does not hold, so by lemma 3.1, $\neg\sigma_R(\mathsf{n}, \mathsf{m})$ is provable. Thus, if $\mathsf{n} \in \mathsf{K}$ is provable but $n \notin K$, all of the following are provable

$$\exists \mathsf{y} \sigma_R(\mathsf{n}, \mathsf{y}), \neg\sigma_R(\mathsf{n}, 0), \neg\sigma_R(\mathsf{n}, 1), \ldots$$

in contradiction of ω-consistency for the statement $\tau(\mathsf{y}) = \sigma_R(\mathsf{n}, \mathsf{y})$. □

We can now present a proof of

3.4. *Theorem* (Gödel's incompleteness theorem [1931])
There is a statement σ of L such that
(*a*) *if Peano arithmetic is consistent, then σ is not provable,*
(*b*) *if Peano arithmetic is ω-consistent, then $\neg\sigma$ is not provable.*

Proof.
(*a*) Recall the sets $\mathrm{Pr}^* = \{n : \mathsf{n} \in \mathsf{K} \text{ is provable}\}$,
$\mathrm{Ref}^* = \{n : \mathsf{n} \in \mathsf{K} \text{ is refutable}\}$,

that we defined in the discussion at the end of the previous section. By corollary 3.2 we have $K \subseteq \mathrm{Pr}^*$; consistency implies that $\mathrm{Pr}^* \cap \mathrm{Ref}^* = \emptyset$, and so $\mathrm{Ref}^* \subseteq \bar{K}$. We can now argue as before: Ref^* is r.e., so take m such that $\mathrm{Ref}^* = W_m$. The situation is illustrated by fig. 8*b*, which should be compared with that in fig. 8*a*.

By the productiveness of $\bar{K}$, we have that $m \in \bar{K} \backslash \mathrm{Ref}^*$; in particular, $m \notin \mathrm{Ref}^*$ means that $\mathsf{m} \notin \mathsf{K}$ is not provable. Hence (*a*) is established, by taking σ to be the statement $\mathsf{m} \notin \mathsf{K}$.

(*b*) The condition of ω-consistency implies (by lemma 3.3) that $\mathrm{Pr}^* \subseteq K$, and hence $\mathrm{Pr}^* = K$. Thus, with ω-consistency, fig. 8*b* is modified to become fig. 8*c*. Thus $m \notin K$ means that $m \notin \mathrm{Pr}^*$; i.e. $\mathsf{m} \in \mathsf{K}$ is not provable. The rules of the predicate calculus tell us immediately that $\neg\sigma$ (i.e. $\neg\mathsf{m} \notin \mathsf{K}$) is not provable. □

Notes

1. The statement σ produced by Gödel's theorem is called an *undecidable* or an *undecided* statement of Peano arithmetic. As discussed at the

Fig. 8*b*. Gödel incompleteness (theorem 3.4(*a*)).

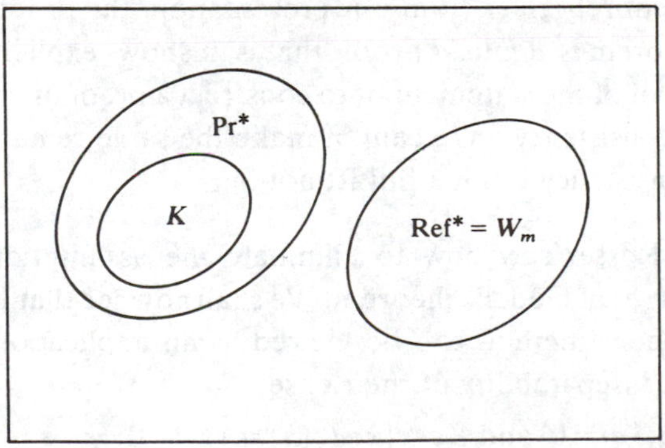

Fig. 8*c*. Gödel incompleteness (theorem 3.4 (b)).

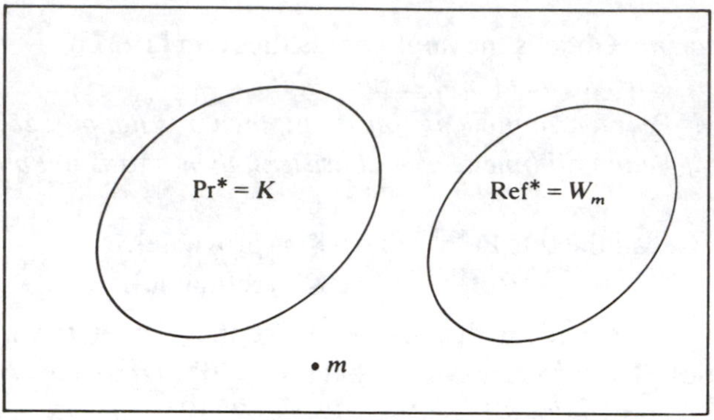

end of § 2, σ has the informal meaning 'I am not provable', and is, on an intuitive level, true.

2. Clearly Gödel's theorem applies to any recursively axiomatised formal system in which all decidable relations can be represented (in the sense of lemma 3.1). In particular, this is true for any such system that is stronger than Peano arithmetic. In consequence, there is no way to avoid the incompleteness phenomenon by adding new axioms: for example σ or $\neg\sigma$. The resulting formal system would have a new undecided statement.

3. Note that the undecided statement σ can be constructed explicitly from a specification of Peano arithmetic, since from such a specification, we could effectively find an index m for Ref*. This constructive aspect of Gödel's theorem is a consequence of the fact that K is *creative*. An analysis of the proof would show that we can demonstrate the mere *existence* of an undecided statement using any non-recursive r.e. set A in place of K.

4. Although not entirely clear from our presentation, the proof of part (a) of Gödel's theorem is a *finitist* proof: that is, it shows explicitly how, given a formal proof of the statement σ, to construct a proof of $\neg\sigma$ (thus demonstrating inconsistency). We cannot make the same remark about (b), because ω-consistency is not a finitist notion.

In 1936 J. B. Rosser saw how to eliminate the assumption of ω-consistency in part (b) of Gödel's theorem. We shall now see that Rosser's refinement of Gödel's method can be viewed as an application of the effective recursive inseparability of the r.e. sets

$$K_0 = \{x : \phi_x(x) = 0\} \text{ and } K_1 = \{x : \phi_x(x) = 1\}$$

(that we discussed in exercise 7-3.13(9)), in place of the use of the creative set K. (Our treatment below does not assume familiarity with this exercise.)

We begin by describing some statements of $\mathcal{S}$ that are formal counterparts of the statements $n \in K_0$ and $n \in K_1$; these are slightly more complex than the formal version of $n \in K$ used earlier. Select decidable predicates $R_0(x, y)$ and $R_1(x, y)$ such that

$$n \in K_0 \Leftrightarrow \text{there is } y \text{ such that } R_0(n, y)$$

and

$$n \in K_1 \Leftrightarrow \text{there is } y \text{ such that } R_1(n, y).$$

Now clearly $K_0 \cap K_1 = \varnothing$, so we also have

(*) $\quad n \in K_0 \Leftrightarrow$ there is y such that (i) $R_0(n, y)$ and
(ii) for all $z \leq y$, $R_1(n, z)$ does not hold,

and there is a similar equivalence for $n \in K_1$. Now take statements σ_{R_0}, σ_{R_1} representing R_0, R_1 in Peano arithmetic as given by lemma 3.1. Rosser's trick was (essentially) to use the following statement (based on (*) above)

(**) $\quad \exists \mathsf{y}(\sigma_{R_0}(\mathsf{n}, \mathsf{y}) \wedge \forall \mathsf{z} \leq \mathsf{y}(\neg \sigma_{R_1}(\mathsf{n}, \mathsf{z})))$

as the formal counterpart of $n \in K_0$, rather than the simpler statement $\exists \mathsf{y} \sigma_{R_0}(\mathsf{n}, \mathsf{y})$. Let us write $\mathsf{n} \in \mathsf{K}_0$ for the statement (**) above. Similarly we write $\mathsf{n} \in \mathsf{K}_1$ for the statement

$$\exists \mathsf{y}(\sigma_{R_1}(\mathsf{n}, \mathsf{y}) \wedge \forall \mathsf{z} \leq \mathsf{y}(\neg \sigma_{R_0}(\mathsf{n}, \mathsf{z}))).$$

Now it is quite straightforward to establish the following key lemma (which should be compared with corollary 3.2):

3.5. *Lemma*

In Peano arithmetic, for any natural number n

(a) *if* $n \in K_0$, *then* $\mathsf{n} \in \mathsf{K}_0$ *is provable,*

(b) *if* $n \in K_1$, *then* $\mathsf{n} \in \mathsf{K}_1$ *is provable,*

(c) *if* $\mathsf{n} \in \mathsf{K}_1$ *is provable, then* $\mathsf{n} \notin \mathsf{K}_0$ *is also provable.*

The proof of this lemma uses some technical properties of Peano arithmetic, and we therefore omit it. It is to obtain 3.5(c) particularly that the more complex formal representations of $n \in K_0$ and $n \in K_1$ are needed. (For those familiar with mathematical logic we should mention that lemma 3.5 is easily established once the following statements have been shown to be provable in Peano arithmetic:

(3.6) (*a*) For any $m \in \mathbb{N}$:
$\forall z \leq m(z = 0 \vee z = 1 \vee \ldots \vee z = m)$,
(*b*) $\forall y \forall z(y \leq z \vee z \leq y)$.)

We can now complete the proof of

3.7. *Theorem* (The Gödel–Rosser incompleteness theorem)
There is a statement τ such that if Peano arithmetic is consistent, neither τ nor $\neg\tau$ is provable.

Proof. Define the sets

$$\mathrm{Pr}^{**} = \{n : \mathsf{n} \in \mathsf{K}_0 \text{ is provable}\}$$
$$\mathrm{Ref}^{**} = \{n : \mathsf{n} \in \mathsf{K}_0 \text{ is refutable}\}$$
$$= \{n : \mathsf{n} \notin \mathsf{K}_0 \text{ is provable}\}.$$

Consistency means that $\mathrm{Pr}^{**} \cap \mathrm{Ref}^{**} = \varnothing$.

From lemma 3.5(*a*) we have

$$K_0 \subseteq \mathrm{Pr}^{**}.$$

Also, for any *n*, combining lemma 3.5(*b*) and (*c*) we have

$$n \in K_1 \Rightarrow \mathsf{n} \notin \mathsf{K}_0 \text{ is provable};$$

i.e.

$$K_1 \subseteq \mathrm{Ref}^{**}.$$

Now Pr^{**} and Ref^{**} are both r.e. (this uses the fact that $\mathscr{P}_{\imath}$ is r.e.) so the recursive inseparability of K_0 and K_1 (exercise 7-2.18(13*b*)) means that there is a number $p \notin \mathrm{Pr}^{**} \cup \mathrm{Ref}^{**}$. The state of affairs is illustrated in fig. 8*d*. Now $p \notin \mathrm{Pr}^{**}$ means that $\mathsf{p} \in \mathsf{K}_0$ is not provable, and $p \notin \mathrm{Ref}^{**}$ means

Fig. 8*d*. Gödel–Rosser incompleteness (theorem 3.7).

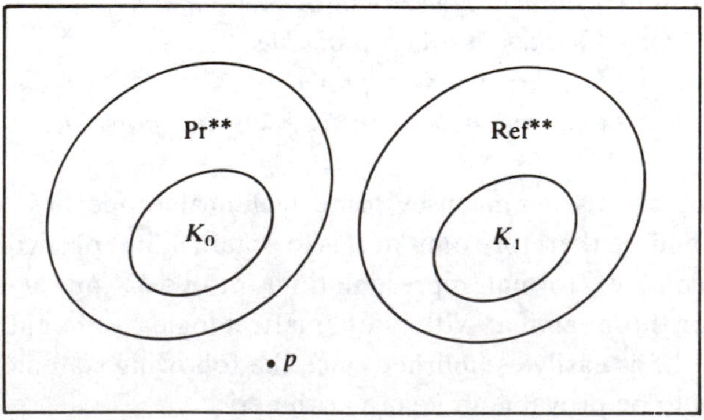

that $p \notin K_0$ is not provable, so the theorem is established, by taking τ to be the statement $p \in K_0$.

Although the proof of the theorem as stated is complete, let us now see how the numper p (hence the statement τ) can be explicitly constructed. From an explicit specification of Peano arithmetic, we can effectively find an index p such that

$$\phi_p(n) = \begin{cases} 1 & \text{if } n \in \text{Pr}^{**}, \\ 0 & \text{if } n \in \text{Ref}^{**}, \\ \text{undefined} & \text{otherwise.} \end{cases}$$

We can now see that $p \notin \text{Pr}^{**} \cup \text{Ref}^{**}$, as follows:

(i) if $p \in \text{Pr}^{**}$, then $\phi_p(p) = 1$, so $p \in K_1$, hence $p \in \text{Ref}^{**}$, contradicting consistency. Hence $p \notin \text{Pr}^{**}$.

(ii) if $p \in \text{Ref}^{**}$, then $\phi_p(p) = 0$, so $p \in K_0$, hence $p \in \text{Pr}^{**}$, another contradiction. Hence $p \notin \text{Ref}^{**}$.

(The fact that p can thus be obtained explicitly uses essentially the *effective* recursive inseparability of K_0 and K_1 (see exercise 7-3.13(9).) □

Notes

1. The statement $\neg\tau$ constructed in this theorem corresponds to the undecided statement σ of theorem 3.4; it is easily seen that $\neg\tau$ also has the informal interpretation 'I am not provable', and is intuitively true.

2. The Gödel–Rosser theorem applies to any recursively axiomatised formal system of arithmetic in which all decidable relations can be represented and for which lemma 3.5 can be established. (Lemma 3.5 always holds for systems in which statements 3.6 (*a*), (*b*) can be proved: such systems are called *Rosser systems*.) Again, there is thus no possibility of avoiding incompleteness by adding new axioms.

3. The Gödel–Rosser theorem is a completely finitist theorem: the proof (when given in full detail) shows how to demonstrate inconsistency explicitly if we were given a proof of either τ or $\neg\tau$.

4. Undecidability

We have already seen that the set $\mathcal{T}$ of true statements of arithmetic is not recursive (theorem 1.5): this is often described by saying that $\mathcal{T}$ is *undecidable*. In general, when considering sets of statements the terms *decidable* and *undecidable* are often used to mean recursive and non-recursive.

We can ask particularly of any formal system of arithmetic, is the set $\mathcal{P}r$ of provable statements decidable? The answer is invariably no, and there are various ways to see this. We confine ourselves to one of the many results in this area, using the ideas of the previous section.

4.1. *Theorem*

Suppose that $(\mathscr{A}, \mathscr{D})$ *is an ω-consistent formal system of arithmetic in which all decidable predicates are representable (in the sense of lemma* 3.1). *Then the set of provable statements is creative.*

Proof. The assumption of the theorem means that Gödel's theorem 3.4 applies, so in particular we have from the proof of theorem 3.4:

$$K = \mathrm{Pr}^* = \{n : \mathsf{n} \in \mathsf{K} \text{ is provable}\}.$$

Now let $\mathrm{Pr} = \{n : \theta_n \text{ is provable}\}$; we can find a computable function h such that $\mathsf{n} \in \mathsf{K}$ is $\theta_{h(n)}$, and then

$$n \in K \Leftrightarrow n \in \mathrm{Pr}^*$$
$$\Leftrightarrow h(n) \in \mathrm{Pr}.$$

So by theorem 7-3.2, Pr is creative. □

4.2. *Corollary*

If Peano arithmetic is ω-consistent then the provable statements form a creative set. (*This is the case in particular if all provable statements are true.*)

The counterpart to theorem 4.1 and corollary 4.2 using Rosser's ideas is given in the following exercise.

4.3. *Exercise*

Suppose that $(\mathscr{A}, \mathscr{D})$ is a consistent recursively axiomatised formal system for which lemmas 3.1 and 3.5 hold. Let Pr** and Ref** be the sets defined in the proof of theorem 3.6.

(*a*) Show that Pr** and Ref** are effectively recursively inseparable.

(*b*) Let $\mathrm{Pr} = \{\mathrm{n}: \theta_n \text{ is provable}\}$ and $\mathrm{Ref} = \{n : \neg\theta_n \text{ is provable}\}$. Prove that Pr and Ref are effectively recursively inseparable. (*Hint.* Extend the idea of theorem 7-3.2 to pairs of effectively recursively inseparable sets.)

The presentation of the results in this chapter is derived largely from the books of Kleene [1967] and Smullyan [1961]. For further discussion of incompleteness and undecidability in arithmetic and related areas, the reader is referred to Bell & Machover [1977], Boolos & Jeffrey [1974], or Rogers [1971].

9
Reducibility and degrees

In earlier chapters we have used the technique of *reducing* one problem to another, often as means of demonstrating undecidability. We did this, for instance, in the proof of theorem 6-1.4 by showing that there is a total computable function k such that $x \in W_x \Leftrightarrow \phi_{k(x)} = \mathbf{0}$, i.e. we used the function k to transform or reduce each instance of the general problem '$x \in W_x$' to an instance of the general problem '$\phi_x = \mathbf{0}$'. In this chapter we consider two ways of making the idea of reducibility precise, and for each we discuss the associated notion of *degree* (of difficulty) that arises.

It is more convenient to deal with reducibility between *sets* rather than between *problems*, remembering that any problem is represented by a set of numbers. The informal idea of a set A being *reducible* to a set B can be expressed in various ways: for instance

(*a*) 'Given a decision procedure for the problem '$x \in B$', we can construct one for '$x \in A$'.'

(*b*) 'For someone who knows all about B, there is a mechanical procedure (that uses his knowledge of B) for deciding questions about A.'

(*c*) 'Questions about A are no harder than questions about B.'

(*d*) 'The degree of difficulty of the problem '$x \in A$' is no greater than that of the problem '$x \in B$'.'

It turns out that there are several non-equivalent ways of making this idea precise. The differences between these consist in the manner and extent to which information about B is allowed to be used to settle questions about A. In §§ 1–3 we shall investigate one of the simplest notions of reducibility, called *many–one reducibility*, which includes all of our earlier uses of the informal idea. In the final sections we shall discuss a more general notion known as *Turing reducibility*.

1. Many–one reducibility

1.1. *Definition*

The set A is *many–one reducible* (abbreviated *m-reducible*) to the set B if there is a total computable function f such that for all x

$$x \in A \quad \text{iff} \quad f(x) \in B.$$

We shall write this $A \le_m B$; and we shall write $f\colon A \le_m B$ to indicate that f is a total computable function demonstrating that $A \le_m B$.

Note. The phrase many–one is used to distinguish this kind of reducibility from a related notion called *one–one reducibility*, for which the function f is required to be injective.

We have used m-reducibility implicitly on many occasions in earlier chapters. The *s–m–n* theorem is often needed to establish many–one reducibility, as we see in the following examples.

1.2. *Examples*

1. In chapter VI we showed that K is m-reducible to each of the following sets:
   (*a*) $\{x : \phi_x = \mathbf{0}\}$ (theorem 6-1.4, quoted above),
   (*b*) $\{x : c \in W_x\}$ (theorem 6-1.6).
2. If we examine the function k given in the proof of theorem 6-1.6 we see that $x \in K \Leftrightarrow \phi_{k(x)}$ is total. Hence
   $k : K \le_m \{x : \phi_x \text{ is total}\}$.
3. Rice's theorem (theorem 6-1.7) is proved by showing that $K \le_m \{x : \phi_x \in \mathscr{B}\}$, where $\mathscr{B}$ is any non-empty subset of $\mathscr{C}_1$ such that $f_\varnothing \notin \mathscr{B}$.
4. $\{x : \phi_x \text{ is total}\} \le_m \{x : \phi_x = \mathbf{0}\}$.
   Proof. Using the *s–m–n* theorem obtain a total computable function k such that $\phi_{k(x)} = \mathbf{0} \circ \phi_x$, for all x. Then
   $k : \{x : \phi_x \text{is total}\} \le_m \{x : \phi_x = \mathbf{0}\}$.

The following theorem gives some of the elementary properties of m-reducibility.

1.3. *Theorem*

Let A, B, C be sets.

(*a*) $\le_m$ *is reflexive* (*i.e.* $A \le_m A$) *and transitive* (*i.e. if* $A \le_m B$ *and* $B \le_m C$ *then* $A \le_m C$),

(*b*) $A \le_m B$ *iff* $\bar{A} \le_m \bar{B}$,

(*c*) *if A is recursive and $B \leq_m A$, then B is recursive,*
(*d*) *if A is recursive and $B \neq \emptyset, \mathbb{N}$, then $A \leq_m B$,*
(*e*) *if A is r.e. and $B \leq_m A$, then B is r.e.,*
(*f*) (i) *$A \leq_m \mathbb{N}$ iff $A = \mathbb{N}$,*
(ii) *$A \leq_m \emptyset$ iff $A = \emptyset$,*
(*g*) (i) *$\mathbb{N} \leq_m A$ iff $A \neq \emptyset$,*
(ii) *$\emptyset \leq_m A$ iff $A \neq \mathbb{N}$.*

Proof

(*a*) *Reflexive.* $\iota: A \leq_m A$, where ι is the identity function. *Transitive.* If $f: A \leq_m B$ and $g: B \leq_m C$, then clearly $g \circ f: A \leq_m C$.
(*b*) If $g: A \leq_m B$, then $x \in A \Leftrightarrow g(x) \in B$; hence $x \in \bar{A} \Leftrightarrow g(x) \in \bar{B}$; hence $g: \bar{A} \leq_m \bar{B}$.
(*c*) Suppose that $g: B \leq_m A$; then $c_B(x) = c_A(g(x))$, so c_B is computable.
(*d*) Choose $b \in B$ and $c \notin B$, and define f by

$$f(x) = \begin{cases} b & \text{if } x \in A, \\ c & \text{if } x \notin A. \end{cases}$$

Then f is computable (since A is recursive), and $x \in A \Leftrightarrow f(x) \in B$; hence $f: A \leq_m B$.
(*e*) Suppose that $g: B \leq_m A$ and $A = \text{Dom}(h)$, with h computable; then $B = \text{Dom}(h \circ g)$, and $h \circ g$ is computable, so B is r.e.
(*f*) (i) By (*a*), $\mathbb{N} \leq_m \mathbb{N}$. Conversely, suppose that $f: A \leq_m \mathbb{N}$; i.e. $x \in A \Leftrightarrow f(x) \in \mathbb{N}$. Then clearly $A = \mathbb{N}$.
(ii) is dual to (i): $A \leq_m \emptyset \overset{(b)}{\Leftrightarrow} \bar{A} \leq_m \mathbb{N} \overset{(i)}{\Leftrightarrow} \bar{A} = \mathbb{N} \Leftrightarrow A = \emptyset$.
(*g*) (i) Suppose that $f: \mathbb{N} \leq_m A$; then $A = \text{Ran}(f)$, so $A \neq \emptyset$ (since f is total). Conversely, suppose that $A \neq \emptyset$, and choose $c \in A$. Then if we define $g(x) = c$ (all x), we have $g: \mathbb{N} \leq_m A$.
(ii) is dual to (i): $\emptyset \leq_m A \overset{(b)}{\Leftrightarrow} \mathbb{N} \leq_m \bar{A} \overset{(i)}{\Leftrightarrow} \bar{A} \neq \emptyset \Leftrightarrow A \neq \mathbb{N}$. □

From (*e*) of this theorem we obtain the following example of non-reducibility:

1.4. *Corollary*

Neither of the sets $\{x : \phi_x$ is total$\}$, $\{x : \phi_x$ is not total$\}$ is m-reducible to K.

Proof. From corollary 7-2.17 neither of these sets is r.e.; apply theorem 1.3(*e*). □

The exceptional behaviour of the sets $\emptyset$, $\mathbb{N}$ as given in theorem 1.3(d), (f), (g) is part of the price that has to be paid for the simplicity of the notion of m-reducibility. Another rather unsatisfactory feature is that the sets A and $\bar{A}$ are not necessarily inter-reducible (contrary to the intuition that the problems '$x \in A$' and '$x \notin A$' should be equally difficult), as we now see:

1.5. *Corollary*

If A is an r.e. set that is not recursive, then $\bar{A} \not\leq_{\mathrm{m}} A$ and $A \not\leq_{\mathrm{m}} \bar{A}$.

Proof. By theorem 1.3(e) if $\bar{A} \leq_{\mathrm{m}} A$, then $\bar{A}$ is r.e., a contradiction. For $A \not\leq_{\mathrm{m}} \bar{A}$, use theorem 1.3($b$). □

The next result shows again the key role played by the r.e. set K.

1.6. *Theorem*

A set A is r.e. if and only if $A \leq_{\mathrm{m}} K$.

Proof. If $A \leq_{\mathrm{m}} K$, then theorem 1.3(e) tells us that A is r.e. Conversely let A be any r.e. set. Define a computable function $f(x, y)$ by

$$f(x, y) = \begin{cases} 1 & \text{if } x \in A, \\ \text{undefined} & \text{if } x \notin A. \end{cases}$$

The s–m–n theorem gives a total computable function $s(x)$ such that $f(x, y) \simeq \phi_{s(x)}(y)$. It is clear from the definition of f that

$$\begin{aligned} x \in A &\Leftrightarrow \phi_{s(x)}(s(x)) \text{ is defined} \\ &\Leftrightarrow s(x) \in K. \end{aligned}$$

I.e. $A \leq_{\mathrm{m}} K$. □

This theorem may be interpreted as saying that the problem '$x \in K$' is the most difficult partially decidable problem.

1.7. *Exercises*

1. Show that K is m-reducible to each of the following sets:
   (a) $\{x : \phi_x(x) = 0\}$,
   (b) $\{x : x \in E_x\}$.
2. Show that for any sets A, B, if $B \neq \emptyset$ then $A \leq_{\mathrm{m}} A \otimes B$. (Recall that $A \otimes B = \{\pi(a, b) : a \in A, b \in B\}$.)
3. Show that
   (a) $\{x : \phi_x = \mathbf{0}\} \leq_{\mathrm{m}} \{x : \phi_x \text{ is total and constant}\}$,
   (b) $\{x : \phi_x \text{ is total}\} \leq_{\mathrm{m}} \{x : W_x \text{ is infinite}\}$.

4. Show that none of the sets in exercise 3 above is m-reducible to an r.e. set.
5. Suppose that A, B are r.e. sets such that $A \cup B = \mathbb{N}$ and $A \cap B \neq \emptyset$. Prove that $A \leq_m A \cap B$.

2. **Degrees**

For any notion of reducibility there is an associated notion of *equivalence* between sets: this corresponds to the informal idea of two sets or problems having the same degree of difficulty. Thus, for m-reducibility we have:

2.1. *Definition*

The sets A and B are *many–one equivalent* (abbreviated *m-equivalent*) if $A \leq_m B$ and $B \leq_m A$. We write this $A \equiv_m B$.

The use of the word equivalent in this definition is justified by

2.2. *Theorem*

The relation $\equiv_m$ *is an equivalence relation.* (See Prologue § 3 for definition.)

Proof. Reflexivity and transitivity follow immediately from theorem 1.3(a); symmetry is obvious from the definition. □

2.3. *Examples*

1. Let c be any number; then $\{x : c \in W_x\} \equiv_m K$, by example 1.2(1$b$) and theorem 1.6.
2. For every recursive set A other than $\emptyset$, $\mathbb{N}$, we have $A \equiv_m \bar{A}$ by theorem 1.3(d).
3. If A is r.e. but not recursive, then $A \not\equiv_m \bar{A}$, by corollary 1.5.
4. $\{x : \phi_x = \mathbf{0}\} \equiv_m \{x : \phi_x \text{ is total}\}$. One half of this is given by example 1.2(4); to see the reverse reduction, use the *s–m–n* theorem to obtain a total computable function k such that

$$\phi_{k(x)}(y) \simeq \begin{cases} 0 & \text{if } \phi_x(y) = 0, \\ \text{undefined} & \text{otherwise.} \end{cases}$$

Then clearly $\phi_x = \mathbf{0} \Leftrightarrow \phi_{k(x)}$ is total.

For any set A, the equivalence class of A under the relation $\equiv_m$ is the class of sets $\mathrm{d_m}(A)$ given by

$$\mathrm{d_m}(A) = \{B : A \equiv_m B\}.$$

This can be thought of as the class of all those sets having the same degree of difficulty (with respect to $\leq_m$) as the set A; hence $d_m(A)$ is called the *m-degree* of A.

2.4. *Definition*

An *m-degree* is an equivalence class of sets under the relation $\equiv_m$; i.e. it is any class of sets of the form $d_m(A)$ for some set A.

It is conventional to use lower case bold face letters such as $\boldsymbol{a}, \boldsymbol{b}, \boldsymbol{c}$ to denote degrees.[1] It is worth making a strong mental note that although lower case letters are used, these are sets of sets. Thus it is meaningful to write $A \in \boldsymbol{a}$, where $\boldsymbol{a}$ is a degree and A is a set, although at first this may appear a little odd.

The relation $\leq_m$ on sets induces a partial ordering (see Prologue § 3 for definition) on m-degrees, also denoted $\leq_m$, as follows:

2.5. *Definition*

Let $\boldsymbol{a}, \boldsymbol{b}$ be m-degrees.

(*a*) $\boldsymbol{a} \leq_m \boldsymbol{b}$ if there are $A \in \boldsymbol{a}$ and $B \in \boldsymbol{b}$ such that $A \leq_m B$,

(*b*) $\boldsymbol{a} <_m \boldsymbol{b}$ if $\boldsymbol{a} \leq_m \boldsymbol{b}$ but $\boldsymbol{a} \neq \boldsymbol{b}$.

Note. It is immediate from the definition of $\equiv_m$ that $\boldsymbol{a} \leq_m \boldsymbol{b}$ iff $A \leq_m B$ for *every* $A \in \boldsymbol{a}$, $B \in \boldsymbol{b}$.

2.6. *Theorem*

The relation $<_m$ *is a partial ordering of m-degrees.*

Proof. From theorem 1.3(*a*) we have immediately that $\boldsymbol{a} \leq_m \boldsymbol{a}$ (reflexivity) and that $\boldsymbol{a} \leq_m \boldsymbol{b}, \boldsymbol{b} \leq_m \boldsymbol{c}$ implies $\boldsymbol{a} \leq_m \boldsymbol{c}$ (transitivity). Suppose now that $\boldsymbol{a} \leq_m \boldsymbol{b}$ and $\boldsymbol{b} \leq_m \boldsymbol{a}$. We have to show that $\boldsymbol{a} = \boldsymbol{b}$. Let $A \in \boldsymbol{a}$ and $B \in \boldsymbol{b}$; then from the definition we have $A \leq_m B$ and $B \leq_m A$, so $A \equiv_m B$. Hence $\boldsymbol{a} = \boldsymbol{b}$. □

The name *recursive m-degree* is given to any m-degree that contains a recursive set; similarly, an *r.e. m-degree* is one that contains an r.e. set. We can translate parts of theorem 1.3 and theorem 1.6 into the language of degrees as follows.

2.7. *Theorem*

(*a*) $\{\emptyset\}$ *and* $\{\mathbb{N}\}$ *are m-degrees, which we denote by* $\mathbf{o}$ *and* $\mathbf{n}$ *respectively*; $\mathbf{o}$ *and* $\mathbf{n}$ *are recursive m-degrees.*

[1] Although we have also used $\boldsymbol{a}$ on occasions to denote an n-tuple $(a_1, \ldots, a_n)$, the context will resolve any possible ambiguity.

(*b*) *There is one other recursive m-degree, denoted* $\mathbf{0}_m$, *that consists of all recursive sets except* $\varnothing$ *and* $\mathbb{N}$, *moreover*, $\mathbf{0}_m \leq_m \boldsymbol{a}$ *for any m-degree* $\boldsymbol{a}$ *other than* $\mathbf{o}, \mathbf{n}$.

(*c*) *For any m-degree* $\boldsymbol{a}$, *we have* $\mathbf{o} \leq_m \boldsymbol{a}$ *provided* $\boldsymbol{a} \neq \mathbf{n}$, *and* $\mathbf{n} \leq_m \boldsymbol{a}$ *provided* $\boldsymbol{a} \neq \mathbf{o}$.

(*d*) *Any r.e. m-degree consists only of r.e. sets.*

(*e*) *If* $\boldsymbol{a} \leq_m \boldsymbol{b}$ *and* $\boldsymbol{b}$ *is an r.e. m-degree, then* $\boldsymbol{a}$ *is also an r.e. m-degree.*

(*f*) *There is a maximum r.e. m-degree, namely* $d_m(K)$, *which is denoted* $\mathbf{0}'_m$.

Proof.

(*a*) Follows from theorem 1.3(*f*);

(*b*) from theorem 1.3(*c*), (*d*);

(*c*) from theorem 1.3(*g*);

(*d*) from theorem 1.3(*e*);

(*e*) from theorem 1.3(*e*);

(*f*) from theorem 1.6. □

Theorem 2.7 gives us a picture of the m-degrees as shown in fig. 9*a*. (In this diagram, we position a degree $\boldsymbol{a}$ below a degree $\boldsymbol{b}$ to indicate that $\boldsymbol{a} \leq_m \boldsymbol{b}$.) We shall see later (as this picture suggests) that there are r.e. m-degrees other than $\mathbf{0}_m$ and $\mathbf{0}'_m$.

The structure of the collection of m-degrees under their partial ordering has been studied extensively. The following theorem means that this structure is what is known as an *upper semi-lattice*.

Fig. 9*a*. The m-degrees.

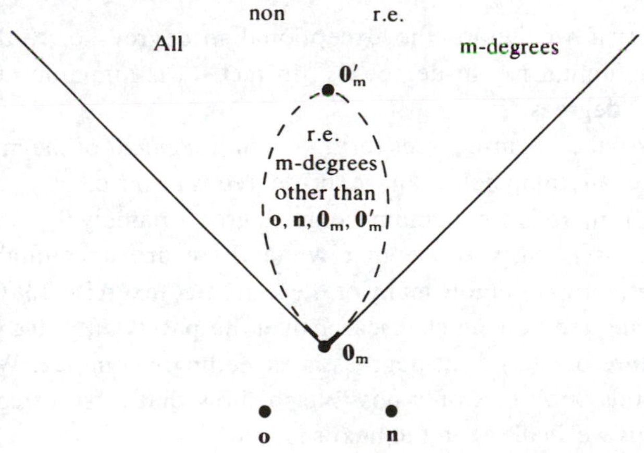

2.8. *Theorem*

Any pair of m-degrees $\boldsymbol{a}, \boldsymbol{b}$ *have a least upper bound; i.e. there is an m-degree* $\boldsymbol{c}$ *such that*

(i) $\boldsymbol{a} \leq_{\mathrm{m}} \boldsymbol{c}$ *and* $\boldsymbol{b} \leq_{\mathrm{m}} \boldsymbol{c}$ *(*$\boldsymbol{c}$ *is an upper bound),*

(ii) $\boldsymbol{c} \leq_{\mathrm{m}}$ *any other upper bound of* $\boldsymbol{a}, \boldsymbol{b}$.

Proof. Pick $A \in \boldsymbol{a}$, $B \in \boldsymbol{b}$ and let $C = A \oplus B$, i.e.

$$C = \{2x : x \in A\} \cup \{2x+1 : x \in B\}.$$

Then $x \in A \Leftrightarrow 2x \in C$, so $A \leq_{\mathrm{m}} C$, and $x \in B \Leftrightarrow 2x+1 \in C$, so $B \leq_{\mathrm{m}} C$. Thus, putting $\boldsymbol{c} = \mathrm{d_m}(C)$ we have that $\boldsymbol{c}$ is an upper bound of $\boldsymbol{a}, \boldsymbol{b}$.

Suppose now that $\boldsymbol{d}$ is an m-degree such that $\boldsymbol{a} \leq_{\mathrm{m}} \boldsymbol{d}$ and $\boldsymbol{b} \leq_{\mathrm{m}} \boldsymbol{d}$. Choose a set $D \in \boldsymbol{d}$, and suppose that $f: A \leq_{\mathrm{m}} D$ and $g: B \leq_{\mathrm{m}} D$. Then we have

$$\begin{aligned} x \in C &\Leftrightarrow (x \text{ is even } \& \tfrac{1}{2}x \in A) \text{ or } (x \text{ is odd } \& \tfrac{1}{2}(x-1) \in B) \\ &\Leftrightarrow (x \text{ is even } \& f(\tfrac{1}{2}x) \in D) \text{ or } (x \text{ is odd } \& g(\tfrac{1}{2}(x-1)) \in D) \end{aligned}$$

Thus we have $h: C \leq_{\mathrm{m}} D$ if we define h by

$$h(x) = \begin{cases} f(\tfrac{1}{2}x) & \text{if } x \text{ is even,} \\ g(\tfrac{1}{2}(x-1)) & \text{if } x \text{ is odd.} \end{cases}$$

Hence $\boldsymbol{c} \leq_{\mathrm{m}} \boldsymbol{d}$. □

It is clear that the least upper bound $\boldsymbol{c}$ of any pair of m-degrees $\boldsymbol{a}, \boldsymbol{b}$ is uniquely determined; moreover, it is easy to see that if $\boldsymbol{a}, \boldsymbol{b}$ are r.e. so is $\boldsymbol{c}$ (see exercise 2.9(5) below).

When considering the structure of the m-degrees, it is natural to examine in particular the structure of the r.e. m-degrees. (These include, of course, the recursive m-degrees $\mathbf{0}_{\mathrm{m}}$, $\mathbf{o}$, $\mathbf{n}$.) We have already seen in theorem 2.7 (and indicated in fig. 9*a*) the following basic facts about r.e. m-degrees:

(*a*) if we ignore the exceptional m-degrees $\mathbf{o}$, $\mathbf{n}$ there is a minimum r.e. m-degree $\mathbf{0}_{\mathrm{m}}$ (in fact $\mathbf{0}_{\mathrm{m}}$ is minimum among all m-degrees);

(*b*) the r.e. m-degrees form an *initial segment* of the m-degrees; i.e. anything below an r.e. m-degree is also r.e.

(*c*) there is a maximum r.e. m-degree – namely $\mathbf{0}'_{\mathrm{m}}$.

Moreover, it is easy to see that while there are uncountably many m-degrees, only countably many of these are r.e. (exercise 2.9(6) below).

It has emerged from much research over the past twenty-five years that the structure of the r.e. m-degrees is exceedingly complex. Within the scope of this book it is only possible to show that it is not completely simple; this we shall see in the next section.

2.9. *Exercises*

1. Show that each of the following sets is m-equivalent to K:
   (*a*) $\{x : x \in E_x\}$,
   (*b*) $\{x : \phi_x(x) = 0\}$.
2. (*a*) Show that $A \equiv_m A \otimes \mathbb{N}$ for any set A,
   (*b*) Let B be a non-empty recursive set. Show that $A \equiv_m A \otimes B$ for any A provided that $A \neq \mathbb{N}$.
3. (Cf. examples 2.3(2, 3).) Is it true that if $A \equiv_m \bar{A}$ then A is recursive? (See exercise 5*d* below.)
4. Show that the following sets all belong to the same m-degree:
   (*a*) $\{x : \phi_x = \mathbf{0}\}$,
   (*b*) $\{x : \phi_x$ is total and constant$\}$,
   (*c*) $\{x : W_x$ is infinite$\}$.
5. Let $\boldsymbol{a}, \boldsymbol{b}$ be m-degrees.
   (*a*) Show that the least upper bound of $\boldsymbol{a}, \boldsymbol{b}$ is uniquely determined; denote this by $\boldsymbol{a} \cup \boldsymbol{b}$;
   (*b*) Show that if $\boldsymbol{a} \leq_m \boldsymbol{b}$ then $\boldsymbol{a} \cup \boldsymbol{b} = \boldsymbol{b}$;
   (*c*) Show that if $\boldsymbol{a}, \boldsymbol{b}$ are r.e., then so is $\boldsymbol{a} \cup \boldsymbol{b}$;
   (*d*) Let $A \in \boldsymbol{a}$ and let $\boldsymbol{a}^*$ denote $d_m(\bar{A})$. (Check that $\boldsymbol{a}^*$ is independent of the choice of $A \in \boldsymbol{a}$.) Show that $(\boldsymbol{a} \cup \boldsymbol{a}^*)^* = \boldsymbol{a} \cup \boldsymbol{a}^*$.
6. (*a*) Show that any m-degree $\boldsymbol{a}$ is denumerable (i.e. there are denumerably many sets $A \in \boldsymbol{a}$).
   (*b*) Show that there are uncountably many m-degrees.
   (*c*) Show that there are countably many r.e. m-degrees.

3. m-complete r.e. sets

We have seen that $\mathbf{0}'_m$, the m-degree of K is maximum among all r.e. m-degrees. This is also described by saying that the set K is an *m-complete r.e. set*, or just an *m-complete set.*[2] (There is a corresponding notion for any other kind of reducibility.)

3.1. *Definition*

A set is *m-complete* if it is r.e. and any r.e. set is m-reducible to it.

From theorem 1.6 we have immediately:

3.2. *Theorem*

(*a*) *K is m-complete,*

[2] It is possible to have a notion of m-complete sets for classes other than the class of r.e. sets; it is then necessary to keep the reference to r.e. here.

(*b*) *A is m-complete iff* $A \equiv_m K$ *iff A is r.e. and* $K \leq_m A$,
(*c*) $\mathbf{0}'_m$ *consists exactly of all m-complete sets.*

Applying this we have the following:

3.3. *Examples*
The following sets are m-complete.
(*a*) $\{x : c \in W_x\}$ (example 1.2(1*b*)),
(*b*) any non-trivial r.e. set of the form $\{x : \phi_x \in \mathscr{B}\}$ where $\mathscr{B} \subseteq \mathscr{C}_1$ (the proofs of theorems 7-3.4 and 3.8 show that $K \leq_m$ such a set),
(*c*) $\{x : \phi_x(x) = 0\}$,
(*d*) $\{x : x \in E_x\}$
(*c*), (*d*): Exercise 1.7(1).

The reader may have realised that m-reducibility appeared implicitly in the statement of theorem 7-3.2, which implies immediately that

3.4. *Theorem*
Any m-complete set is creative.

Proof. If A is m-complete, then $K \leq_m A$, so $\bar{K} \leq_m \bar{A}$, and by Theorem 7-3.2 $\bar{A}$ is productive. □

It is very pleasing to find that the converse of this theorem is also true, giving us a precise characterisation of m-complete sets:

3.5. *Theorem* (Myhill)
Creative sets are m-complete.

We must wait until chapter 11 for a new tool – the Second Recursion theorem – with which to prove this result. Note, however, that we have already established it for creative sets of indices in example 3.3(*b*).

As an immediate corollary to theorem 3.4 we can use simple sets to show that $\mathbf{0}_m$ and $\mathbf{0}'_m$ are not the only r.e. degrees:

3.6. *Corollary* (to theorem 3.4)
Simple sets are not m-complete; *hence if* $\boldsymbol{a}$ *is the m-degree of any simple set, then* $\mathbf{0}_m <_m \boldsymbol{a} <_m \mathbf{0}'_m$.

Proof. Simple sets are designed to be neither recursive nor creative. □

This corollary justifies the inclusion of *something* between $\mathbf{0}_m$ and $\mathbf{0}'_m$ in fig. 9*a*; it does not, however, justify the suggestion in that picture that there is more than one non-recursive r.e. m-degree other than $\mathbf{0}'_m$. In fact there are infinitely many such m-degrees, although we shall not prove this here.

It is beyond the scope of this book to investigate further the structure of the m-degrees under their partial ordering $\leq_m$, which, as already mentioned, is very complex. Much of this complexity can be deduced from results about the complex nature of the Turing degrees, which we discuss in the next sections.

4. Relative computability

We saw in § 1 that m-reducibility has two rather unsatisfactory features: the exceptional behaviour of $\varnothing$ and $\mathbb{N}$, and the fact that we do not always have $A \equiv_m \bar{A}$. These features stem from the restricted nature of m-reducibility: we have $A \leq_m B$ only if each question '$x \in A$?' can be settled by answering a single prescribed question about B in a prescribed way. The idea of *Turing reducibility*, which we shall define in § 5, is that '$x \in A$?' can be settled in a mechanical way by answering several questions about B, the nature and (finite) number of which are not necessarily known in advance. This idea is made precise in terms of *relative computability*, which we describe in this section.

Suppose that χ is any total unary function. Informally we say that a function f is *computable relative to* χ, or just χ*-computable*, if f can be computed by an algorithm that is effective in the usual sense, except that from time to time during computations we are allowed access to values of the function χ. Such an algorithm is called a χ*-algorithm*. We can think of a χ-algorithm as being linked to some external agent or *oracle* that can supply values of χ on demand. The χ-algorithm operates in a purely mechanical fashion, and a value $\chi(n)$ is requested from the oracle only as dictated by the algorithm.

We can formulate a precise definition of relative computability using a modification of our URM, called an Unlimited Register Machine with Oracle, or URMO for short.

4.1. *Definition*

The URMO is like the URM in all respects except that it can recognize a fifth kind of instruction $O(n)$ for every $n \geq 1$. The instruction $O(n)$ is called an *oracle instruction.*

To be able to obey oracle instructions the URMO must be linked to an *oracle*, which supplies values of some given function χ on demand. We say then that the URMO has the function χ in its oracle. The function χ is *not* thought of as part of the URMO itself.

The response of the URMO to an oracle instruction $O(n)$ is as follows: if χ is in the oracle, then replace r_n (the contents of register R_n) by $\chi(r_n)$.

This is denoted in flow diagrams by

$$r_n := \chi(r_n) \quad \text{or} \quad \chi(r_n) \rightarrow \mathrm{R}_n.$$

The URMO, with χ in its oracle and obeying the instruction $\mathrm{O}(n)$ may be envisaged as shown in fig. 9*b*.

A program is, as before, a finite sequence of instructions. The URMO operates under a URMO program P in the same way as the URM, with the following additional stipulation: after obeying an oracle instruction I_k in P the next instruction is I_{k+1}.

We emphasise that in a URMO program P no particular function χ is mentioned. Thus the meaning of P varies according to the function supplied in the oracle. However, a computation under P can be carried out only when a particular function χ is supplied, so we write P^χ to denote the program P when used with the function χ in the oracle. Thus we write

$$P^\chi(a_1, \ldots, a_n)$$

for the computation by P, with χ in the oracle, and with initial configuration $a_1, a_2, \ldots, a_n, 0, 0, \ldots$; and we write

$$P^\chi(\boldsymbol{a})\downarrow b$$

to mean that the computation $P^\chi(\boldsymbol{a})$ stops with the number b in register R_1.

We can now make the following definitions (parallel with definition 1-3.1).

Fig. 9*b*.

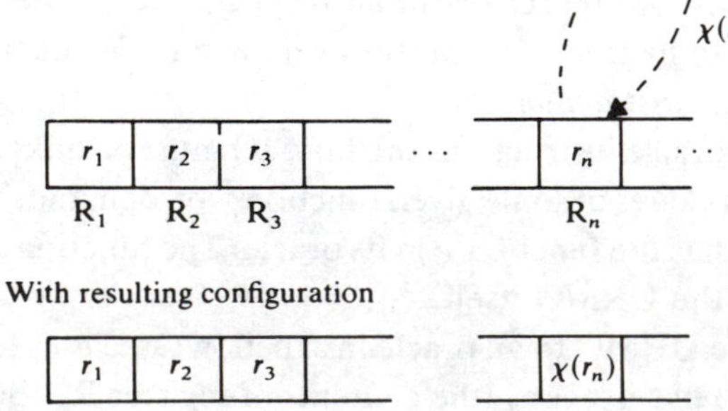

4.2. *Definition*

Let χ be a unary total function, and suppose that f is a partial function from $\mathbb{N}^n$ to $\mathbb{N}$.

(*a*) Let P be a URMO program. Then *P URMO-computes f relative to* χ (or *f is* χ*-computed by P*) if, for every $\boldsymbol{a} \in \mathbb{N}^n$ and $b \in \mathbb{N}$,

$P^\chi(\boldsymbol{a})\downarrow b \quad \text{iff} \quad f(\boldsymbol{a}) \simeq b.$

(*b*) The function f is *URMO-computable relative to* χ (or just χ*-computable*) if there is a URMO program that URMO-computes it relative to χ.

We write $\mathscr{C}^\chi$ to denote the class of all χ-computable functions.

We are now in a position where we could define Turing-reducibility. However, to aid a better understanding of this concept when we come to it, we shall first outline a little of the development of the theory of relative computability.

Most methods and results from unrelativised computability have counterparts in relative computability. Thus in many of the theorems that follow we supply only a sketch proof or a reference to the unrelativised version of the same result. Throughout this section χ stands for a total unary function.

4.3. *Theorem*

(*a*) $\chi \in \mathscr{C}^\chi$,

(*b*) $\mathscr{C} \subseteq \mathscr{C}^\chi$,

(*c*) *if* χ *is computable, then* $\mathscr{C} = \mathscr{C}^\chi$,

(*d*) $\mathscr{C}^\chi$ *is closed under substitution, recursion and minimalisation,*

(*e*) *if* ψ *is a total unary function that is* χ*-computable, then* $\mathscr{C}^\psi \subseteq \mathscr{C}^\chi$.

Proof.

(*a*) Use the URMO program O(1).

(*b*) Any URM program is a URMO program.

(*c*) In view of (*b*), we need only show that $\mathscr{C}^\chi \subseteq \mathscr{C}$. Suppose that f is χ-computable and that χ is computable. Proceeding informally, we can compute any value of f as follows: use the χ-algorithm for f, and whenever a value of χ is requested simply compute it using the algorithm for χ. This is an effective procedure, so by Church's thesis f is computable. (We leave the reader to provide a formal proof of this result; see exercise 4.10(3).)

(*d*) The proofs are identical to those of theorems 2-3.1, 2-4.4 and 2-5.2.

(*e*) The proof is similar to that for (*c*) (which is really a special case of (*e*)). □

Other approaches to relativised computability Any alternative approach to computability can be modified to provide a corresponding notion of relative computability. A relativised version of the Fundamental result (theorem 3-1.1) can then be proved, and this leads to the formulation of Church's thesis for relativised computability.

We mention here only the relativised notion of partial recursive function:

4.4. *Definition*

The class $\mathcal{R}^\chi$ of *χ-partial recursive functions* is the smallest class of functions such that

(*a*) the basic functions are in $\mathcal{R}^\chi$,

(*b*) $\chi \in \mathcal{R}^\chi$,

(*c*) $\mathcal{R}^\chi$ is closed under substitution, recursion and minimalisation.

The phrases *partial recursive in χ* or *partial recursive relative to χ* are also used with the same meaning as χ-partial recursive.

The notions *χ-recursive* (or *recursive in*, or *relative to*, χ) and *χ-primitive recursive* (or *primitive recursive in*, or *relative to*, χ) are defined in the obvious way.

Corresponding to theorem 3-2.2 (and proved in the same way) we have

4.5. *Theorem*

For any χ, $\mathcal{R}^\chi = \mathcal{C}^\chi$.

Numbering programs and functions URMO programs can be effectively numbered or coded by an easy adaptation of the method used in chapter 4 for URM programs. Let us assume that this has been done, so that we have a fixed effective enumeration (without repetitions)

$$Q_0, Q_1, Q_2, \ldots$$

of all URMO programs.[3] Then we write

$\phi_m^{\chi,n}$ for the n-ary function χ-computed by Q_m,

[3] Each URM program P appears in this list ; in most cases, however, its number here will be different from that assigned to it in chapter 4.

ϕ_m^χ for $\phi_m^{\chi,1}$,
W_m^χ for $\mathrm{Dom}(\phi_m^\chi)$,
E_m^χ for $\mathrm{Ran}(\phi_m^\chi)$.

The *s–m–n* theorem (4-4.3) has a relativised counterpart with identical proof:

4.6. *Theorem* (The relativised *s–m–n* theorem)
For each $m, n \geq 1$ there is a total computable $(m+1)$-ary function $s_n^m(e, \boldsymbol{x})$ such that for any χ

$$\phi_e^{\chi,(m+n)}(\boldsymbol{x}, \boldsymbol{y}) \simeq \phi_{s_n^m(e,\boldsymbol{x})}^{\chi,n}(\boldsymbol{y}).$$

Note. The function s_n^m here differs, of course, from the function given the same name in theorem 4-4.3. Note, however, that s_n^m here is still computable (not merely χ-computable) and does not depend on χ.

Universal programs for relative computability Relativisation of the proof of theorem 5-1.2 gives immediately:

4.7. *Theorem*
For each n, the universal function $\psi_U^{\chi,n}$ for n-ary χ-computable functions given by

$$\psi_U^{\chi,n}(e, \boldsymbol{x}) \simeq \phi_e^{\chi,n}(\boldsymbol{x})$$

is χ-computable.

Remark. A careful examination of the full formal proof of theorem 5-1.2 would show that there is a URMO program $Q_U^{(n)}$, independent of χ, that χ-computes $\psi_U^{\chi,n}$ for any χ.

χ-recursive and χ-r.e. sets The relativised notions of recursive and r.e. sets are given by:

4.8. *Definition*
Let A be a set
(*a*) A is *χ-recursive* (or *recursive in χ*) if c_A is χ-computable,
(*b*) A is *χ-r.e.* (or *r.e. in χ*) if the partial characteristic function

$$f(x) = \begin{cases} 1 & \text{if } x \in A, \\ \text{undefined} & \text{if } x \notin A, \end{cases}$$

is χ-computable.

The following selection of basic results about χ-recursive and χ-r.e. sets is proved by the addition of the prefix χ- at the appropriate places in the proofs of the corresponding unrelativised results in chapter 7:

4.9. *Theorem*

(*a*) *For any set A, A is χ-recursive iff A and $\bar{A}$ are χ-r.e.*

(*b*) *For any set A, the following are equivalent*

(i) *A is χ-r.e.,*

(ii) *$A = W_m^\chi$ for some m,*

(iii) *$A = E_m^\chi$ for some m,*

(iv) *$A = \emptyset$ or A is the range of a total χ-computable function,*

(v) *for some χ-decidable predicate $R(x, y)$,*

$$x \in A \Leftrightarrow \exists y\, R(x, y)$$

(R is *χ-decidable* if its characteristic function is χ-computable).

(*c*) *Let $K^\chi = \{x : x \in W_x^\chi\}$; then K^χ is χ-r.e. but not χ-recursive.*

Computability relative to a set For any set A, we define *computability relative to A* (or just *A-computability*) to mean computability relative to c_A, the characteristic function of A. Thus we write

P^A for P^{c_A} (if P is a URMO program),

$\mathscr{C}^A$ for $\mathscr{C}^{c_A}$,

ϕ_m^A for $\phi_m^{c_A}$,

W_m^A for $W_m^{c_A}$,

E_m^A for $E_m^{c_A}$,

K^A for K^{c_A},

A-recursive for c_A-recursive,

A-r.e. for c_A-r.e.,

etc.

In the next section we shall define Turing reducibility in terms of computability relative to a set. For a set A, we can summarise the basic idea that we have presented in this section, in a nutshell, as follows: A-computability is computability for anyone who knows all about A. To be a little more precise, we should expand this to: for anyone who can answer any question of the form '$x \in A$?'. This excludes knowledge of 'infinite' facts about A, such as whether A has infinitely many even members.

4.10. *Exercises*

1. Let χ, ψ be total unary functions, and suppose that ϕ_e^χ is total. Is ϕ_e^ψ necessarily total?
2. Suppose that $\chi_1, \chi_2, \ldots, \chi_k$ are total unary functions. Define $\mathcal{R}^{\chi_1,\chi_2,\ldots,\chi_k}$ to be the smallest class of functions containing the basic functions and $\chi_1, \ldots, \chi_k$, and closed under substitutions, recursion and minimalisation. Formulate a definition of the set $\mathcal{C}^{\chi_1,\ldots,\chi_k}$ of functions computable relative to $\chi_1, \ldots, \chi_k$ such that $\mathcal{C}^{\chi_1,\ldots,\chi_k} = \mathcal{R}^{\chi_1,\ldots,\chi_k}$. (*Hint. Either* define a machine having k oracles, *or* find a single unary function χ such that $\mathcal{R}^{\chi_1,\ldots,\chi_k} = \mathcal{R}^\chi$.)
3. Provide a full formal proof of theorem 4.3(*c*): if χ is computable, then $\mathcal{C} = \mathcal{C}^\chi$.
4. Show that there is a total computable function k (independent of χ) such that $W_{k(a,b)}^\chi = W_a^\chi \cup W_b^\chi$ for all indices a, b.
5. Verify theorem 4.9.
6. Let A be any set.
   (*a*) Show that for any r.e. set B, there is an index e such that $B = W_e^A$,
   (*b*) Show that if A is recursive , then W_e^A is r.e. for all e,
   (*c*) Show that if A is recursive, then K^A is r.e. but not recursive.
7. Let A, B, C, be sets. Prove that
   (*a*) if A is B-recursive and B is C-recursive, then A is C-recursive,
   (*b*) if A is B-r.e. and B is C-recursive, then A is C-r.e.,
   (*c*) if A is B-recursive and B is C-r.e., then A is not necessarily C-r.e.
8. (Relativisation of theorem 1.6.) Let A be any set. Show that for any set B,

   B is A-r.e. $\Leftrightarrow B \leq_m K^A$.

9. Show that there is a single number d such that

   $K^A = W_d^A$ for all sets A.

10. (a) We say that a set A is χ-*simple* if (i) A is χ-r.e., (ii) $\bar{A}$ is infinite, (iii) $\bar{A}$ contains no infinite χ-r.e. subset. Show that there is a χ-simple set.
    (*b*) Formulate the definition of a χ-creative set. Show that a χ-simple set is not χ-creative.

5. Turing reducibility and Turing degrees

Using relative computability we make the following definitions:

5.1. *Definitions*

(*a*) The set A is *Turing reducible* (or just *T-reducible*) to the set B if A is B-recursive (equivalently, if c_A is B-computable). This is written $A \leq_T B$.

(*b*) The sets A, B are *Turing equivalent* (or *T-equivalent*) if $A \leq_T B$ and $B \leq_T A$. (The use of the word equivalent is justified in theorem 5.2(*b*) below.) We write this $A \equiv_T B$.

Let us consider informally the meaning of Turing reducibility. Suppose that $A \leq_T B$ and that P is a URMO program that computes c_A relative to B. Then for any x, $P^B(x)$ converges and

$$P^B(x)\downarrow 1 \quad \text{if } x \in A,$$
$$P^B(x)\downarrow 0 \quad \text{if } x \notin A.$$

During any completed computation $P^B(x)$ there will have been a finite number of requests to the oracle for a value $c_B(n)$ of c_B, as dictated by P and the progress of the computation. These requests amount to a finite number of questions of the form '$n \in B$?'. So for any x, '$x \in A$?' is settled in a mechanical way by answering a finite number of questions about B. Thus we see that Turing reducibility accords with the informal notion of reducibility discussed at the beginning of § 4.

Some of the basic properties of the relations $\leq_T$ and $\equiv_T$ are given in the next theorem.

5.2. *Theorem*

(*a*) *$\leq_T$ is reflexive and transitive,*
(*b*) *$\equiv_T$ is an equivalence relation,*
(*c*) *if $A \leq_m B$ then $A \leq_T B$,*
(*d*) *$A \equiv_T \bar{A}$ for all A,*
(*e*) *if A is recursive, then $A \leq_T B$ for all B,*
(*f*) *if A is recursive and $B \leq_T A$ then B is recursive,*
(*g*) *if A is r.e. then $A \leq_T K$.*

Proof.

(*a*) and (*b*) follow immediately from the observation that

$$A \leq_T B \Leftrightarrow \mathscr{C}^A \subseteq \mathscr{C}^B \quad \text{(by theorem 4.3(}a\text{), (}e\text{))}$$

and hence

$$A \equiv_T B \Leftrightarrow \mathscr{C}^A = \mathscr{C}^B.$$

(*c*) Suppose that $f: A \leq_m B$, and let P be a URM program in standard form that computes f. Then the URMO program P, O(1) is easily seen to B-compute c_A.
(*d*) Since $c_{\bar{A}} = \overline{\text{sg}} \circ c_A$, $\bar{A}$ is A-recursive (by substitution); hence $\bar{A} \leq_T A$; and $A \leq_T \bar{A}$ similarly.
(*e*) By theorem 4.3(*b*).
(*f*) By theorem 4.3(*c*).
(*g*) By (*c*) above and theorem 1.6. □

Remarks

1. From (*d*), (*e*), (*f*) of this theorem we see that T-reducibility does not have the defects of m-reducibility; this also shows us that these two notions are distinct.
2. Part (*g*) of the above theorem shows that K is a *T-complete* (r.e.) set, according to the following definition:

5.3. *Definition*

A set A is *T-complete* if A is r.e. and $B \leq_T A$ for every r.e. set B.

The name *Turing degree* is given to any equivalence class of sets under the relation $\equiv_T$: again, we think of a degree as a collection of sets all having the same degree of difficulty.

5.4. *Definitions*

(*a*) Let A be a set; the equivalence class

$\mathrm{d_T}(A) = \{B : B \equiv_T A\}$

is called the *Turing degree* of A, abbreviated the *T-degree* of A.
(*b*) Any T-degree containing a recursive set is called a *recursive T-degree*.
(*c*) Any T-degree containing an r.e. set is called an *r.e. T-degree*.

The notions of Turing reducibility and Turing degree are widely accepted as the most basic among all other similar notions. Hence the term *reducible* without qualification is often used to mean Turing reducible; similarly, Turing degrees are often referred to merely as degrees, or *degrees of unsolvability*. We shall adopt this practice in the remainder of our chapter. As before, the letters $\boldsymbol{a}$, $\boldsymbol{b}$, $\boldsymbol{c}$, etc. are used for degrees.

The relation $\leq_T$ on sets induces a partial ordering on degrees, as with $\leq_m$:

5.5. *Definition*

Let $\boldsymbol{a}, \boldsymbol{b}$ be degrees.

(*a*) $\boldsymbol{a} \leq \boldsymbol{b}$ if for some (equivalently, for all) $A \in \boldsymbol{a}$ and $B \in \boldsymbol{b}$, $A \leq_T B$;

(*b*) $\boldsymbol{a} < \boldsymbol{b}$ if $\boldsymbol{a} \leq \boldsymbol{b}$ and $\boldsymbol{a} \neq \boldsymbol{b}$.

(We leave it as an easy exercise for the reader to verify that $<$ is a partial ordering on degrees (cf. theorem 2.6).)

We can reformulate much of theorem 5.2 in terms of degrees as follows:

5.6. *Theorem*

(*a*) *There is a single recursive degree, which is denoted* $\mathbf{0}$; $\mathbf{0}$ *consists of all the recursive sets, and is the unique minimum degree.*

(*b*) *Let* $\mathbf{0}'$ *denote the degree of* K; *then* $\mathbf{0} < \mathbf{0}'$ *and* $\mathbf{0}'$ *is a maximum among all r.e. degrees.*

(*c*) *For any sets A, B*

(i) $\mathrm{d_m}(A) \subseteq \mathrm{d_T}(A)$,

(ii) *if* $\mathrm{d_m}(A) \leq_{\mathrm{m}} \mathrm{d_m}(B)$, then $\mathrm{d_T}(A) \leq \mathrm{d_T}(B)$.

Proof.

(*a*) This is immediate from theorem 5.2(*e*) and (*f*).

(*b*) From (*a*) $\mathbf{0} \leq \mathbf{0}'$; and $\mathbf{0} \neq \mathbf{0}'$ since K is not recursive. By theorem 5.2(*g*), if $\boldsymbol{a}$ is any r.e. degree, $\boldsymbol{a} \leq \mathbf{0}'$.

(*c*) Immediate from theorem 5.2(*c*). □

There are two fundamental features of the structure of Turing degrees under their partial ordering that we should now mention.

The jump operation We have seen that the step from recursive sets to T-complete sets such as K is a definite increase in degree of difficulty, expressed in the language of T-degrees by writing $\mathbf{0} < \mathbf{0}'$. We now show that for *any* degree $\boldsymbol{a}$ there is a corresponding step or jump to a higher degree $\boldsymbol{a}'$, known as the *jump* of $\boldsymbol{a}$. This is defined using the set $K^A = \{x : x \in W_x^A\}$ (for any set $A \in \boldsymbol{a}$): but first we need the following theorem.

5.7. *Theorem*

Let A, B be any sets.

(*a*) (i) K^A *is A-r.e.,*

(ii) *if B is A-r.e., then* $B \leq_T K^A$.

(*b*) *If A is recursive then* $K^A \equiv_T K$.
(*c*) $A <_T K^A$.
(*d*) (i) *If* $A \leq_T B$ *then* $K^A \leq_T K^B$,
(ii) *if* $A \equiv_T B$ *then* $K^A \equiv_T K^B$.

Proof.

(*a*) (i) is given by theorem 4.9(*c*); for (ii), a straightforward relativisation of theorem 1.6 (using the relativised *s–m–n* theorem) shows that if B is A-r.e. then $B \leq_m K^A$.

(*b*) Clearly $K \leq_T K^A$, since K is A-r.e. for any A; on the other hand, if A is recursive then the A-computable partial characteristic function of K^A is actually computable (theorem 4.3(*c*)); hence K^A is r.e. Thus $K^A \leq_T K$.

(*c*) $A \leq_T K^A$ is given by (*a*)(ii); $A \not\equiv_T K^A$ is given by theorem 4.9(*c*).

(*d*) (i) If $A \leq_T B$, then since K^A is A-r.e. it is also B-r.e. (see exercise 4.10(7*b*)). Hence $K^A \leq_T K^B$ by (*a*)(ii).

(ii) follows immediately from (i). □

Part (*a*) of this theorem tells us that K^A is what we would call a *T-complete A-r.e.* set; it is sometimes called the *completion* of A, but usually it is called the *jump* of A and denoted A'.

Notice that for any $A \in \mathbf{0}$, the degree of K^A is $\mathbf{0}'$ (by (*b*) of the above theorem). This leads to the following definition of the *jump operator* on degrees.

5.8. *Definition*

For any degree $\boldsymbol{a}$, the *jump* of $\boldsymbol{a}$, denoted $\boldsymbol{a}'$, is the degree of K^A for any $A \in \boldsymbol{a}$.

Remarks

1. Theorem 5.7(*d*) tells us that this is a valid definition because the degree of K^A is the same for every $A \in \boldsymbol{a}$.
2. By theorem 5.7(*b*) the new definition of $\mathbf{0}'$ here as the jump of $\mathbf{0}$ accords with our earlier definition of $\mathbf{0}'$ as the degree of K (theorem 5.6).

We can immediately write down the basic properties of the jump operator:

5.9. *Theorem*

For any degrees $\boldsymbol{a}$, $\boldsymbol{b}$

(*a*) $\boldsymbol{a} < \boldsymbol{a}'$,
(*b*) if $\boldsymbol{a} \leq \boldsymbol{b}$ then $\boldsymbol{a}' \leq \boldsymbol{b}'$,
(*c*) $\mathbf{0}' \leq \boldsymbol{a}'$,
(*d*) if $B \in \boldsymbol{b}$, $A \in \boldsymbol{a}$ and B is A-r.e., then $\boldsymbol{b} \leq \boldsymbol{a}'$.

Proof.
(*a*) By theorem 5.7(*c*).
(*b*) By theorem 5.7(*d*).
(*c*) From (*b*), since $\mathbf{0} \leq \boldsymbol{a}$.
(*d*) By theorem 5.7(*a*). □

The second fundamental feature of the structure of the Turing degrees is one we have seen already for the m-degrees: they form an upper semi-lattice:

5.10. *Theorem*

Any degrees $\boldsymbol{a}$, $\boldsymbol{b}$ *have a unique least upper bound.*

Proof. We merely mention that the least upper bound of $\boldsymbol{a}$, $\boldsymbol{b}$ is (as with m-degrees) the degree of $A \oplus B$ for any sets $A \in \boldsymbol{a}$, $B \in \boldsymbol{b}$, and leave the rest of the proof as an exercise, which is similar to the proof of theorem 2.8. □

The least upper bound of degrees $\boldsymbol{a}$, $\boldsymbol{b}$ is denoted by $\boldsymbol{a} \cup \boldsymbol{b}$: it is clear from the construction that if $\boldsymbol{a}$, $\boldsymbol{b}$ are r.e. then so is $\boldsymbol{a} \cup \boldsymbol{b}$.

The structure of the Turing degrees under their partial ordering, and equipped with the operations $'$ and $\cup$, has been studied extensively, and is still by no means fully understood. Particular attention has been given to the structure of the r.e. degrees (these do *not* form an initial segment of the Turing degrees, as was the case with the r.e. m-degrees: see theorem 5.18 below). It is now known that the structure of the T-degrees and the r.e. T-degrees is extremely rich and complex. For a long time, however, even the following simply posed question was unsettled:

5.11. *Post's problem*

Is there an r.e. degree $\boldsymbol{a}$ such that $\mathbf{0} < \boldsymbol{a} < \mathbf{0}'$?

This problem was posed by Post in 1944. The simple sets, invented by Post, did not provide an answer, as they did with corresponding question for m-degrees (corollary 3.6). One reason for this is seen in the following result of Dekker, which shows in particular that $\mathbf{0}'$ contains a simple set.

5.12. *Theorem*

Any non-recursive r.e. degree contains a simple set.

Proof (sketch). Let B be an r.e. set that is not recursive, and let $B = \mathrm{Ran}(f)$ where f is a total injective computable function (exercise 7-2.18(7)). Let A be the set given by

$$A = \{x : \exists y (y > x \text{ and } f(y) < f(x))\}.$$

In exercise 7-4.4(2) we gave the hint for showing that A is simple. We leave the proof that $A \equiv_T B$ as an exercise (exercise 5.21(6) below). □

This theorem underlines the difference between m-degrees and T-degrees, since it shows that $\mathbf{0}'$, unlike $\mathbf{0}'_m$, contains many r.e. sets that are not m-complete.

The breakthrough on Post's problem came in 1956 when Friedberg and Muchnik independently proved:

5.13. *Theorem*

There are r.e. sets A, B such that $A \not\leq_T B$ and $B \not\leq_T A$. Hence, if $\boldsymbol{a}, \boldsymbol{b}$ are $d_T(A)$, $d_T(B)$ respectively, $\boldsymbol{a} \not\leq \boldsymbol{b}$ and $\boldsymbol{b} \not\leq \boldsymbol{a}$, and thus $\mathbf{0} < \boldsymbol{a} < \mathbf{0}'$ and $\mathbf{0} < \boldsymbol{b} < \mathbf{0}'$.

(Degrees $\boldsymbol{a}$, $\boldsymbol{b}$ such that $\boldsymbol{a} \not\leq \boldsymbol{b}$ and $\boldsymbol{b} \not\leq \boldsymbol{a}$ are called *incomparable* degrees; this is written $\boldsymbol{a} \mid \boldsymbol{b}$.)

For a proof of the Friedberg–Muchnik theorem, which is well beyond the scope of this book, we refer the reader to books such as Rogers [1967] or Shoenfield [1971]. Friedberg and Muchnik used a new technique known as the *priority method*, which opened the way to the discovery of the complex nature of the structure of the Turing-degrees.

There are many results about degrees that, like the Friedberg–Muchnik theorem, are easy to formulate but difficult to prove. We give below a sample of these, to illustrate the complexity of the T-degrees.

5.14. *Theorem*

For any r.e. degree $\boldsymbol{a} > \mathbf{0}$, there is an r.e. degree $\boldsymbol{b}$ such that $\boldsymbol{b} \mid \boldsymbol{a}$.

5.15. *Sacks' Density theorem*

For any r.e. degrees $\boldsymbol{a} < \boldsymbol{b}$ there is an r.e. degree $\boldsymbol{c}$ with $\boldsymbol{a} < \boldsymbol{c} < \boldsymbol{b}$.

5.16. *Sacks' Splitting theorem*

For any r.e. degree $\boldsymbol{a} > \mathbf{0}$ there are r.e. degrees $\boldsymbol{b}, \boldsymbol{c}$ such that $\boldsymbol{b} < \boldsymbol{a}$, $\boldsymbol{c} < \boldsymbol{a}$ and $\boldsymbol{a} = \boldsymbol{b} \cup \boldsymbol{c}$ (hence $\boldsymbol{b} \mid \boldsymbol{c}$).

5.17. *Theorem* (Lachlan, Yates)
(*a*) *There are r.e. degrees* $\boldsymbol{a}, \boldsymbol{b} > \mathbf{0}$ *such that* $\mathbf{0}$ *is the greatest lower bound of* $\boldsymbol{a}$ *and* $\boldsymbol{b}$.
(*b*) *There are r.e. degrees* $\boldsymbol{a}$, $\boldsymbol{b}$ *having no greatest lower bound (either among all degrees or among r.e. degrees).*

Turning to non r.e. degrees, a surprising result is

5.18 *Theorem* (Shoenfield)
There is a non-r.e. degree $\boldsymbol{a} < \mathbf{0}'$.

A *minimal degree* is a degree $\boldsymbol{m} > \mathbf{0}$ such that there is no degree $\boldsymbol{a}$ with $\mathbf{0} < \boldsymbol{a} < \boldsymbol{m}$. By Sacks' Density theorem there can be no minimal r.e. degree. However, Spector proved:

5.19. *Theorem*
There is a minimal degree.

For proofs of these and other results about degrees we refer the reader again to the books of Rogers and Shoenfield. The article by Simpson [1977] gives a very readable survey of more recent results that are not included in these books.

T-degrees and m-degrees Often results about T-degrees give information about the structure of the m-degrees almost immediately, via theorem 5.6(*c*). We illustrate with

5.20. *Corollary* (to theorem 5.14)
For any r.e. m-degree $\boldsymbol{a} >_{\mathrm{m}} \mathbf{0}_{\mathrm{m}}$, *there is an r.e. m-degree* $\boldsymbol{b}$ *such that* $\boldsymbol{b} \mid \boldsymbol{a}$.

Proof. Let $A \in \boldsymbol{a}$; A is r.e. so by theorem 5.14 take an r.e. T-degree $\boldsymbol{c}$ such that $\mathrm{d_T}(A) \mid \boldsymbol{c}$. Let B be an r.e. set in $\boldsymbol{c}$, and let $\boldsymbol{b} = \mathrm{d_m}(B)$. Then if $\boldsymbol{a} \leq_{\mathrm{m}} \boldsymbol{b}$ or $\boldsymbol{b} \leq_{\mathrm{m}} \boldsymbol{a}$, by theorem 5.6(*c*) we have $\mathrm{d_T}(A) \leq \boldsymbol{c}$ or $\boldsymbol{c} \leq \mathrm{d_T}(A)$, contradicting $\mathrm{d_T}(A) \mid \boldsymbol{c}$. Hence $\boldsymbol{a} \mid \boldsymbol{b}$. □

Other reducibilities There are other notions of reducibility that lie between the restricted notion of m-reducibility and the broader T-reducibility. The book of Rogers [1967] provides a full and detailed discussion of these.

5.21. *Exercises*

1. Show that each of the following sets is T-complete:
   (*a*) $\{x : x \in E_x\}$,
   (*b*) $\{x : W_x = \emptyset\}$.
2. Improve theorem 5.7(*d*) by showing that $A \leq_T B$ iff $K^A \leq_m K^B$, and $A \equiv_T B$ iff $K^A \equiv_m K^B$.
3. Show that the previous question can be made effective in the following sense: there is a total computable function f such that for any A, B, if $c_A = \phi_e^B$, then $\phi_{f(e)}: K^A \leq_m K^B$.
   (*Hint.* Find total computable functions g, h such that (i) if $c_A = \phi_e^B$ then $K^A = W_{g(e)}^B$, (ii) $\phi_{h(e)}: W_e^B \leq_m K^B$, for all e.)
4. For any set A define a sequence of sets $A^{(n)}$ by
   $A^{(0)} = A; \qquad A^{(n+1)} = K^{A^{(n)}}$,
   and let $A^{(\omega)} = \{\pi(m, n) : m \in A^{(n)}\}$.
   (*a*) Show that $A^{(n)} <_T A^{(\omega)}$ for all n.
   (*b*) Show that there is a total computable function h such that $c_{A^{(n)}} = \phi_{h(n)}^{A^{(\omega)}}$ for all n.
   (*c*) Suppose that B is a set such that $A^{(n)} \leq_T B$ for all n in the following strong way: there is a total computable function f such that $c_{A^{(n)}} = \phi_{f(n)}^B$, all n. Show that $A^{(\omega)} \leq_T B$.
   (*d*) Show that if $A \leq_T B$ then $A^{(n)} \leq_T B^{(n)}$ all n, and $A^{(\omega)} \leq_T B^{(\omega)}$.
   (*Hint.* Use question 3 above, together with (*b*) and (*c*).)
5. Prove theorem 5.10.
6. Complete the proof of theorem 5.12.
7. Prove as a corollary to theorem 5.17(*a*) that there are r.e. m-degrees such that $\mathbf{0}_m$ is the greatest lower bound of $\boldsymbol{a}$ and $\boldsymbol{b}$.

10
Effective operations on partial functions

Once we have studied effectively computable operations on *numbers* it is natural to ask whether there is a comparable notion for operations on *functions*. The essential difference between functions and numbers as basic objects is that functions are usually infinite rather than finite. With this in mind, in § 1 of this chapter we discuss the features we might reasonably expect of an *effective* operator on partial functions: this leads to the formulation of the definition of *recursive operators* on partial functions.

In § 2 we shall see that there is a close connection between recursive operators and those effective operations on computable functions that we discussed in Chapter 5 § 3. In § 3 we prove the important fixed point theorem for recursive operators known as the first Recursion theorem. The final part of this chapter provides a discussion of some of the applications of this theorem in computability and the theory of programming.

1. **Recursive operators**

Let us denote by $\mathscr{F}_n$ $(n \geq 1)$ the class of all partial functions from $\mathbb{N}^n$ to $\mathbb{N}$. We use the word *operator* to describe a function $\Phi: \mathscr{F}_m \rightarrow \mathscr{F}_n$; the letters Φ, Ψ, . . . will invariably denote operators in this chapter. We shall confine our attention to totally defined operators $\Phi: \mathscr{F}_m \rightarrow \mathscr{F}_n$; i.e. such that the domain of Φ is the whole of $\mathscr{F}_m$.

The chief problem when trying to formulate the idea of a computable (or effective) operator $\Phi: \mathscr{F}_1 \rightarrow \mathscr{F}_1$, say, is that both an 'input' function f and the 'output' function $\Phi(f)$ are likely to be infinite objects, and hence incapable of being given in a finite time. Yet our intuition about effective processes is that in some sense they should be completed within a finite time.

To see how this problem can be overcome, consider the following operators from $\mathscr{F}_1$ to $\mathscr{F}_1$:

(*a*) $\Phi_1(f)=2f$.

(*b*) $\Phi_2(f)=g$, where $g(x)=\sum_{y\leq x} f(y)$.

These operators are certainly down to earth and explicit. Intuitively we might regard them as effective operators: but why? Let $f\in\mathscr{F}_1$ and let $g_1=\Phi_1(f)$; notice that any particular value $g_1(x)$ (if defined) can be calculated in finite time from the single value $f(x)$ of f; if we set $g_2=\Phi_2(f)$, then to calculate $g_2(x)$ (if defined) we need to know the *finite* number of values $f(0), f(1), \ldots, f(x)$. Thus in both cases any defined value of the output function ($\Phi_1(f)$ or $\Phi_2(f)$) can be effectively calculated in a *finite* time using only a *finite* part of the input function f. This is essentially the definition of a recursive operator given below.

One consequence of the definition will be the following: suppose that $\Phi(f)(x)=y$ is calculated using only a finite part θ of f; then if g is any other function having θ as a finite part we must expect that $\Phi(g)(x)=y$ also.

To frame our definition precisely there are some technical considerations. First, let us agree that by a 'finite part' of a function f we mean a finite function θ extended by f. (We say that θ is a *finite function* if its domain is a finite set.) For convenience we adopt the convention

θ always denotes a finite function in this chapter.

The above discussion shows that the definition of recursive operator will involve effective calculations with finite functions. We make this precise by coding each finite function θ by a number $\tilde{\theta}$ and using ordinary computability. A suitable coding for our purposes is defined as follows: suppose that $\theta\in\mathscr{F}_n$. The n-tuple $\boldsymbol{x}=(x_1,\ldots,x_n)$ is coded by the number $\langle\boldsymbol{x}\rangle=p_1^{x_1+1}p_2^{x_2+1}\ldots p_n^{x_n+1}$; then define the code $\tilde{\theta}$ for θ by

$$\tilde{\theta}=\prod_{\boldsymbol{x}\in\mathrm{Dom}(\theta)} p_{\langle\boldsymbol{x}\rangle}^{\theta(\boldsymbol{x})+1}\quad\text{provided that }\mathrm{Dom}(\theta)\neq\varnothing,$$

$$\tilde{\theta}=0\quad\text{if }\mathrm{Dom}(\theta)=\varnothing\ \text{(in which case }\theta=f_\varnothing).$$

There is a simple effective procedure to decide for any number z whether $z=\tilde{\theta}$ for some finite function θ; and if so, to decide whether a given $\boldsymbol{x}$ belongs to $\mathrm{Dom}(\theta)$, and calculate $\theta(\boldsymbol{x})$ if it does.

Now we have our definition:

1.1. *Definition*

Let $\Phi:\mathscr{F}_m\to\mathscr{F}_n$. Then Φ is a *recursive operator* if there is a computable function $\phi(z,\boldsymbol{x})$ such that for all $f\in\mathscr{F}_m$ and $\boldsymbol{x}\in\mathbb{N}^n$, $y\in\mathbb{N}$

$\Phi(f)(\boldsymbol{x}) \simeq y$ iff there is finite $\theta \subseteq f$ such that $\phi(\tilde{\theta}, \boldsymbol{x}) \simeq y$.
(Note that ϕ is not required to be total.)

1.2. *Example*

The operator $\Phi(f) = 2f$ is a recursive operator: to see this define $\phi(z, x)$ by

$$\phi(z, x) = \begin{cases} 2\theta(x) & \text{if } z = \tilde{\theta} \text{ and } x \in \text{Dom}(\theta), \\ \text{undefined} & \text{otherwise.} \end{cases}$$

By Church's thesis, ϕ is computable: now for any f, x, y we have

$$\begin{aligned} \Phi(f)(x) \simeq y &\Leftrightarrow x \in \text{Dom}(f) \text{ and } y = 2f(x) \\ &\Leftrightarrow \text{there is } \theta \subseteq f \text{ with } x \in \text{Dom}(\theta) \text{ and } y = 2\theta(x) \\ &\Leftrightarrow \text{there is } \theta \subseteq f \text{ such that } \phi(\tilde{\theta}, x) \simeq y. \end{aligned}$$

Hence Φ is a recursive operator.

Further examples will be given in 1.6 below.

An important feature of recursive operators is that they are *continuous* and *monotone* in the following sense.

1.3. *Definition*

Let $\Phi: \mathcal{F}_m \to \mathcal{F}_n$ be an operator.

(*a*) Φ is *continuous* if for any $f \in \mathcal{F}_m$, and all $\boldsymbol{x}$, y:
$\Phi(f)(\boldsymbol{x}) \simeq y$ iff there is finite $\theta \subseteq f$ with $\Phi(\theta)(\boldsymbol{x}) \simeq y$;

(*b*) Φ is *monotone* if whenever $f, g \in \mathcal{F}_m$ with $f \subseteq g$, then $\Phi(f) \subseteq \Phi(g)$.

These properties are easily established for recursive operators, and as we shall see they aid the recognition of such operators.

1.4. *Theorem*

A recursive operator is continuous and monotone.

Proof. Let $\Phi: \mathcal{F}_m \to \mathcal{F}_n$ be a recursive operator, with computable function ϕ as required by the definition. Suppose that $\Phi(f)(\boldsymbol{x}) \simeq y$, and let $\theta \subseteq f$ such that $\phi(\tilde{\theta}, \boldsymbol{x}) \simeq y$. Since $\theta \subseteq \theta$, it follows immediately that $\Phi(\theta)(\boldsymbol{x}) \simeq y$. Conversely, if $\theta \subseteq f$ and $\Phi(\theta)(\boldsymbol{x}) \simeq y$, there is $\theta_1 \subseteq \theta$ such that $\phi(\tilde{\theta}_1, \boldsymbol{x}) \simeq y$; but then $\theta_1 \subseteq f$, so we have that $\Phi(f)(\boldsymbol{x}) \simeq y$. Hence Φ is continuous.

Monotonicity follows directly from continuity: suppose that $f \subseteq g$ and $\Phi(f)(\boldsymbol{x}) \simeq y$. Take $\theta \subseteq f$ such that $\Phi(\theta)(\boldsymbol{x}) \simeq y$; then $\theta \subseteq g$, so by continuity, $\Phi(g)(\boldsymbol{x}) \simeq y$. □

The use of the term *continuous* to describe the property 1.3(a) is justified informally as follows. Suppose that $\Phi: \mathscr{F}_1 \to \mathscr{F}_1$ satisfies 1.3(a) and $f \in \mathscr{F}_1$. Then given any $x_1, \ldots, x_k$ for which $\Phi(f)(x_i)$ $(1 \le i \le k)$ are defined, using 1.3(a) we can obtain a finite $\theta \subseteq f$ such that $\Phi(\theta)(x_i) = \Phi(f)(x_i)$ $(1 \le i \le k)$. Thus, whenever $g \supseteq \theta$, by 1.3(a) again, we have $\Phi(g)(x_i) = \Phi(f)(x_i)$ $(1 \le i \le k)$. i.e. if g is 'near' to f (in the sense that they agree on the finite set Dom(θ)) then $\Phi(g)$ is 'near' to $\Phi(f)$ (in the sense that they agree on the finite set $x_1, \ldots, x_k$). Thus, informally, Φ is continuous.

The continuity property 1.3(a) specifies that a value $\Phi(f)(\boldsymbol{x})$ is determined (if at all) by a finite amount of *positive* information about f. This means information asserting that f is defined at certain points and takes certain values there, as opposed to *negative* information that would indicate points where f is not defined. Using this idea the term continuous can be rigorously justified as follows.

The *positive information topology*[1] on $\mathscr{F}_m$ is defined by taking as base of open neighbourhoods sets of the form

$$U_\theta = \{f: \theta \subseteq f\} \quad (\theta \in \mathscr{F}_m, \text{ finite}).$$

Thus f belongs to U_θ iff θ is correct positive information about f. It is then an easy exercise to see that an operator is continuous with respect to the positive information topology precisely when it possesses property 1.3(a).

The following characterisation of recursive operators using continuity will make it easy to establish recursiveness of various operators.

1.5. *Theorem*

Let $\Phi: \mathscr{F}_m \to \mathscr{F}_n$ be an operator. Then Φ is a recursive operator iff

(a) *Φ is continuous,*

(b) *the function $\phi(z, \boldsymbol{x})$ given by*

$$\begin{cases} \phi(\tilde{\theta}, \boldsymbol{x}) \simeq \Phi(\theta)(\boldsymbol{x}) & \text{for } \theta \in \mathscr{F}_m, \\ \phi(z, \boldsymbol{x}) \text{ is undefined} & \text{for all other } z, \end{cases}$$

is computable.

Proof. Suppose that Φ is recursive with computable function ϕ_1 such that

$$\Phi(f)(\boldsymbol{x}) \simeq y \text{ iff } \exists \theta(\theta \subseteq f \text{ and } \phi_1(\tilde{\theta}, \boldsymbol{x}) \simeq y).$$

[1] The reader unfamiliar with topology will lose nothing in further development by omitting this paragraph.

Then taking ϕ as given in the theorem, we have

$$\phi(\tilde{\theta}, \boldsymbol{x}) \simeq y \Leftrightarrow \exists \theta_1(\theta_1 \subseteq \theta \text{ and } \phi_1(\tilde{\theta}_1, \boldsymbol{x}) \simeq y);$$

the relation on the right is partially decidable, so ϕ is computable by theorem 6-6.13.

Conversely, suppose that conditions (a) and (b) of the theorem hold: then

$$\begin{aligned}\Phi(f)(\boldsymbol{x}) \simeq y &\Leftrightarrow \exists \theta(\theta \subseteq f \text{ and } \Phi(\theta)(\boldsymbol{x}) \simeq y) \text{ (by } (a))\\ &\Leftrightarrow \exists \theta(\theta \subseteq f \text{ and } \phi(\tilde{\theta}, \boldsymbol{x}) \simeq y) \text{ (by } (b)),\end{aligned}$$

whence Φ is a recursive operator. □

This theorem enables us to show quite easily that the following operators are all recursive:

1.6. *Examples*

(a) (The diagonalisation operator) $\Phi(f)(x) \simeq f(x, x)$ $(f \in \mathscr{F}_2)$. Φ is obviously continuous, and $\phi(\tilde{\theta}, x) \simeq \theta(x, x)$ is computable.

(b) $\Phi(f)(x) \simeq \sum_{y \leq x} f(y)$ $(f \in \mathscr{F}_1)$

This is the second example discussed at the beginning of this section. We saw there that Φ is continuous; and clearly $\phi(\tilde{\theta}, x) \simeq \sum_{y \leq x} \theta(y)$ is computable.

(c) Let $g \in \mathscr{F}_1$ be computable. Define $\Phi: \mathscr{F}_n \to \mathscr{F}_n$ by $\Phi(f) = g \circ f$. Obviously Φ is continuous, and $\phi(\tilde{\theta}, x) \simeq g(\theta(x))$ is computable.

(d) (The Ackermann operator). Let $\Phi: \mathscr{F}_2 \to \mathscr{F}_2$ be given by

$$\Phi(f)(0, y) = y + 1,$$

$$\Phi(f)(x+1, 0) \simeq f(x, 1),$$

$$\Phi(f)(x+1, y+1) \simeq f(x, f(x+1, y)).$$

To see that Φ is continuous, note that $\Phi(f)(x, y)$ depends on at most two particular values of f. For recursiveness, it is immediate by Church's thesis that the function ϕ given by

$$\phi(\tilde{\theta}, 0, y) = y + 1$$

$$\phi(\tilde{\theta}, x+1, 0) \simeq \theta(x, 1)$$

$$\phi(\tilde{\theta}, x+1, y+1) \simeq \theta(x, \theta(x+1, y))$$

is computable.

(e) (The μ-operator.) Consider Φ: $\mathscr{F}_{n+1} \to \mathscr{F}_n$, given by $\Phi(f)(\boldsymbol{x}) \simeq \mu y(f(\boldsymbol{x}, y) = 0)$. It is immediate that this operator is continuous, and that the function ϕ given by

$$\phi(\tilde{\theta}, \boldsymbol{x}) \simeq \mu y(\theta(\boldsymbol{x}, y) = 0)$$

is computable.

When the definition 1.1 of a recursive operator $\Phi:\mathcal{F}_m\to\mathcal{F}_n$ is extended to the case $n=0$, we have what is called a *recursive functional*. The members of $\mathcal{F}_0$ are 0-ary functions; i.e. constants. Just as $\mathcal{F}_n$ $(n\geq 1)$ includes the function that is defined nowhere, $\mathcal{F}_0$ includes the 'undefined' constant, which is denoted by ω. Thus $\mathcal{F}_0=\mathbb{N}\cup\{\omega\}$, and an operator $\Phi:\mathcal{F}_m\to\mathcal{F}_0$ is a *recursive functional* if there is a computable function $\phi(x)$ such that for any $f\in\mathcal{F}_m$, and $y\in\mathbb{N}$:

$$\Phi(f)\simeq y \text{ iff } \exists\theta(\theta\subseteq f \text{ and } \phi(\tilde{\theta})\simeq y).$$

We write $\Phi(f)=\omega$ if $\Phi(f)$ is undefined; this emphasises that Φ is still thought of as being a total operator.

We should point out that in some texts the term *partial recursive functional* $\mathcal{F}_m\to\mathcal{F}_n$ is used to describe recursive operators, including the case $n=0$. In such contexts the word partial describes the kind of object being operated on rather than the domain of definition of the operation.

We shall not discuss here the extension of the ideas of this section to partially defined operators and the corresponding *partial recursive operators* $\Phi:\mathcal{F}_m\to\mathcal{F}_n$. The reader is referred to Rogers [1967] for a full discussion of these and related matters.

1.7. *Exercises*

1. Show that the following operators are recursive.

   (*a*) $\Phi(f)=f^2$ $(f\in\mathcal{F}_1)$,

   (*b*) $\Phi(f)=g$ $(f\in\mathcal{F}_n)$, where g is a fixed computable function in $\mathcal{F}_1$,

   (*c*) $\Phi(f)=f\circ g$ $(f\in\mathcal{F}_1)$ where g is a fixed computable function in $\mathcal{F}_n$,

   (*d*) Let $h\in\mathcal{F}_{n+1}$ be a fixed computable function; define $\Phi:\mathcal{F}_{n+1}\to\mathcal{F}_{n+1}$ by

   $$\Phi(f)(x,\mathbf{y})\simeq\begin{cases}0 & \text{if } h(x,\mathbf{y})=0,\\ f(x+1,\mathbf{y})+1 & \text{if } h(x,\mathbf{y}) \text{ is defined and } \neq 0,\\ \text{undefined} & \text{otherwise}\end{cases}$$

   (The significance of this operator will be seen later.)

2. Prove that if Φ is a recursive operator and f is computable then so is $\Phi(f)$.

3. Decide whether the following operators $\Phi:\mathcal{F}_1\to\mathcal{F}_1$ are (i) monotonic, (ii) continuous, (iii) recursive.

   $$(a)\ \Phi(f)(x)\simeq\begin{cases}f(x) & \text{if Dom}(f) \text{ is finite},\\ \text{undefined} & \text{if Dom}(f) \text{ is infinite}.\end{cases}$$

(*b*) $\Phi(f)(x) = \begin{cases} 0 & \text{if } f(x) \text{ is defined,} \\ \text{undefined} & \text{otherwise.} \end{cases}$

(*c*) $\Phi(f)(x) = \begin{cases} \left.\begin{array}{l} 0 \text{ if } f(x) \in K \\ 1 \text{ if } f(x) \notin K \end{array}\right\} & \text{if } f(x) \text{ is defined,} \\ \text{undefined} & \text{otherwise.} \end{cases}$

(*d*) $\Phi(f)(x) \simeq \begin{cases} \text{undefined} & \text{if Dom}(f) \text{ is finite,} \\ f(x) & \text{if Dom}(f) \text{ is infinite.} \end{cases}$

4. Suppose that $\Phi: \mathcal{F}_m \to \mathcal{F}_n$ and $\Psi: \mathcal{F}_n \to \mathcal{F}_p$ are recursive operators. Prove that $\Psi \circ \Phi: \mathcal{F}_m \to \mathcal{F}_p$ is recursive.
5. Show how to extend the definition of recursive operator to include operators $\Phi: \mathcal{F}_{m_1} \times \mathcal{F}_{m_2} \times \ldots \times \mathcal{F}_{m_k} \to \mathcal{F}_n$, and prove appropriate versions of theorems 1.4 and 1.5 for your definition. Prove that the following operators are recursive:
(*a*) $\Phi: \mathcal{F}_1 \times \mathcal{F}_n \to \mathcal{F}_n$ given by $\Phi(f, g) = f \circ g$ (cf. question 1*c* above);
(*b*) $\Phi: \mathcal{F}_{n+1} \times \mathcal{F}_{n+1} \to \mathcal{F}_{n+1}$ given by
$$\Phi(f, h)(x, \mathbf{y}) \simeq \begin{cases} 0 & \text{if } h(x, \mathbf{y}) = 0, \\ f(x+1, \mathbf{y}) + 1 & \text{if } h(x, \mathbf{y}) \text{ is defined and is not } 0, \\ \text{undefined} & \text{otherwise} \end{cases}$$
(cf. 1*d* above).
6. (For those who know some topology.)
(*a*) Prove that an operator is continuous in the sense of definition 1.3(*a*) iff it is continuous in the positive information topology.
(*b*) Prove that the following are equivalent for $V \subseteq \mathcal{F}_n$:
(i) V is open in the positive information topology,
(ii) $f \in V$ iff $\exists \theta(\theta \subseteq f$ and $\theta \in V)$.
7. Let $\Phi: \mathcal{F}_m \to \mathcal{F}_n$ and $\Psi: \mathcal{F}_n \to \mathcal{F}_p$ be continuous operators; prove that $\Psi \circ \Phi: \mathcal{F}_m \to \mathcal{F}_p$ is continuous.
8. Let $\mathcal{P}(\mathbb{N})$ denote the class of all subsets of $\mathbb{N}$; formulate a definition of a recursive operator $\Phi: \mathcal{P}(\mathbb{N}) \to \mathcal{P}(\mathbb{N})$ that parallels the notion of a recursive operator from $\mathcal{F}_1 \to \mathcal{F}_1$. Frame and prove theorems corresponding to theorems 1.4 and 1.5.
(*Hint.* The question of membership $x \in \Phi(A)$ should depend effectively on a finite amount of positive information about membership of the set A.)

   (Effective operators $\mathcal{P}(\mathbb{N}) \to \mathcal{P}(\mathbb{N})$ are called *enumeration operators* and are discussed in full in Rogers [1967].)

2. Effective operations on computable functions

In chapter 5 § 3 we considered that certain operations on *computable* functions should be called effective because they can be given by total computable functions acting on indices. For instance, in example 5-3.1(2) we saw that there is a total computable function g such that for all $e \in \mathbb{N}$, $(\phi_e)^2 = \phi_{g(e)}$.

We shall see in this section that any recursive operator Φ, when restricted to computable functions, yields an effective operation of this kind on indices. This is the first part of a theorem of Myhill and Shepherdson. They proved, moreover, that *all* such operations on indices of computable functions arise in this way.

We shall prove the two parts of the Myhill–Shepherdson result separately, taking the easier part first.

2.1. *Theorem* (Myhill–Shepherdson, part I)

Suppose that $\Psi: \mathscr{F}_m \to \mathscr{F}_n$ *is a recursive operator. Then there is a total computable function h such that*

$$\Psi(\phi_e^{(m)}) = \phi_{h(e)}^{(n)} \quad (e \in \mathbb{N}).$$

Proof. Let ψ be a computable function showing that Ψ is a recursive operator according to definition 1.1. Then for any e we have

$$\Psi(\phi_e^{(m)})(\mathbf{x}) \simeq y \Leftrightarrow \exists \theta(\theta \subseteq \phi_e^{(m)} \text{ and } \psi(\tilde{\theta}, \mathbf{x}) \simeq y).$$

We shall show that the function g defined by

$$g(e, \mathbf{x}) \simeq \Psi(\phi_e^{(m)})(\mathbf{x})$$

is computable, by showing that the relation $g(e, \mathbf{x}) \simeq y$ is partially decidable. To this end, consider the relation $R(z, e, \mathbf{x}, y)$ given by

$$R(z, e, \mathbf{x}, y) \equiv \exists \theta(z = \tilde{\theta} \text{ and } \theta \subseteq \phi_e^{(m)} \text{ and } \psi(\tilde{\theta}, \mathbf{x}) \simeq y).$$

Then R is partially decidable, with the following informal partial decision procedure.

(1) Decide whether $z = \tilde{\theta}$ for some θ; if so obtain $\mathbf{x}_1, \ldots, \mathbf{x}_k \in \mathbb{N}^m$ and $y_1, \ldots, y_k$ such that $\mathrm{Dom}(\theta) = \{\mathbf{x}_1, \ldots, \mathbf{x}_k\}$ and $\theta(\mathbf{x}_i) = y_i$ $(1 \le i \le k)$; then

(2) for $i = 1, \ldots, k$ compute $\phi_e^{(m)}(\mathbf{x}_i)$; if, for $1 \le i \le k$, $\phi_e^{(m)}(\mathbf{x}_i)$ is defined and equals y_i, then

(3) compute $\psi(z, \mathbf{x})$ and if defined check whether it equals y.

If $R(z, e, \mathbf{x}, y)$ holds, this is a mechanical procedure that will tell us so in finite time, as required.

Since $R(z, e, \mathbf{x}, y)$ is partially decidable, so is the relation $\exists z\, R(z, e, \mathbf{x}, y)$ (by theorem 6-6.5): but

$$\begin{aligned}\exists z\, R(z, e, \mathbf{x}, y) &\Leftrightarrow \Psi(\phi_e^{(m)})(\mathbf{x}) \simeq y \text{ (from the definition of } R)\\ &\Leftrightarrow g(e, \mathbf{x}) \simeq y \text{ (from the definition of } g).\end{aligned}$$

Thus $g(e, \mathbf{x}) \simeq y$ is partially decidable, so by theorem 6-6.13 g is computable.

Now the s–m–n theorem provides a total computable function h such that

$$\begin{aligned}\phi_{h(e)}^{(n)}(\mathbf{x}) &\simeq g(e, \mathbf{x})\\ &\simeq \Psi(\phi_e^{(m)})(\mathbf{x}),\end{aligned}$$

from which we have $\phi_{h(e)}^{(n)} = \Psi(\phi_e^{(m)})$. □

Notice that the function h given by this theorem for a recursive operator $\Psi: \mathcal{F}_1 \to \mathcal{F}_1$ is *extensional* in the following sense.

2.2. *Definition*

A total function $h: \mathbb{N} \to \mathbb{N}$ is *extensional* if for all a, b, if $\phi_a = \phi_b$ then $\phi_{h(a)} = \phi_{h(b)}$.

Now we can state the other half of Myhill and Shepherdson's result.

2.3. *Theorem* (Myhill–Shepherdson, part II)

Suppose that h is an extensional total computable function. Then there is a unique recursive operator Ψ such that $\Psi(\phi_e) = \phi_{h(e)}$ for all e.

Proof. At the heart of our proof lies an application of the Rice–Shapiro theorem (theorem 7-2.16).

Let h be an extensional total computable function. Then h defines an operator $\Psi_0: \mathscr{C}_1 \to \mathscr{C}_1$ by

$$\Psi_0(\phi_e) = \phi_{h(e)};$$

Ψ_0 is well defined since h is extensional. We have to show that there is a unique recursive operator $\Psi: \mathcal{F}_1 \to \mathcal{F}_1$ that extends Ψ_0.

First note that $\Psi_0(\theta)$ is defined for all finite θ, since finite functions are computable. Thus any recursive operator Ψ extending Ψ_0, being continuous, *must* be defined by

(2.4) $\Psi(f)(x) \simeq y \equiv \exists \theta(\theta \subseteq f \text{ and } \Psi_0(\theta)(x) \simeq y)$.

So such a Ψ, if it exists, is unique. To prove the theorem we must now show that

(i) (2.4) *does* define an operator Ψ,

(ii) Ψ extends Ψ_0,

(iii) Ψ is recursive.

We first use the Rice–Shapiro theorem to show that Ψ_0 is continuous in the following sense: for *computable* functions f

(2.5) $\quad \Psi_0(f)(x) \simeq y \Leftrightarrow \exists\theta(\theta \subseteq f \text{ and } \Psi_0(\theta)(x) \simeq y).$

To see this, fix x, y and let $\mathscr{A} = \{f \in \mathscr{C}_1 : \Psi_0(f)(x) \simeq y\}$. Then the set $A = \{e : \phi_e \in \mathscr{A}\} = \{e : \phi_{h(e)}(x) \simeq y\}$ is r.e.; so by the Rice–Shapiro theorem, if f is computable then

$$f \in \mathscr{A} \Leftrightarrow \exists\theta(\theta \subseteq f \text{ and } \theta \in \mathscr{A}),$$

which is precisely (2.5).

Now we establish (i), (ii), (iii) above.

(i) Let f be any partial function; we must show that for any x, (2.4) defines $\Psi(f)(x)$ uniquely (if at all). Suppose then that $\theta_1, \theta_2 \subseteq f$ and $\Psi_0(\theta_1)(x) \simeq y_1$ and $\Psi_0(\theta_2)(x) \simeq y_2$. Take a finite function $\theta \supseteq \theta_1, \theta_2$ (say, $\theta = f|\mathrm{Dom}(\theta_1) \cup \mathrm{Dom}(\theta_2)$); by (2.5)

$$y_1 \simeq \Psi_0(\theta_1)(x) \simeq \Psi_0(\theta)(x) \simeq \Psi_0(\theta_2)(x) \simeq y_2.$$

Thus (2.4) defines an operator Ψ unambiguously.

(ii) This is immediate from (2.5) and the definition (2.4).

(iii) We show that Ψ satisfies the conditions of theorem 1.5. Clearly Ψ is continuous, from the definition. For the other condition we must show that the function ψ given by

$$\psi(\tilde{\theta}, x) \simeq \Psi(\theta)(x),$$
$$\psi(z, x) \text{ is undefined if } z \neq \tilde{\theta},$$

is computable. Now it is easily seen by using Church's thesis that there is a computable function c such that for any finite function θ, $c(\tilde{\theta})$ is an index for θ; i.e. $\theta = \phi_{c(\tilde{\theta})}$. Thus

$$\psi(\tilde{\theta}, x) \simeq \Psi(\phi_{c(\tilde{\theta})})(x)$$
$$\simeq \phi_{h(c(\tilde{\theta}))}(x),$$

so ψ is computable, since h and c are. Hence Ψ is a recursive operator. □

Remarks

1. The proof of theorem 2.3 actually shows that for any extensional computable h there is a unique *continuous* operator $\Psi: \mathscr{F}_1 \to \mathscr{F}_1$ such that $\Psi(\phi_e) = \phi_{h(e)}$, all e, and that this operator is recursive.

2. Theorem 2.3 extends in a natural way to cover operators from $\mathscr{F}_m \to \mathscr{F}_n$. The proof is almost identical, using the natural extension of the Rice–Shapiro theorem to subsets of $\mathscr{C}_m$; see exercise 2.6(2) below.

2.6. *Exercises*

1. Suppose that Φ, Ψ are recursive operators $\mathscr{F}_1 \to \mathscr{F}_1$; knowing that $\Phi \circ \Psi$ is continuous (exercise 1.7(7)) use the two parts of the Myhill–Shepherdson theorem together with the first remark above to show that $\Phi \circ \Psi$ is recursive.
2. State and prove a general version of theorem 2.3 for operators from $\mathscr{C}_m \to \mathscr{C}_n$.
3. Formulate and prove versions of the Myhill–Shepherdson theorem (both parts) appropriate for the operators you have defined (*a*) in exercise 1.7(5), (*b*) in exercise 1.7(8).

3. The first Recursion theorem

The first Recursion theorem of Kleene is a fixed point theorem for recursive operators, and is often referred to as the Fixed point theorem (of recursion theory). We shall see later that it is a very useful result.

3.1. *The first Recursion theorem* (Kleene)

Suppose that $\Phi: \mathscr{F}_m \to \mathscr{F}_m$ is a recursive operator. Then there is a computable function f_Φ that is the least fixed point of Φ; i.e.

(*a*) $\Phi(f_\Phi) = f_\Phi$,

(*b*) *if* $\Phi(g) = g$, *then* $f_\Phi \subseteq g$.

Hence, if f_Φ is total, it is the only fixed point of Φ.

Proof. We use the continuity and monotonicity of Φ to construct the least fixed point f_Φ as follows. Define a sequence of functions $\{f_n\}$ $(n \in \mathbb{N})$ by

$$f_0 = f_\varnothing \text{ (the function with empty domain)},$$
$$f_{n+1} = \Phi(f_n).$$

Then $f_0 = f_\varnothing \subseteq f_1$; and if $f_n \subseteq f_{n+1}$, by monotonicity we have that $f_{n+1} = \Phi(f_n) \subseteq \Phi(f_{n+1}) = f_{n+2}$. Hence $f_n \subseteq f_{n+1}$ for all n. Now let

$$f_\Phi = \bigcup_{n \in \mathbb{N}} f_n,$$

by which we mean

$$f_\Phi(\mathbf{x}) \simeq y \text{ iff } \exists n \text{ such that } f_n(\mathbf{x}) \simeq y.$$

We shall show that f_Φ is a fixed point for Φ.

For all n,

$$f_n \subseteq f_\Phi$$

hence

$$f_{n+1}=\Phi(f_n)\subseteq\Phi(f_\Phi);$$

thus

$$f_\Phi\subseteq\Phi(f_\Phi).$$

Conversely, suppose that $\Phi(f_\Phi)(\mathbf{x})\simeq y$; then there is finite $\theta\subseteq f_\Phi$ such that $\Phi(\theta)(\mathbf{x})\simeq y$; take n such that $\theta\subseteq f_n$; then by continuity $\Phi(f_n)(\mathbf{x})\simeq y$. That is, $f_{n+1}(\mathbf{x})\simeq y$. Hence $f_\Phi(\mathbf{x})\simeq y$. Thus $\Phi(f_\Phi)\subseteq f_\Phi$, and so $\Phi(f_\Phi)=f_\Phi$ as required.

To see that f_Φ is the *least* fixed point of Φ, suppose that $\Phi(g)=g$; then clearly $f_0=f_\varnothing\subseteq g$, and by induction we see that $f_n\subseteq g$ for all n. Hence $f_\Phi\subseteq g$, as required. Moreover, if f_Φ is total, then $f_\Phi=g$, so f_Φ is the only fixed point of Φ.

Finally we show that f_Φ is computable. Use theorem 2.1 to obtain a total computable function h such that for all e

$$\Phi(\phi_e)=\phi_{h(e)}.$$

Let e_0 be an index for f_0; define a computable function k by

$$k(0)=e_0$$
$$k(n+1)=h(k(n)).$$

Then $f_n=\phi_{k(n)}$ for each n; thus

$$f_\Phi(\mathbf{x})\simeq y\Leftrightarrow\exists n(\phi_{k(n)}(\mathbf{x})\simeq y).$$

The relation on the right hand side is partially decidable, and hence f_Φ is computable. □

Remark. The recursiveness of the operator Φ was used in this proof only in showing that f_Φ is computable. The first part of the proof shows that any *continuous* operator has a least fixed point.

We shall see in the following examples that a recursive operator may have many fixed points, and that the least fixed point is not necessarily a total function.

3.2. *Examples*

1. Let Φ be the recursive operator given by

$$\Phi(f)(0)=1,$$
$$\Phi(f)(x+1)\simeq f(x+2).$$

Then the least fixed point is $\begin{cases} f_\Phi(0)=1,\\ f_\Phi(x+1)=\text{undefined}.\end{cases}$

Other fixed points of Φ take the form $\begin{cases} f(0)=1,\\ f(x+1)=a.\end{cases}$

2. Recall the definition of the Ackermann function ψ in example 2-5.5:

   $\psi(0, y) = y + 1,$

   $\psi(x+1, 0) \simeq \psi(x, 1),$

   $\psi(x+1, y+1) \simeq \psi(x, \psi(x+1, y)).$

   The first Recursion theorem gives a neat proof that these equations do define a unique function ψ and that ψ is total and computable. Let Φ be the Ackermann operator given in example 1.6(d). The fixed points of Φ are the functions that satisfy the above equations. Let $\psi = f_\Phi$; then ψ is a *computable* function satisfying these equations, so we have only to show that ψ is total. Clearly, $\psi(0, y)$ is defined for all y; if $\psi(x, y)$ is defined for all y, then by induction on y we see that $\psi(x+1, y)$ is defined for all y. Hence $\psi(x, y)$ is defined for all x, y; i.e. ψ is total.
3. Let $h(x, \mathbf{y})$ be a fixed computable function and let Φ be the recursive operator given in exercises 1.7(1d). Then the least fixed point f_Φ is a computable function satisfying

   $$f_\Phi(x, \mathbf{y}) \simeq \begin{cases} 0 & \text{if } h(x, \mathbf{y}) = 0, \\ f_\Phi(x+1, \mathbf{y}) + 1 & \text{if } h(x, \mathbf{y}) \text{ is defined and not } 0, \\ \text{undefined} & \text{otherwise.} \end{cases}$$

   But what is this rather strange looking function? We can quite easily check that

   $f_\Phi(x, \mathbf{y}) \simeq \mu z(h(x+z, \mathbf{y}) = 0)$

   as follows. First suppose that $\mu z(h(x+z, \mathbf{y}) = 0) = m$; then $h(x+z, \mathbf{y})$ is defined and not 0 for all $z < m$, and $h(x+m, \mathbf{y}) = 0$. Hence

   $$\begin{aligned} f_\Phi(x, \mathbf{y}) &= f_\Phi(x+1, \mathbf{y}) + 1 = \ldots = f_\Phi(x+z, \mathbf{y}) + z \quad (z \leq m) \\ &= f_\Phi(x+m, y) + m = 0 + m = m. \end{aligned}$$

   Suppose on the other hand that $f_\Phi(x, \mathbf{y}) = m$; then from the equations this must be because

   $m = f_\Phi(x, \mathbf{y}) = f_\Phi(x+1, \mathbf{y}) + 1 = \ldots = f_\Phi(x+m, \mathbf{y}) + m$

   and $h(x+z, \mathbf{y})$ is defined and not 0 for $z < m$; then $f_\Phi(x+m, \mathbf{y}) = 0$, so $h(x+m, \mathbf{y}) = 0$. Thus $m = \mu z(h(x+z, \mathbf{y}) = 0)$.

We can infer from this example that the function $f_\Phi(0, \mathbf{y}) \simeq \mu z(h(z, \mathbf{y}) = 0)$ is computable; of course, there is no use pretending that we have a new and clever proof of the closure of $\mathscr{C}$ under the μ-operator, since we have used this property of $\mathscr{C}$ implicitly in our proof of the first

Recursion theorem. (In Kleene's equation calculus approach (see chapter 3 § 1), however, the first Recursion theorem is proved without the use of the μ-operator, so closure under the μ-operator is established by this example.)

We can see from the above examples why the first Recursion theorem is so called. The general idea of recursion is that of defining a function 'in terms of itself'. A simple instance of this is primitive recursion, discussed in chapter 2. We have seen more general forms of recursion in the definitions of Ackerman's function, and the function f_Φ in example 3.2(3) above.

We were able to see quite easily in chapter 2 that primitive recursive definitions are meaningful, but with more complex recursive definitions this is not so obvious; conceivably there are no functions satisfying the proposed definition. This is where the first Recursion theorem comes in. Very general kinds of definition by recursion are represented by an equation of the form

(3.3) $\quad f=\Phi(f)$

where Φ is a recursive operator. The first Recursion theorem shows that such a definition *is* meaningful; there is even a *computable* function satisfying it. Since in mathematics we require that definitions define things uniquely, we can say that the recursive definition (3.3) defines the least fixed point of the operator Φ. Thus, according to the first Recursion theorem, the class of computable functions is closed under a very general form of definition by recursion.

3.4. *Exercises*

1. Find the least fixed point of the following operators:

   (*a*) $\Phi(f)=f \quad (f\in\mathscr{F}_1)$;

   (*b*) $\Phi(f)(x)=\begin{cases}0 & \text{if } x=0, \quad (f\in\mathscr{F}_1)\\ 2x-1+f(x-1) & \text{if } x>0;\end{cases}$

   (*c*) $\Phi(f)(x, y)=\begin{cases}0 & \text{if } x=0,\\ f(x-1, f(x, y)) & \text{if } x>0.\end{cases}$

2. (McCarthy) Show that the function $m(x)$ given by

   $$m(x)=\begin{cases}91 & \text{if } x\leq 100,\\ x-10 & \text{otherwise,}\end{cases}$$

   is the only fixed point of the recursive operator Φ given by

   $$\Phi(f)(x)=\begin{cases}f(f(x+11)) & \text{if } x\leq 100,\\ x-10 & \text{otherwise.}\end{cases}$$

3. Suppose that Φ and Ψ are recursive operators $\mathscr{F}_1 \times \mathscr{F}_1 \to \mathscr{F}_1$ (in the sense you have defined in exercise 1.7(5)). Show that there is a least pair of functions f, g such that

   $f = \Phi(f, g)$

   $g = \Psi(f, g)$

   and f, g are computable.
4. Suppose that $\Phi: \mathscr{F}_n \times \mathscr{F}_m \to \mathscr{F}_n$ is a recursive operator (in the sense you have defined in exercise 1.7(5)). For each $g \in \mathscr{F}_m$ let $\Phi_g: \mathscr{F}_n \to \mathscr{F}_n$ be the operator given by $\Phi_g(f) = \Phi(f, g)$.
   Show that the operator $\Psi(g) =$ least fixed point of Φ_g is a recursive operator $\mathscr{F}_m \to \mathscr{F}_n$.

4. An application to the semantics of programming languages

We shall see in this section how the first Recursion theorem helps to resolve a problem in the semantics of computer programming languages – the area that deals with the question of giving *meaning* to programs. Our discussion is necessarily given in terms of a general and unspecified programming language, but this is adequate to explain the basic idea.

Suppose, then, that L is a general programming language. The basic symbols of L will have been chosen with a particular meaning in mind, so that the meaning of compound expressions built from them is also clear. We may then envisage a simple program for a function as follows. Suppose that $\tau(\mathbf{x})$ is an expression of L such that whenever the variables $\mathbf{x}$ are given particular values $\mathbf{a}$, then $\tau(\mathbf{a})$ can be unambiguously evaluated according to the semantics of L. If we now take a function symbol f of L that does not occur in τ, then

$$f(\mathbf{x}) = \tau(\mathbf{x}) \tag{4.1}$$

is a simple program for a function f_τ, that has the obvious meaning: for any numbers $\mathbf{a}$, $f_\tau(\mathbf{a})$ is obtained by evaluating the expression $\tau(\mathbf{a})$ according to the semantics of L.

Suppose now that τ is an expression in which the symbol f *does* occur. We indicate this by writing $\tau(f, \mathbf{x})$. Then the program (4.1) becomes

$$f(\mathbf{x}) = \tau(f, \mathbf{x}). \tag{4.2}$$

This is now what is called a *recursive program*. Situations occur where this is the most natural and economical way to describe a function that we may desire the computer to compute. Yet the meaning of the 'program' (4.2) is not entirely clear. The fundamental problem with any recursive program is: how do we give it a precise meaning? It can hardly be called a program until this question is settled.

There are basically two approaches that provide an answer to this question:

(*a*) *The computational approach.* Here the function taken to be defined by a recursive program is given in terms of a method of computing it. This approach reflects the fact that the computer scientist needs to know not only what a program means, but also how to implement it.

(*b*) *The fixed point approach* gives a meaning to a recursive program by an application of the first Recursion theorem. The fixed point theory also resolves some problems raised by the computational approach, and actually shows that the two approaches may be viewed as complementary rather than competing.

Let us now briefly explain these two approaches and see how first Recursion theorem enters the picture.

The computational approach This is best described by giving some examples. Consider the recursive program

$$(4.3)\qquad f(x)=\begin{cases}1 & \text{if } x=0,\\ 2f(x-1) & \text{if } x>0.\end{cases}$$

(We are assuming that in L we can formulate conditional expressions such as this.) Using the equation (4.3) we can formally evaluate the value $f(3)$, for instance, as follows:

$$f(3)\simeq 2\times f(2)\simeq 2\times 2\times f(1)\simeq 2\times 2\times 2\times f(0)\simeq 8;$$

here we have made successive substitutions and simplifications using the formal equation (4.3). Hence if f_τ is the function deemed to be given by the program (4.3) we would have $f_\tau(3)=8$.

With more complicated recursive programs there may be more than one way to use the formal equation $f(\boldsymbol{x})=\tau(f,\boldsymbol{x})$ in such an evaluation procedure. Consider, for instance, the recursive program

$$(4.4)\qquad f(x,y)=\begin{cases}1 & \text{if } x=0,\\ f(x-1,f(x,y)) & \text{if } x>0.\end{cases}$$

Suppose that we try formally to evaluate $f(1,0)$. We have

$$(4.5)\qquad f(1,0)\simeq f(0,f(1,0)).$$

But now there is a choice of occurrences of f for which to substitute

$\tau(f, \boldsymbol{x})$. Choosing the leftmost one and simplifying we have

$$f(1,0) \simeq f(0, f(1,0)) = 1 \text{ (since } x = 0).$$

If, on the other hand, we substitute for the rightmost occurrence of f each time, we obtain from (4.5)

$$f(1,0) \simeq f(0, f(1,0)) \simeq f(0, f(0, f(1,0)))$$
$$\simeq f(0, f(0, f(0, f(1,0)))) \simeq \ldots$$

and in this case no 'value' for $f(1, 0)$ emerges.

A *computation rule* is a rule R that specifies how to proceed when confronted with such a choice of possible substitutions during any formal evaluation procedure. The computational rules we considered for the recursive program (4.4) were 'leftmost' (LM) and 'rightmost' (RM). There are many other possible rules. For any computation rule R, and recursive program $f(\boldsymbol{x}) = \tau(f, \boldsymbol{x})$ we define the function $f_{\tau,R}$ by: $f_{\tau,R}(\boldsymbol{a})$ is the value obtained when $f(\boldsymbol{a})$ is formally evaluated using the rule R. If no value is thus obtained, $f_{\tau,R}(\boldsymbol{a})$ is undefined. (Thus for the recursive program (4.4) we have $f_{\tau,\mathrm{LM}}(1, 0) = 1$, and $f_{\tau,\mathrm{RM}}(1, 0)$ is undefined.)

So we see that each computation rule gives a meaning to any recursive program (and, at the same time, a method of implementing it).

The above example demonstrates that different computation rules may give different meanings to any particular recursive program. The problem now for the computer scientist who chooses this computational approach is to decide which computation rule to choose. Moreover, for any rule R, there is the question of determining in what sense, if any, the function $f_{\tau,R}$ satisfies the equation

$$f(\boldsymbol{x}) \simeq \tau(f, \boldsymbol{x}).$$

The fixed point approach, using the first Recursion theorem, avoids these problems, and in fact sheds light on both of them, as we shall see.

The fixed point approach An expression $\tau(f, \boldsymbol{x})$ of L gives rise to an operator $\Phi: \mathscr{F}_n \to \mathscr{F}_n$ by setting

$$\Phi(g)(\boldsymbol{x}) \simeq \tau(g, \boldsymbol{x})$$

for any $g \in \mathscr{F}_n$. Moreover, in most programming languages the finite and explicit nature of the expression $\tau(f, \boldsymbol{x})$ ensures that Φ is a *recursive* operator. The first Recursion theorem now tells us that Φ has a computable least fixed point, which we may denote by f_τ. Thus we may *define* the function given by the program (4.2) as f_τ. This is quite reasonable, because f_τ *is* computable, and moreover we know that $f_\tau(\boldsymbol{x}) \simeq \tau(f_\tau, \boldsymbol{x})$, which is surely what the programmer intended.

There remains the matter of finding good practical procedures for *implementing* the program (4.2) with its meaning defined in this way. It can be shown that for any computation rule R, $f_{\tau,R} \subseteq f_\tau$; further, there are computation rules R for which $f_{\tau,R} = f_\tau$ for all τ. Any one of these may be chosen as a practical way of implementing recursive programs. Then we can say that the computational and fixed point approaches are complementary rather than opposed to each other: the fixed point approach, via the first Recursion theorem, gives theoretical justification for the particular computation rule chosen.

There are further advantages in adopting the fixed point approach (or a computation rule equivalent to it): there is a variety of useful induction techniques for proving correctness, equivalence, and other properties of recursive programs with fixed point semantics, and these can all be rigorously justified.

For a full discussion of this whole topic the reader is referred to the books of Bird [1976] and Manna [1974]. Here we have slightly simplified the framework within which the computer scientist works; in fact the fixed point f_τ he chooses is least in a slightly different sense (but still given by a version of the first Recursion theorem).

11
The second Recursion theorem

The first Recursion theorem, together with the Myhill–Shepherdson theorem in the previous chapter, shows that for any *extensional* total computable function f there is a number n such that

$$\phi_{f(n)} = \phi_n.$$

The *second* Recursion theorem says that there is such an n even when f is *not* extensional: we shall prove this in § 1 of this chapter.

This theorem (and its proof) may seem a little strange at first. Nevertheless it plays an important role in more advanced parts of the theory of computability. We shall use it in the promised proof of Myhill's theorem (theorem 9-3.5) and in the proof of the Speed-up theorem in the next chapter.

In § 1, after proving the simplest version of the second Recursion theorem, we describe some applications and interpretations of it; § 2 is devoted to a discussion of the idea underlying the proof of the theorem, and other matters, including the relationship between the two Recursion theorems. A more general version of the second Recursion theorem is proved in § 3, and is used to give the proof of Myhill's theorem.

1. The second Recursion theorem

First let us prove the theorem, and then see how we can understand it.

1.1. *Theorem* (The second Recursion theorem)

Let f be a total unary computable function; then there is a number n such that

$$\phi_{f(n)} = \phi_n.$$

Proof. By the s–m–n theorem there is a *total* computable function $s(x)$ such that for all x

(*) $\qquad \phi_{f(\phi_x(x))}(y) \simeq \phi_{s(x)}(y).$

(If $\phi_x(x)$ is undefined, we mean the expression on the left of (*) to be undefined; alternatively, we can take the left of (*) to denote $\psi_U(f(\phi_x(x)), y)$.)

Now take any m such that $s = \phi_m$; rewriting (*) we have

$$\phi_{f(\phi_x(x))}(y) \simeq \phi_{\phi_m(x)}(y).$$

Then, putting $x = m$ and taking $n = \phi_m(m)$ (which is defined, since ϕ_m is total) we have

$$\phi_{f(n)}(y) \simeq \phi_n(y)$$

as required. □

In spite of its appearance, for non-extensional functions f this is not a genuine fixed-point theorem: there is no induced mapping $\phi_x \to \phi_{f(x)}$ of computable functions for which ϕ_n could be called a fixed point. However, we *do* have an induced mapping f^* of *programs* given by

$$f^*(P_x) = P_{f(x)}.$$

To expect a fixed point for f^* in general would be too much: this would be a program P_n such that $f^*(P_n)$ and P_n are the *same*; i.e. $f(n) = n$. But what theorem 1.1 says is that there is a program P_n such that $f^*(P_n)$ and P_n have the *same effect* (when computing unary functions); i.e. $\phi_{f(n)} = \phi_n$. Thus the second Recursion theorem is loosely called a *pseudo*-fixed point theorem; and for convenience, any number n such that $\phi_{f(n)} = \phi_n$ is called a *fixed point* or *fixed point value* for f.

The second Recursion theorem is a result about indices for computable functions; it may be thought therefore that the proof rests on some special feature of the particular numbering of programs that has been chosen. Inspection of the proof shows, however, that we used only the *s–m–n* theorem and the computability of the universal function; neither of these results depends in any essential way on the details of our numbering. Moreover, theorem 1.1 can be used to establish the second Recursion theorem corresponding to any suitable numbering of programs; see exercise 1.10(9) below.

There are various ways in which theorem 1.1 can be generalised, although the idea underlying the proof remains the same. In exercise 1.10(7) we have the generalisation to k-ary functions for $k > 1$; in theorem 3.1 it is shown that a fixed point can be calculated effectively from various parameters that may be connected with f.

We continue this section with some corollaries and applications of the second Recursion theorem.

1.2. *Corollary*

If f is a total computable function, there is a number n such that $W_{f(n)}=W_n$ and $E_{f(n)}=E_n$.

Proof. If $\phi_{f(n)}=\phi_n$, then $W_{f(n)}=W_n$ and $E_{f(n)}=E_n$. □

1.3. *Corollary*

If f is a total computable function there are arbitrarily large numbers n such that $\phi_{f(n)}=\phi_n$.

Proof. Pick any number k; take a number c such that

$$\phi_c \neq \phi_0, \phi_1, \ldots, \phi_k.$$

Define a function g by

$$g(x)=\begin{cases} c & \text{if } x \leq k, \\ f(x) & \text{if } x > k. \end{cases}$$

Then g is computable; let n be a fixed point for g. If $n \leq k$, then $\phi_{g(n)}=\phi_c \neq \phi_n$, a contradiction. Hence $n > k$, so $f(n)=g(n)$ and n is a fixed point for f. □

(In exercise 1.10(8) we shall indicate how the proof of theorem 1.1 can be modified to obtain an increasing effective enumeration of fixed points for f.)

The following corollary summarises the way that the second Recursion theorem is often applied, in conjunction with the *s–m–n* theorem.

1.4. *Corollary*

Let $f(x, y)$ be any computable function; then there is an index e such that

$$\phi_e(y) \simeq f(e, y).$$

Proof. Use the *s–m–n* theorem to obtain a total computable function s such that $\phi_{s(x)}(y) \simeq f(x, y)$; now apply theorem 1.1, taking e as a fixed point for s. □

As simple applications of this corollary, we have

1.5. *Examples*

(*a*) There is a number n such that $\phi_n(x)=x^n$, all x: apply corollary 1.4 with $f(m, x)=x^m$;

(*b*) there is a number n such that $W_n = \{n\}$: apply corollary 1.4 with

$$f(x, y) \simeq \begin{cases} 0 & \text{if } y = x, \\ \text{undefined} & \text{otherwise,} \end{cases}$$

obtaining an index n such that $\phi_n(y)$ is defined iff $y = n$.

The second Recursion theorem received its name because, like the first Recursion theorem, it justifies certain very general definitions 'by recursion'. Consider, for example, the following 'definition' of a function ϕ_e, in terms of a given total computable function f:

$$\phi_e = \phi_{f(e)}.$$

The function ϕ_e is 'defined' effectively in terms of an algorithm for computing itself (coded by the number e). In spite of its appearance as a circular definition, we are told by the second Recursion theorem that there *are* computable functions ϕ_e satisfying such a definition.

It is often useful in advanced computability theory to be able to make an even more general definition of a function ϕ_e 'by recursion' of the kind

$$\phi_e(x) \simeq g(e, x),$$

where g is a given total computable function. Again, think of ϕ_e as 'defined' effectively in terms of a code for its own algorithm. Then the second Recursion theorem, in the guise of corollary 1.4, makes this kind of definition meaningful also. We shall use this fact in the Speed-up theorem in the next chapter.

We continue this section with some further straightforward, but sometimes surprising, consequences of theorem 1.1. First, we show how it can be used to give a simple proof of Rice's theorem (6-1.7).

1.6. *Theorem* (Rice).

Suppose that $\emptyset \subset \mathcal{A} \subset \mathscr{C}_1$, *and let* $A = \{x : \phi_x \in \mathcal{A}\}$. *Then* A *is not recursive.*

Proof. Let $a \in A$ and $b \notin A$. If A is recursive, then the function f given by

$$f(x) = \begin{cases} a & \text{if } x \notin A, \\ b & \text{if } x \in A, \end{cases}$$

is computable. Further, f has the property that $x \in A \Leftrightarrow f(x) \notin A$, for all x.

On the other hand, by theorem 1.1, there is a number n such that $\phi_{f(n)} = \phi_n$, so $f(n) \in A \Leftrightarrow n \in A$, a contradiction. □

Another application of the second Recursion theorem shows, as promised in chapter 4 § 2, that the 'natural' enumeration of computable functions without repetitions is not computable.

1.7. *Theorem*

Suppose that f is a total increasing function such that

(a) if $m \neq n$, then $\phi_{f(m)} \neq \phi_{f(n)}$,

(b) $f(n)$ is the least index of the function $\phi_{f(n)}$.

Then f is not computable.

Proof. Suppose that f satisfies the conditions of the theorem. By (a), f cannot be the identity function, so there must be a number k such that

$$f(n) > n \quad (n \geq k),$$

whence, by (b)

$$\phi_{f(n)} \neq \phi_n \quad (n \geq k).$$

On the other hand, if f is computable, then by corollary 1.3 there is a number $n \geq k$ such that $\phi_{f(n)} = \phi_n$, a contradiction. □

Applications of the second Recursion theorem such as the following can be interpreted in anthropomorphic terms.

Let P be a program. We can regard the code number $\gamma(P)$ as a *description* of P. We could regard the program P as capable of *self-reproduction* if for all inputs x the computation $P(x)$ gave as output its own description, $\gamma(P)$. At first glance, it would seem difficult to construct a self-reproducing program P, since to construct P we would need to know $\gamma(P)$, and hence P itself, in advance. Nevertheless, the second Recursion theorem shows that there are such programs.

1.8. *Theorem*

There is a program P such that for all x, $P(x)\downarrow \gamma(P)$; i.e. P is self-reproducing.

Proof. If we write n for $\gamma(P)$, the theorem says that there is a number n such that

$$\phi_n(x) = n \text{ (for all } x).$$

To establish this, simply apply corollary 1.4 to the function $f(m, x) = m$. □

We turn now to psychology! Recall the notation and terminology of chapter 5. There we defined a total computable function $\sigma(e, x, t)$ that codes the state of the computation $P_e(x)$ after t steps; $\sigma(e, x, t)$ contains information about the contents of the registers and the number of the next instruction to be obeyed at stage t. It is clear, then, that complete details of the first t steps of the computation $P_e(x)$ are encoded by the number

$$\sigma^*(e, x, t) = \prod_{i \le t} \mathrm{p}_{i+1}^{\sigma(e,x,i)}.$$

Let us call the number $\sigma^*(e, x, t)$ the *code of the computation* $P_e(x)$ *to* t *steps*. Clearly σ^* is computable.

Suppose now that we are given a total computable function ψ and a program P. By the *ψ-analysis of the computation $P(x)$* we mean the code of the computation $P(x)$ to $\psi(x)$ steps. We call a program P *ψ-introspective at x* if $P(x)$ converges and gives as output its own ψ-analysis; we call P *totally ψ-introspective* if it is ψ-introspective at all x.

1.9. *Theorem*

There is a program P that is totally ψ-introspective.

Proof. Simply apply corollary 1.4 to the computable function $f(e, x) = \sigma^*(e, x, \psi(x))$, obtaining a number n such that

$$\phi_n(x) = f(n, x) = \text{the } \psi\text{-analysis of } P_n(x). \quad \square$$

We close this section with a tale in which the second Recursion theorem appears in military dress.

'We are at war. An operation is mounted to sabotage the enemy's central computer facility. Our special agents have penetrated the enemy defences and found a means of entry to the high security building that houses all the programs

$$P_0, P_1, P_2, \ldots$$

for the central computer. The mission will be accomplished if our agents can systematically sabotage all of these programs, ensuring that subsequently no program will operate as the enemy thinks it will. Simply to destroy the programs is not sufficient: the enemy would soon discover this and set about rewriting them. What is needed is a subtle alteration to each program, so that, unknown to the enemy, the computer will give wrong results. Swiftly and silently our men move into action . . .

Alas, defeat at the hands of the second Recursion theorem! Whatever systematic plan is devised to modify the programs, it will define an effectively computable function f by

$$f(x) = \text{the code of the modification of } P_x.$$

The second Recursion theorem springs into action, producing a number n such that P_n and its transform $P_{f(n)}$ have the same effect (on unary inputs, at least). The operation was bound to fail.

(Sometime later, back at HQ, our master strategists consider recruiting a chimpanzee whose mission is to alter the programs in random fashion . . .)'

1.10. *Exercises*

1. Show that there is a number n such that $\phi_n(x) = [\sqrt[n]{x}]$.
2. Show that there is a number n such that $W_n = E_n = n\mathbb{N}$.
3. Show that there is a number e such that $\phi_e(x) = e^2$ for all x.
4. Is there a number n such that $W_n = \{x : \phi_n(x)\uparrow\}$?
5. Suppose that $\mathscr{A} \subseteq \mathscr{C}_1$, and let $A = \{x : \phi_x \in \mathscr{A}\}$. Show that $A \not\leq_{\mathrm{m}} \bar{A}$. Deduce theorem 1.6.
6. Give an example of a total computable function f such that (i) if ϕ_x is total, then so is $\phi_{f(x)}$, (ii) there is no fixed point n for f with ϕ_n total.
7. Prove the second Recursion theorem for k-ary computable functions: if f is a total computable function there is a number n such that

   $\phi^{(k)}_{f(n)} = \phi^{(k)}_n$.
8. Show that theorem 1.1 may be improved to: For any total computable function f, there is an increasing recursive function $n(t)$ such that for every t, $\phi_{n(t)} = \phi_{f(n(t))}$. (*Hint.* Examine the proof of theorem 1.1; note first that from our proof of the s–m–n theorem we have $s(x) \geq x$ for all x (or else show that by adding some redundant instructions to the end of $P_{s(x)}$ an equally suitable computable function $s'(x)$ can be found, with $s'(x) \geq x$). Now observe that given any number k we can effectively find an index m for $s(x)$ with $m \geq k$. Then, following the proof of theorem1.1, we have that $n = s(m)$ is a fixed point for f, and $n = s(m) \geq m \geq k$. It is now a simple matter to construct a function $n(t)$ as required.)
9. Prove that the second Recursion theorem does not depend on the particular effective numbering of programs that is chosen. (*Hint.* Let δ be another effective numbering of programs; let Q_m = program given code number m by δ; let ψ_m = the unary function computed by Q_m. We have to prove that for any total computable function f there is a number n such that $\psi_{f(n)} = \psi_n$.

For this, show that there is a computable bijection r such that $P_x = Q_{r(x)}$; then show that it is sufficient to establish that there is a number m such that $\phi_{r^{-1}fr(m)} = \phi_m$.)

10. Suppose that in the tale just before these exercises, our special agents find that the enemy's computer operators have become extremely sophisticated – they have only one program, a *universal* program. Can our men now completely accomplish their task?
11. Could a chimpanzee succeed where the special agents failed? (A philosophical problem.)

2. Discussion

The second Recursion theorem and its proof may seem a little mysterious at first. We shall see, however, that it is essentially a simple diagonal argument applied to effective enumerations of computable functions.

Suppose that h is a computable function. If h is total, then the enumeration $\boldsymbol{E}$ given by

$$\boldsymbol{E}: \phi_{h(0)}, \phi_{h(1)}, \phi_{h(2)}, \ldots$$

is an effective enumeration of computable functions. If h is *not* total, we can still regard h as enumerating a sequence of computable functions $\boldsymbol{E}$ by adopting the convention that for any x the expression $\phi_{h(x)}$ denotes the function given by

$$\phi_{h(x)}(y) \simeq \psi_U(h(x), y)$$
$$= \begin{cases} \phi_{h(x)}(y) & \text{if } h(x) \text{ is defined,} \\ \text{undefined} & \text{if } h(x) \text{ is undefined.} \end{cases}$$

Thus, if $h(x)$ is undefined, $\phi_{h(x)}$ is the function that is nowhere defined.

The following lemma shows that the sequence $\boldsymbol{E}$ thus enumerated by h is an *effective* enumeration even when h is not total.

2.1. *Lemma*

Suppose that h is a computable function. There is a total computable function h' such that h and h' enumerate the same sequence of computable functions.

Proof. The *s–m–n* theorem gives a *total* h' such that

$$\phi_{h'(x)}(y) \simeq \psi_U(h(x), y). \quad \square$$

We can now explain the idea underlying the proof of the Recursion theorem. For any k, let us denote by $\boldsymbol{E}_k$ the sequence of computable functions effectively enumerated by ϕ_k; then the list $\boldsymbol{E}_0, \boldsymbol{E}_1, \boldsymbol{E}_2, \ldots$ includes *all* possible effective enumerations of computable functions. We can display the details of these enumerations as follows (ignore the circles):

$$\begin{array}{lcccccc}
\boldsymbol{E}_0: & \bigcirc\!\!\!\!\!\phi_{\phi_0(0)} & \phi_{\phi_0(1)} & \phi_{\phi_0(2)} & \ldots & \phi_{\phi_0(k)} & \ldots \\
\boldsymbol{E}_1: & \phi_{\phi_1(0)} & \bigcirc\!\!\!\!\!\phi_{\phi_1(1)} & \phi_{\phi_1(2)} & \ldots & \phi_{\phi_1(k)} & \ldots \\
\boldsymbol{E}_2: & \phi_{\phi_2(0)} & \phi_{\phi_2(1)} & \bigcirc\!\!\!\!\!\phi_{\phi_2(2)} & \ldots & \phi_{\phi_2(k)} & \ldots \\
\vdots & \vdots & \vdots & \vdots & & \vdots & \\
\boldsymbol{E}_k: & \phi_{\phi_k(0)} & \phi_{\phi_k(1)} & \phi_{\phi_k(2)} & \ldots & \bigcirc\!\!\!\!\!\phi_{\phi_k(k)} & \ldots \\
\vdots & \vdots & \vdots & \vdots & & \vdots &
\end{array}$$

Then the *diagonal enumeration*, $\boldsymbol{D}$, circled on this array, is given by

$$\boldsymbol{D}: \phi_{\phi_0(0)}, \phi_{\phi_1(1)}, \phi_{\phi_2(2)}, \ldots$$

Thus $\boldsymbol{D}$ is an *effective* enumeration, given by the computable function $h(x) \simeq \phi_x(x)$. Moreover, $\boldsymbol{D}$ has an entry in common with each effective enumeration $\boldsymbol{E}$; in fact, for each k, $\boldsymbol{D}$ and $\boldsymbol{E}_k$ have their $(k+1)$th entry $\phi_{\phi_k(k)}$ in common.

Suppose now that f is a total computable function. Then we can 'operate' on $\boldsymbol{D}$ to give an enumeration $\boldsymbol{D}^*$ given by

$$\boldsymbol{D}^*: \phi_{f(\phi_0(0))}, \phi_{f(\phi_1(1))}, \phi_{f(\phi_2(2))}, \ldots$$

Now $\boldsymbol{D}^*$ is an effective enumeration of computable functions (given by $f(h(x))$) so there is a number m such that $\boldsymbol{D}^* = \boldsymbol{E}_m$. By lemma 2.1 we may assume that ϕ_m is total. As noted above, $\boldsymbol{D}$ and $\boldsymbol{E}_m$ have their $(m+1)$th entry in common, i.e.

$$\phi_{\phi_m(m)} = \phi_{f(\phi_m(m))}.$$

Since ϕ_m is total, the number $\phi_m(m) = n$, say, is defined, and

$$\phi_n = \phi_{f(n)}.$$

The argument is simply illustrated as follows:

$$\begin{array}{llllll}
\boldsymbol{D}: \searrow & & & & & \\
\quad \boldsymbol{E}_0: & \phi_{\phi_0(0)} & \ldots & & & \\
\quad \boldsymbol{E}_1: & \vdots & \phi_{\phi_1(1)} & \ldots & & \\
 & & \vdots & \phi_{\phi_2(2)} & \ldots & \\
 & & & \vdots & \ddots & \\
\boldsymbol{D}^* = \boldsymbol{E}_m: & \phi_{f(\phi_0(0))} & \phi_{f(\phi_1(1))} & \phi_{f(\phi_2(2))} & \ldots & \phi_{f(\phi_m(m))} = \phi_{\phi_m(m)}
\end{array}$$

So $n = \phi_m(m)$ is a fixed point.

Note. This proof can be rephrased to appear similar to standard diagonal arguments as follows. Suppose that f is a total function such that $\phi_{f(n)} \neq \phi_n$

for all n: then using f on the diagonal enumeration $\boldsymbol{D}$, the enumeration $\boldsymbol{D}^*$ is constructed so as to differ from $\boldsymbol{E}_k$ at k (fulfilling the requirements of the diagonal motto). Hence $\boldsymbol{D}^*$ is *not* an effective enumeration, so f cannot be computable.

The second Recursion theorem can thus be viewed as a generalisation of many earlier diagonal arguments. To illustrate this, we show how to use the second Recursion theorem to prove that K is not recursive, one of the fundamental diagonal arguments.

2.2. *Theorem*

K is not recursive.

Proof. Let a, b be indices such that $W_a = \emptyset$ and $W_b = \mathbb{N}$. If K is recursive, then the function g defined by

$$g(x) = \begin{cases} a & \text{if } x \in K, \\ b & \text{if } x \notin K, \end{cases}$$

is computable. Notice that g has the property that for all x

$$W_{g(x)} \neq W_x$$

(since $x \in W_{g(x)} \Leftrightarrow W_{g(x)} = \mathbb{N} \Leftrightarrow g(x) = b \Leftrightarrow x \notin W_x$). This is in contradiction to the second Recursion theorem. □

Remark. We have, of course, used a sledge hammer to crack a nut. The point about this proof is that all diagonalisation is hidden inside the application of the Second Recursion theorem. We are *not* suggesting that the earlier proof should be replaced by this one.

The relationship between the two Recursion theorems Suppose that $\Phi: \mathcal{F}_1 \to \mathcal{F}_1$ is a recursive operator, and that h is a total computable function such that $\Phi(\phi_x) = \phi_{h(x)}$ for all x (as given by the Myhill–Shepherdson theorem). If n is a fixed point for h, then $\phi_{h(n)} = \phi_n$, i.e. $\Phi(\phi_n) = \phi_n$. Thus the second Recursion theorem tells us (as does the first theorem) that Φ has a computable fixed point; it does *not* tell us, however, that Φ has a computable *least* fixed point. So, for recursive operators the first Recursion theorem gives us more information.

On the other hand, the second Recursion theorem applies to non-extensional computable functions as well; i.e. functions that do not arise from recursive operators. Thus the second theorem has a wider range of application than the first theorem, although in the area of overlap it generally gives less information. Thus, these two theorems are best regarded as complementary, although a case is made by Rogers [1967] for the view that the second theorem is the more general of the two.

3. Myhill's theorem

Let us now formulate and prove the generalisation of theorem 1.1 needed for Myhill's theorem. Suppose we have a total computable function $f(x, z)$; theorem 1.1 shows that for any particular value of the parameters z there is a number n such that $\phi_{f(n,z)} = \phi_n$. We now show that n can be obtained effectively from z.

3.1. *Theorem* (The second Recursion theorem)
Suppose that $f(x, z)$ is a total computable function. There is a total computable function $n(z)$ such that for all z

$$\phi_{f(n(z),z)} = \phi_{n(z)}.$$

Proof. We simply introduce the parameter at appropriate points in the proof of theorem 1.1.

By the s–m–n theorem there is a total computable function $s(x, z)$ such that

$$(*) \qquad \phi_{f(\phi_x(x),z)} = \phi_{s(x,z)}.$$

Then, again by using the s–m–n theorem, there is a total computable function $m(z)$ such that $s(x, z) = \phi_{m(z)}(x)$. Rewriting (*) we have

$$\phi_{f(\phi_x(x),z)} = \phi_{\phi_{m(z)}(x)}.$$

Then, putting $x = m(z)$ and setting $n(z) = \phi_{m(z)}(m(z))$ we have

$$\phi_{f(n(z),z)} = \phi_{n(z)}.$$

as required. □

We proceed immediately with the proof of Myhill's theorem (theorem 9-3.5).

3.2. *Myhill's theorem*
Any creative set is m-complete.

Proof. Suppose that A is creative and B is r.e.; we must prove that $B \leq_m A$.

Let p be a productive function for $\bar{A}$. Define a function $f(x, y, z)$ by

$$f(x, y, z) = \begin{cases} 0 & \text{if } z = p(x) \text{ and } y \in B, \\ \text{undefined} & \text{otherwise.} \end{cases}$$

Then f is computable, so by the s–m–n theorem there is a total computable function $s(x, y)$ such that

$$\phi_{s(x,y)}(z) \simeq f(x, y, z).$$

Then, in particular

$$W_{s(x,y)} = \begin{cases} \{p(x)\} & \text{if } y \in B, \\ \varnothing & \text{otherwise.} \end{cases}$$

By the second Recursion theorem (theorem 3.1) there is a total computable function $n(y)$ such that

$$W_{s(n(y),y)} = W_{n(y)}$$

for all y. Thus, for all y

$$W_{n(y)} = \begin{cases} \{p(n(y))\} & \text{if } y \in B, \\ \varnothing & \text{otherwise.} \end{cases}$$

We claim now that

(**) $$y \in B \text{ iff } p(n(y)) \in A.$$

(*a*) Suppose that $y \in B$; then $W_{n(y)} = \{p(n(y))\}$. If $p(n(y)) \notin A$, then $W_{n(y)} \subseteq \bar{A}$, so by the productive property of p, $p(n(y)) \notin W_{n(y)}$. This is a contradiction. Hence $p(n(y)) \in A$.

(*b*) Suppose that $y \notin B$; then $W_{n(y)} = \varnothing \subseteq \bar{A}$. By the productive property of p, $p(n(y)) \in \bar{A}$.

The claim (**) is thus established, so $B \leq_m A$ since $p(n(y))$ is computable. □

3.3. *Corollary*
The m-degree $\mathbf{0}'_m$ *consists of all creative sets.*

3.4. *Exercises*

1. Prove the following generalisation of theorem 3.1: For any number k there is a total computable function $n(e, \mathbf{z})$ (where $\mathbf{z} = (z_1, \ldots, z_k)$) with the following property: if $\mathbf{z}$ is such that $\phi_e^{(k+1)}(x, \mathbf{z})$ is defined for all x, then
$$\phi_{\phi_e^{(k+1)}(n(e,\mathbf{z}),\mathbf{z})} = \phi_{n(e,\mathbf{z})}.$$
(*Hint.* This can in fact be derived as a corollary to theorem 3.1.)
2. Formulate and prove the result that improves theorem 3.1 in the same way that exercise 1.10(8) improves theorem 1.1.

12
Complexity of computation

In the real world of computing, the critical question about a function f is *not* Is f computable?, but rather Is f computable in *practical* terms? In other words, Is there a program for f that will compute f in the time (or space) we have available? The answer depends partly on our skill in writing programs and the sophistication of our computers; but intuitively we feel that there is an additional factor which can be described as the 'intrinsic complexity' of the function f itself. The theory of *computational complexity*, which we introduce in this chapter, has been developed in order to be able to discuss such questions and to aid the study of the more practical aspects of computability.

Using the URM approach, we can measure the time taken to compute each value of a function f by a particular program, on the assumption that each step of a URM computation is performed in unit time. The *time of computation* thus defined is an example of a *computational complexity measure* that reflects the complexity or efficiency of the program being used. (Later we shall mention other complexity measures.)

With a notion of complexity of computation made precise, it is possible to pursue questions such as How intrinsically complex is a computable function f? and Is it possible to find a 'best' program for computing f?

The theory of computational complexity is a relatively new field of research; we shall present a small sample of results that have a bearing on the questions raised above. At the end of the chapter we shall provide suggestions for the reader wishing to pursue this topic further.

We begin in § 1 by defining some notation; after some discussion we proceed to show that there are arbitrarily complex computable functions. Section 2 is devoted to the surprising and curious Speed-up theorem of M. Blum, which shows in particular that there are computable functions having no 'best' program. In § 3 we introduce the idea of complexity classes and prove Borodin's Gap theorem; in the final section we show how we can use complexity classes to give a pleasant characterisation of the *elementary functions* – an important subclass of the primitive recursive functions.

1. Complexity and complexity measures

We begin by establishing some notation.

1.1. *Notation*

(*a*) For any program P, we write $t_P^{(n)}$ for the function given by

$$t_P^{(n)}(\boldsymbol{x}) = \begin{cases} \text{the number of steps taken} & \\ \text{by } P \text{ to compute } f_P^{(n)}(\boldsymbol{x}), & \text{if } f_P^{(n)}(\boldsymbol{x}) \text{ is defined,} \\ \text{undefined} & \text{otherwise,} \end{cases}$$
$$= \mu t(P(\boldsymbol{x})\downarrow \text{ in } t \text{ steps}).$$

(*b*) For any index e we write $t_e^{(n)}(\boldsymbol{x})$ for $t_{P_e}^{(n)}(\boldsymbol{x})$. We shall write t_P for $t_P^{(1)}$ and t_e for $t_e^{(1)}$ as is customary.

The collection of time functions $t_e^{(n)}$ constitutes an example of a *computational complexity measure*. Some simple but important properties of these functions are given in the following lemma.

1.2. *Lemma*

(*a*) $\text{Dom}(t_e^{(n)}) = \text{Dom}(\phi_e^{(n)})$, *all* n, e.

(*b*) *For each* n *the predicate* $M(e, \boldsymbol{x}, y)$ *defined by* $M(e, \boldsymbol{x}, y) \equiv t_e^{(n)}(\boldsymbol{x}) \simeq y$ *is decidable.*

Proof. (*a*) is obvious; (*b*) follows from corollary 5-1.3(*b*). □

Remark. The property (*b*) is used frequently in complexity theory; it stands in marked contrast to the fact that $\phi_e^{(n)}(\boldsymbol{x}) \simeq y$ is an *undecidable* predicate.

Often in complexity theory a property holds for all sufficiently large numbers n, though not necessarily for all n. Thus we make the following definition.

1.3. *Definition*

A predicate $M(n)$ holds for *almost all* n, or *almost everywhere* (a.e.) if $M(n)$ holds for all but finitely many natural numbers n (or, equivalently, if there is a number n_0 such that $M(n)$ holds whenever $n \geq n_0$).

We can now state our first theorem, which shows that there are arbitrarily complex computable functions.

1.4. *Theorem*

Let b be a total computable function. There is a total computable function f, taking only the values 0, 1, *such that if e is any index for f, then*

$$t_e(n) > b(n) \text{ a.e.}$$

Proof. The reader should not be surprised to find that f is obtained by a diagonal construction. The essence of the construction is to ensure that if $t_i(m) \leq b(m)$ for infinitely many values m, then f differs from ϕ_i at one of those values. We define f by recursion as follows.

At each stage n in the construction of f we shall either define an index i_n, or decide in a finite amount of time that i_n is to be undefined. We then ensure that $f(n)$ differs from $\phi_{i_n}(n)$ if i_n is defined. In detail, assuming that $f(0), \ldots, f(n-1)$ have been thus defined, we put

$$i_n = \begin{cases} \mu i[i \leq n \text{ and } i \text{ differs from all previously} \\ \quad \text{defined } i_k \text{ and } t_i(n) \leq b(n)] & \text{if such an } i \text{ exists,} \\ \text{undefined} & \text{otherwise.} \end{cases}$$

$$f(n) = \begin{cases} 1 & \text{if } i_n \text{ is defined and } \phi_{i_n}(n) = 0, \\ 0 & \text{otherwise.} \end{cases}$$

There is a finite procedure that tells us for a given i whether $t_i(n) \leq b(n)$, since

$$t_i(n) \leq b(n) \Leftrightarrow \exists y \leq b(n)(t_i(n) \simeq y),$$

and the right hand side is decidable by lemma 1.2(b). Hence there is an effective procedure to decide whether i_n is defined, and if so, to find its value. Moreover, if i_n is defined, then so is $\phi_{i_n}(n)$. Hence f is a well-defined total computable function.

Suppose now that $f \simeq \phi_e$; by construction $e \neq i_n$ whenever i_n is defined. We shall show that if i is any index such that $t_i(m) \leq b(m)$ for infinitely many m, then $i = i_n$ for some n, and hence $i \neq e$. This is sufficient to show that $t_e(m) > b(m)$ for almost all m.

Suppose then that $t_i(m) \leq b(m)$ for infinitely many m. Let $p = 1 + \max\{k : i_k \text{ is defined and } i_k < i\}$ (put $p = 0$ if there are no defined $i_k < i$). Choose n such that $n \geq i, p$ and $t_i(n) \leq b(n)$. If $i = i_k$ for some $k < n$, there is nothing further to prove. Assuming then that $i \neq i_k$ for all $k < n$, we have at stage n:

$$i \leq n \text{ and } i \text{ differs from all previously defined } i_k \text{ and } t_i(n) \leq b(n).$$

Thus, from the definition of i_n, i_n is defined and $i_n \leq i$. But since $n \geq p$, we must have $i_n \geq i$. Hence $i_n = i$, as required. □

We cannot in general improve this theorem to obtain the conclusion $t_e(n) > b(n)$ for *all* n; this is because for any f we can always write a program that computes f quickly for some particular value a, simply by specifying the value of $f(a)$ in a preface to the program. For example, suppose that $f(a) = 1$; let F be a program that computes f. Then the program F' based on the flow diagram in fig. 12*a* also computes f. Clearly we have $t_{F'}(a) = a + 3$. Thus, if b is a computable function such that $b(x) > x + 3$ for some x, then we cannot obtain the conclusion of theorem 1.4 with $t_e(n) > b(n)$ for *all* n.

Using a similar idea we can write a program that computes f quickly for any given finite number of values: see exercise 1.8(1) below. This shows that $t_e(n) > b(n)$ a.e. is the best possible conclusion in theorem 1.4.

Other computational complexity measures There are many other natural ways to measure the complexity of a computation, of which the following are a few examples. For simplicity we restrict our discussion to unary computations.

Fig. 12*a*.

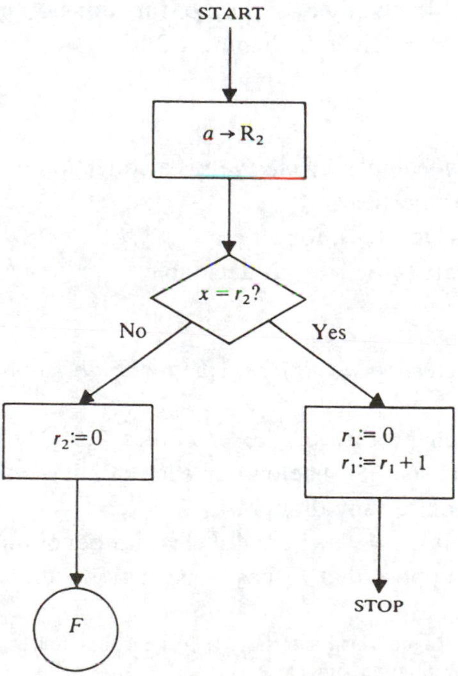

1.5. *Examples*

1. $$\Phi_e(x)=\begin{cases}\text{number of jumps made}^1 \text{ in executing } P_e(x), \\ \qquad\qquad \text{if } P_e(x)\downarrow, \\ \text{undefined} \quad \text{otherwise.}\end{cases}$$

This measure is closely associated with the number of loops performed when executing $P_e(x)$, which is in turn related to the time of computation $t_e(x)$.

2. $$\Phi_e(x)=\begin{cases}\text{the maximum number held in any of the registers} \\ \text{at any time during the computation } P_e(x) \\ \qquad\qquad \text{if } P_e(x)\downarrow, \\ \text{undefined} \quad \text{otherwise.}\end{cases}$$

This measure obviously relates to the amount of storage space needed to carry out the computation $P_e(x)$ on a real computer.

3. With the Turing machine approach, two natural complexity measures are (i) the number of steps needed to perform a Turing computation and (ii) the amount of tape used to perform a computation.

In general, an abstract computational complexity measure (for unary computations) is *defined* to be any collection of functions Φ_e having the abstract properties that were given by lemma 1.2 for t_e.

1.6. *Definition*

A *computational complexity measure* is a collection of functions Φ_e with the following properties:

(*a*) $\text{Dom}(\Phi_e)=\text{Dom}(\phi_e)$, for all e;

(*b*) The predicate '$\Phi_e(x)\simeq y$' is decidable.

1.7. *Lemma*

The functions given in examples 1.5 *above are computational complexity measures.*

Proof. We give sketch proofs for the examples 1.5(1) and 1.5(2), leaving 1.5(3) as an exercise (1.8(3) below). In each case it is only part (*b*) of definition 1.6 that requires any thought.

(1) To decide '$\Phi_e(x)\simeq y$', where $\Phi_e(x)$ = number of jumps made during $P_e(x)$. Suppose that P_e has s instructions; then at most s

[1] We mean here that if a jump instruction $J(m, n, p)$ is encountered, then a jump (to I_p) is *made* if $r_m = r_n$; but not otherwise.

consecutive steps of $P_e(x)$ can be performed without making a jump. So run $P_e(x)$ for up to $1+(y+1)s$ steps. If $P_e(x)$ stops in fewer than this number of steps, then count the number of jumps made to see if it is y. Otherwise (i.e. if $P_e(x)$ has not stopped after $1+(y+1)s$ steps) $P_e(x)$ will have performed at least $y+1$ jumps, so we conclude that $\Phi_e(x) \neq y$.

(2) To decide '$\Phi_e(x) \simeq y$', where $\Phi_e(x)$ = maximum number held in any register during $P_e(x)$. Let $u = \rho(P_e)$, and consider all possible non-halting states under the program P_e with $r_1, \ldots, r_u \leq y$. There are $s(y+1)^u$ such states that are distinct. Run $P_e(x)$ for up to $1+s(y+1)^u$ steps. If $P_e(x)$ stops after this number of steps or fewer, then find the maximum number that has occurred in any of the registers and see if it is y. Otherwise (if $P_e(x)$ has not stopped) one of two possibilities will have occurred: (i) the computation has been in the same state on two separate occasions, so $P_e(x)$ is in a loop and $\Phi_e(x)$ is undefined; (ii) there has been no repetition of states, in which case some register has contained a number greater than y. In both cases we conclude that $\Phi_e(x) \neq y$. □

Note that in proving theorem 1.4 we used only the properties of t_e given by lemma 1.2. Thus theorem 1.4 holds for *any* computational complexity measure. There are many other results in complexity theory which do not depend on any particular measure of complexity. Such results are said to be *machine independent*. The Speed-up theorem of the next section and the Gap theorem of § 3 are further examples of such results.

1.8. *Exercises*

1. Let f be a total computable function that takes only the values 0, 1. Show that for any m there is a program F for f such that $t_F(x) \leq 2x+3$ for all $x \leq m$. Deduce that if b is a computable function such that $b(x) > 2x+3$, then the restriction to almost all n in theorem 1.4 cannot be improved.
2. Let Φ_e be the complexity measure given in example 1.5(2). Show that whenever $\phi_e(x)$ is defined, then $\Phi_e(x) \geq \max(x, \phi_e(x))$.

   Let f be any total computable function, and let X be a finite subset of Dom(f). Prove that there is a program P_e for f that is the best possible on X (for this measure); i.e. $\Phi_e(x) = \max(x, \phi_e(x))$ for $x \in X$.

3. For the complexity measures given in example 1.5(3), verify lemma 1.6, expressed in the following terms. For any Turing machine M, let f_M be the unary function computed by M. Then show that
(*a*) $\mathrm{Dom}(\Phi_M) = \mathrm{Dom}(f_M)$,
(*b*) '$\Phi_M(x) \simeq y$' is decidable
(i) when

$$\Phi_M(x) = \begin{cases} \text{the number of steps taken in computing } f_M(x) \\ \text{using } M, \quad \text{if } f_M(x) \text{ is defined,} \\ \text{undefined} \quad \text{otherwise.} \end{cases}$$

(ii) when

$$\Phi_M(x) = \begin{cases} \text{the length of tape actually used}^2 \text{ in the} \\ \text{computation of } f_M(x) \text{ by } M, \quad \text{if } f_M(x) \text{ is defined,} \\ \text{undefined} \quad \text{otherwise.} \end{cases}$$

4. Suppose that $\Phi_e(x)$ and $\Psi_e(x)$ are two abstract computational complexity measures. Show that Φ_e and Ψ_e are *recursively related* in the following sense: there is a recursive function r such that for any e

$\Psi_e(n) \leq r(n, \Phi_e(n))$ and $\Phi_e(n) \leq r(n, \Psi_e(n))$

for almost all n for which $\Phi_e(n)$ and $\Psi_e(n)$ are defined. (*Hint.* Consider the function r defined by $r(n, m) = \max\{\Phi_e(n), \Psi_e(n)$: $e \leq n$ and $\Phi_e(n) = m$ or $\Psi_e(n) = m\}$.)

Show further that if $\Phi_e(n), \Psi_e(n) \geq n$ whenever defined, there is a recursive function r such that $\Psi_e(n) \leq r(\Phi_e(n))$ and $\Phi_e(n) \leq r(\Psi_e(n))$ whenever $\Phi_e(n)$ and $\Psi_e(n)$ are defined.

2. The Speed-up theorem

Suppose that P and Q are programs for computing a total function f, such that for any x

$2t_Q(x) < t_P(x)$.

We would naturally say that Q is more than twice as fast as P. One instance of the Speed-up theorem tells us that there is a total function f with the following property: if P is any program for f, then there is another program for f that is more than twice as fast on almost all inputs. Thus, in particular, there can be no *best* program for computing f.

[2] We say that a square on the tape is *used* if it is scanned during the computation or lies between the outermost non-blank squares on the initial tape (including these outermost squares).

The Speed-up theorem will give speed-up by any preassigned (computable) factor: the example above represents speed-up by a factor of 2, given by the computable function $r(x)=2x$. The proof of this theorem is probably the most difficult in this book. First we prove a pseudo-speed-up theorem, which contains most of the work. The Speed-up theorem then follows quite easily.

2.1. *The pseudo-Speed-up theorem* (Blum)

Let r be a total computable function. There is a total computable function f such that given any program P_i for f, we can find a P_j with the properties

(*a*) *ϕ_j is total and $\phi_j(x)=f(x)$ a.e.,*

(*b*) *$r(t_j(x))<t_i(x)$ a.e.*

(*Note*. This is *pseudo*-speed-up in that we do not necessarily have $\phi_j(x)=f(x)$ for *all* x, as will be the case in the Speed-up theorem.)

Proof. First we must fix a particular total computable function s given by the s–m–n theorem, such that $\phi_e^{(2)}(u,x)\simeq\phi_{s(e,u)}(x)$.

We shall find a particular index e such that $\phi_e^{(2)}$ is total and has the following properties, where we write g_u for the function given by $g_u(x)=\phi_e^{(2)}(u,x)$:

(*a*) $g_0=f$, the function required in the statement of the theorem,

(*b*) for any u, $g_u(x)=g_0(x)$ a.e.,

(*c*) if $f=\phi_i$ then there is an index j for g_{i+1} such that $r(t_j(x))<t_i(x)$ a.e.; in fact we can take $j=s(e,i+1)$.

Clearly this is sufficient to prove the theorem.

For the moment think of e as arbitrary but fixed. Thinking of u as a parameter, we shall define a computable function $g(u,x)$, which will also depend implicitly on e in an effective way. For a particular e which will be chosen later, g will be the function $\phi_e^{(2)}$ above. The definition of g is by recursion on x, with u fixed, as follows.

For any x, $g(u,x)$ is defined only if $g(u,0),\dots,g(u,x-1)$ have all been defined, and in the process some finite sets of *cancelled indices* $C_{u,0},C_{u,1},\dots,C_{u,x-1}$ have been defined. Suppose that this is the case. Now set

$$C_{u,x}=\begin{cases}\{i: u\le i<x,\ i\notin\bigcup_{y<x}C_{u,y}\text{ and }t_i(x)\le r(t_{s(e,i+1)}(x))\}\\ \qquad\qquad\qquad\text{if } t_{s(e,i+1)}(x)\text{ is defined for } u\le i<x,\\ \text{undefined}\quad\text{otherwise.}\end{cases}$$

(Of course, if $x\le u$ then $C_{u,x}=\varnothing$ and is defined). Note that for any i, if $t_{s(e,i+1)}(x)$ is defined, we can decide whether $t_i(x)\le r(t_{s(e,i+1)}(x))$ (using lemma 1.2(*b*)), whether or not $t_i(x)$ is defined.

Then $g(u, x)$ is given by

$$g(u, x) = \begin{cases} 1 + \max\{\phi_i(x) : i \in C_{u,x}\} & \text{if } C_{u,x} \text{ is defined,} \\ \text{undefined} & \text{otherwise.} \end{cases}$$

(If $C_{u,x}$ is defined, then for any $i \in C_{u,x}$ we must have $\phi_i(x)$ defined, so $g(u, x)$ is certainly defined in this case.)

By Church's thesis, g, as thus defined, is a computable partial function which depends implicitly and effectively on the value of e. Hence, by corollary 11-1.4 to the second Recursion theorem (slightly generalised) there is an index e such that

$$(*) \qquad g(u, x) \simeq \phi_e^{(2)}(u, x).$$

From now on let e be a fixed index such that (*) holds; then e is the index mentioned at the beginning of the proof. We must verify that it has the required properties.

First we show that (*) implies that g is total. Fix x; for $u \geq x$, $C_{u,x} = \emptyset$ so $g(u, x) = 1$ immediately from the definition. For $u < x$ we show that $g(u, x)$ is defined by reverse induction on u. Suppose then that $g(x, x)$, $g(x-1, x), \ldots, g(u+2, x), g(u+1, x)$ are all defined. Then from (*) and the definition of s we have $\phi_{s(e,x)}(x), \phi_{s(e,x-1)}(x), \ldots, \phi_{s(e,u+1)}(x)$ are all defined; hence so are $t_{s(e,i+1)}(x)$ for $u \leq i < x$. This in turn means that $C_{u,x}$ is defined, hence $g(u, x)$ is defined also. Thus $g(u, x)$ is a total function.

Now, writing g_u for the function given by $g_u(x) = g(u, x)$ we have

$$\begin{aligned} g_u(x) &= g(u, x) \\ &= \phi_e^{(2)}(u, x) \text{ (from (*))} \\ &= \phi_{s(e,u)}(x) \text{ (by definition of } s\text{).} \end{aligned}$$

We must verify the properties (a)–(c) above.

(a) If we put $f = g_0$, then f is certainly total, as required by the theorem.

(b) Fix a number u; we must show that $g(0, x)$ and $g(u, x)$ differ for only finitely many x. It is clear from the construction of the sets $C_{u,x}$ that for any x

$$C_{u,x} = C_{0,x} \cap \{u, u+1, \ldots, x-1\}.$$

Since the sets $C_{0,x}$ are all disjoint (by construction) we can find the number $v = \max\{x : C_{0,x} \text{ contains an index } i < u\}$. Then for $x > v$ we have $C_{0,x} \subseteq \{u, u+1, \ldots, x-1\}$, and hence $C_{0,x} = C_{u,x}$. This means that $g(0, x) = g(u, x)$ for $x > v$. Thus $g_0(x) = g_u(x)$ a.e.

(*c*) Suppose that i is an index for f; taking $j = s(e, i+1)$ we have that $\phi_j = \phi_{s(e,i+1)} = g_{i+1}$ (from above), so j is an index for g_{i+1}. We can prove that

$$r(t_j(x)) = r(t_{s(e,i+1)}(x)) < t_i(x) \quad \text{for all } x > i.$$

If this were not the case, then i would have been cancelled in the definition of $g(0, x)$ for some $x > i$; i.e. there would have been $x > i$ with $i \in C_{0,x}$. But then, by construction of g, we would have $g(0, x) \neq \phi_i(x)$, a contradiction. This completes the proof. □

Note that the pseudo-Speed-up theorem is *effective*: given a program P for f we can effectively find another program that computes f almost everywhere, and is almost everywhere faster than P.

We now show how to modify the above proof to obtain

2.2. *The Speed-up theorem* (Blum)

Let r be any total computable function. There is a total computable function f such that, given any program P_i for f, there is another program P_k for f such that $r(t_k(x)) < t_i(x)$ a.e.

Proof. We may assume without any loss of generality that r is an increasing function (or else replace r by a larger increasing computable function). First, by a slight modification of the proof of theorem 2.1 we obtain a total computable function f such that given any program P_i for f, there is a program P_j such that

(*a*) ϕ_j is total and $\phi_j(x) = f(x)$ a.e.,

(*b*) $r(t_j(x) + x) < t_i(x)$ a.e.

To do this, simply rewrite the definition of $C_{u,x}$ replacing '. . . and $t_i(x) \leq r(t_{s(e,i+1)}(x))$' by '. . . and $t_i(x) \leq r(t_{s(e,i+1)}(x) + x)$'. We shall show that the function f so obtained is the function required by the theorem.

Suppose then that $f = \phi_i$ and j is chosen with the properties (*a*), (*b*) above. Our aim now is to modify P_j to produce a program P_{j^*} that computes f for *all* x. Suppose that $\phi_j(x) = f(x)$ for all $x > v$. Let $f(m) = b_m$ for $m \leq v$. We modify P_j by writing some extra instructions at the beginning designed to give these values for $m \leq v$. Specifically, let P_{j^*} be the program that embodies the flow diagram given in fig. 12*b*. Clearly P_{j^*} computes f; moreover, there is a number c such that the extra instructions add at most c steps to any computation; i.e. for all x

$$t_{j^*}(x) \leq t_j(x) + c.$$

Fig. 12*b*. Speed-up from pseudo-Speed-up.

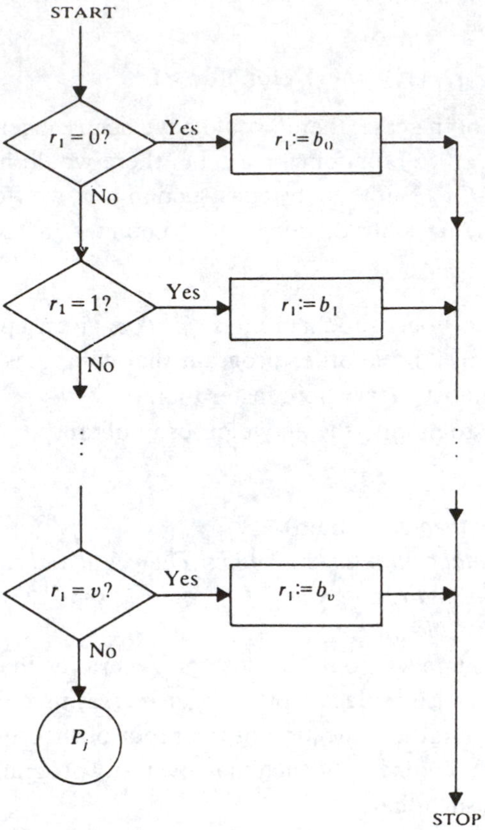

Thus we have

$$\begin{aligned} r(t_{j^*}(x)) &\leq r(t_j(x)+c) \text{ (since } r \text{ is increasing)} \\ &\leq r(t_j(x)+x) \text{ for } x \geq c \\ &< t_i(x) \text{ a.e.} \end{aligned}$$

Hence, taking $k = j^*$ the theorem is proved. □

Remarks

1. The above proofs of the pseudo-Speed-up and Speed-up theorems are adapted from Young [1973]. Both results hold for arbitrary complexity measures; in the case of theorem 2.1 it is clear that our proof uses only the abstract properties of the time measure $t_i(x)$; in the proof of theorem 2.2, however, we have used some special details of the URM time measure, in estimating the relationship between t_{j^*} and t_j. In Young's paper the above proof is generalised so as to work for any complexity measure.

2. It can be shown that the Speed-up theorem is *not* in general effective.

The Speed-up theorem pinpoints a problem when we try to define the complexity of a computable function f (rather than the complexity of any particular algorithm for f). We cannot define this as the complexity of the best, or fastest, algorithm for f simply because f may not have a best program.

We conclude this section with an amusing consequence of the Speed-up theorem. Suppose that we have a URM that performs 1 step per second, and we replace this with a new super-improved machine that is 100 times as fast. Then a computation $P_i(x)$ that took $t_i(x)$ seconds to perform on the old machine will be performed in $t_i(x)/100$ seconds on the new model. Consider now the function f given by the Speed-up theorem with speed-up factor of 100. Suppose that f is being computed by P_i on the new fast machine. By the Speed-up theorem there is a program P_j for f such that $100t_j(x) < t_i(x)$ a.e.; i.e. $t_j(x) < t_i(x)/100$. Thus for almost all x, the *old* machine using P_j computes f faster than the new machine using P_i. We conclude that for some functions at least the new machine is no superior to the old one (on most inputs)!

2.3. *Exercises*

1. Show that in general the limitation of the inequality $r(t_k(x)) < t_i(x)$ in the Speed-up theorem to *almost all* x cannot be improved.
2. Why should we regard the conclusion of the discussion in the preceding paragraph (about new and old URMs) as of theoretical rather than practical significance?

3. Complexity classes

Suppose that b is any total computable function. From the point of view of complexity, a natural class of functions comprises those functions having a program whose running time is bounded by b. Thus we define

3.1. *Definition*

Let b be a total computable function. The *complexity class* of b, $\mathfrak{C}_b$ is defined by

$$\begin{aligned}\mathfrak{C}_b &= \{\phi_e : \phi_e \text{ is total and } t_e(x) \leq b(x) \text{ a.e.}\}\\ &= \{f : f \text{ is total, computable and has a program } P_e \text{ with } t_e(x) \leq b(x) \text{ a.e.}\}.\end{aligned}$$

Remark. The class $\mathfrak{C}_b$, as thus defined, is the complexity class of b relative to the time measure $t_e(x)$; for any measure $\Phi_e(x)$, we could define the complexity class $\mathfrak{C}_b^\Phi$ in the obvious way.

If b' is another total computable function, with $b'(x) \geq b(x)$ for all x, of course $\mathfrak{C}_{b'} \supseteq \mathfrak{C}_b$; if $b'(x) > b(x)$ for all x, we would naturally expect that $\mathfrak{C}_{b'}$ contains some new functions not in $\mathfrak{C}_b$, especially if $b'(x)$ is much larger than $b(x)$. The next theorem shows that this intuition is false: we can find b, b' with b' greater than b by any preassigned computable factor, such that $\mathfrak{C}_{b'} = \mathfrak{C}_b$; in fact, the theorem shows that b, b' can be chosen so that there is no running time $t_e(x)$ that lies between $b(x)$ and $b'(x)$ for more than finitely many x. Thus the theorem is called the Gap theorem.

3.1. *The Gap theorem* (Borodin)

Let r be a total computable function such that $r(x) \geq x$. Then there is a total computable function b such that

(*a*) *for any e and $x > e$, if $t_e(x)$ is defined and $t_e(x) \geq b(x)$, then $t_e(x) > r(b(x))$; hence*

(*b*) $\mathfrak{C}_b = \mathfrak{C}_{r\circ b}$.

Proof. We define $b(x)$ informally as follows. Define a sequence of numbers $k_0 < k_1 < \ldots < k_x$ by

$$k_0 = 0,$$

$$k_{i+1} = r(k_i) + 1 \ (i < x).$$

Consider the disjoint intervals[3] $[k_i, r(k_i)]$ for $0 \leq i \leq x$. There are $x+1$ such intervals, so there is at least one that does not contain any of the numbers $t_e(x)$ for $e < x$, since there are at most x such numbers that are defined. Choose i_x = the least i such that

$$t_e(x) \notin [k_i, r(k_i)] \text{ for all } e < x,$$

and set $b(x) = k_{i_x}$.

Now, given that i_x as defined above exists on theoretical grounds, there is an effective procedure which will find it; we simply make repeated use of lemma 1.2(*b*) to check $t_e(x) \in [k_i, r(k_i)]$ for various e and i. We conclude that b is a computable function, by Church's thesis.

For the conclusion of the theorem, (*a*), suppose that $x > e$ and $t_e(x) \geq b(x)$; by construction of $b(x)$, we have $t_e(x) \notin [b(x), r(b(x))]$. Hence $t_e(x) > r(b(x))$.

[3] By the *interval* $[c, d]$ we mean the set of natural numbers $\{x : c \leq x \leq d\}$.

For part (b), we obviously have $\mathfrak{C}_b \subseteq \mathfrak{C}_{r \circ b}$; now note that if $f \in \mathfrak{C}_{r \circ b} \backslash \mathfrak{C}_b$, then f has a program P_e with

$$t_e(x) \leq r(b(x)) \text{ a.e.}$$

but

$$t_e(x) > b(x) \text{ infinitely often (otherwise } f \in \mathfrak{C}_b).$$

This clearly contradicts (a). Hence $\mathfrak{C}_b = \mathfrak{C}_{r \circ b}$. □

Note. This proof is based on that given by Young [1973]. It is easy to see that the function b in the theorem can be made larger than any pre-assigned computable function c, simply by setting $k_0 = c(x)$ instead of $k_0 = 0$ in the proof. It is also clear from the proof that the Gap theorem is machine independent.

4. The elementary functions

In this final section we introduce the class of *elementary functions* as an example of a class of computable functions that can be characterised very neatly in terms of the complexity classes corresponding to time of computation. The elementary functions form a natural and extensive subclass of the primitive recursive functions, as we shall see. They have been studied in some depth, and are of interest in their own right, quite apart from complexity theory.

4.1. *Definition*

(a) The class $\mathscr{E}$ of *elementary functions* is the smallest class such that

(i) the functions $x+1$, $U_i^n (1 \leq i \leq n)$, $x \dot{-} y$, $x+y$, xy are all in $\mathscr{E}$,

(ii) $\mathscr{E}$ is closed under substitution,

(iii) $\mathscr{E}$ is closed under the operations of forming bounded sums and bounded products (i.e. if $f(\boldsymbol{x}, z)$ is in $\mathscr{E}$ then so are the functions $\sum_{z<y} f(\boldsymbol{x}, z)$ and $\prod_{z<y} f(\boldsymbol{x}, z)$, as defined in chapter 2 § 4).

(b) A predicate $M(\boldsymbol{x})$ is *elementary* if its characteristic function c_M is elementary.

Roughly speaking, $\mathscr{E}$ is the class of functions that can be obtained by iteration of the operations of ordinary arithmetic. It is clear that elementary functions are computable; in fact they are all primitive recursive, by the results of chapter 2 § 4. The next lemma helps to compile some examples of elementary functions and predicates.

4.2. *Lemma*

(*a*) $\mathscr{E}$ *is closed under bounded minimalisation.*

(*b*) *Elementary predicates are closed under 'not', 'and', 'or', and the bounded quantifiers '$\forall z<y$' and '$\exists z<y$'.*

Proof.

(*a*) Suppose that $f(\boldsymbol{x}, z)$ is elementary; recall from the proof of theorem 2-4.12 that

$$\mu z < y(f(\boldsymbol{x}, z) = 0) = \sum_{v<y} \prod_{u \leq v} \operatorname{sg}(f(\boldsymbol{x}, u)).$$

To see that this is elementary, just notice that sg is elementary, since $\operatorname{sg}(x) = x \dot{-} (x \dot{-} 1)$, and $1 = (x+1) \dot{-} x$.

(*b*) We leave the proof as an easy exercise. □

The next theorem gives an indication of the fact that $\mathscr{E}$ is quite extensive.

4.3. *Theorem*

The functions $\boldsymbol{m}$ *(for* $m \in \mathbb{N}$*), and all of the functions listed in theorems* 2-4.5 *and* 4.15 *are elementary.*

Proof. We shall sketch proofs for a few functions where the proof is non-trivial or differs significantly from that given in chapter 2. The terminology of chapter 2 is used throughout.

(i) x^y. $x^y = \prod_{i<y} x = \prod_{i<y} U_1^2(x, i)$.

(ii) qt. $\operatorname{qt}(x, y) = \mu z \leq y(x = 0 \text{ or } x(z+1) > y)$
$= \mu z \leq y(x\, \overline{\operatorname{sg}}((x(z+1) \dot{-} y)) = 0)$.

(iii) rm. $\operatorname{rm}(x, y) = y \dot{-} x \operatorname{qt}(x, y)$.

(iv) p_x. Assuming that the function $\Pr(x)$ (the characteristic function of 'x is prime') has been proved elementary, we have

$$p_x = \mu y \leq 2^{2^x} (x = 0 \text{ or } y \text{ is the } x\text{th prime})$$

$$= \mu y \leq 2^{2^x}\Big(x = \sum_{z \leq y} \Pr(z)\Big)$$

$$= \mu y \leq 2^{2^x}\Big(\Big|x - \sum_{z \leq y} \Pr(z)\Big| = 0\Big).$$

(The bound $p_x \leq 2^{2^x}$ is easily proved by induction, using the fact that $p_{x+1} \leq p_1 p_2 \ldots p_x + 1$.)

We leave the proofs for the other functions as an exercise for the reader. □

We now show that $\mathscr{E}$ is even closed under definitions by primitive recursion, provided that we know in advance some elementary bound on the function being defined by the recursion equations.

4.4. *Theorem*

Let $f(\mathbf{x})$ and $g(\mathbf{x}, y, z)$ be elementary and let h be the function defined from f, g by

$$h(\mathbf{x}, 0) = f(\mathbf{x}),$$
$$h(\mathbf{x}, y+1) = g(\mathbf{x}, y, h(\mathbf{x}, y)).$$

Suppose that there is an elementary function $b(\mathbf{x}, y)$ such that $h(\mathbf{x}, y) \leq b(\mathbf{x}, y)$ for all $\mathbf{x}$, y. Then h is elementary.

Proof. Fix $\mathbf{x}$, y; then the calculation of $h(\mathbf{x}, y)$ in the usual way requires the calculation of the sequence of numbers $h(\mathbf{x}, 0), h(\mathbf{x}, 1), \ldots, h(\mathbf{x}, y)$. These can be coded by the single number s where:

$$\begin{aligned} s &= 2^{h(\mathbf{x},0)} 3^{h(\mathbf{x},1)} \ldots \mathrm{p}_{y+1}^{h(\mathbf{x},y)} \\ &= \prod_{z \leq y} \mathrm{p}_{z+1}^{h(\mathbf{x},z)} \\ &\leq \prod_{z \leq y} \mathrm{p}_{z+1}^{b(\mathbf{x},z)} = c(\mathbf{x}, y), \text{ say,} \end{aligned}$$

where $c(\mathbf{x}, y)$ is an elementary function. The key facts about s are (i) $(s)_1 = h(\mathbf{x}, 0) = f(\mathbf{x})$, (ii) for $z < y$, $(s)_{z+2} = h(\mathbf{x}, z+1) = g(\mathbf{x}, z, (s)_{z+1})$ and (iii) $h(\mathbf{x}, y) = (s)_{y+1}$. Thus we have

$$h(\mathbf{x}, y) = [\mu s \leq c(\mathbf{x}, y)((s)_1 = f(\mathbf{x}) \text{ and } \forall z < y((s)_{z+2} = g(\mathbf{x}, z, (s)_{z+1})))]_{y+1}.$$

This expression for h shows that h is elementary, by the results proved above. □

The principle of definition described in this theorem is called *limited (primitive) recursion*. We shall see later that this is a weaker principle than primitive recursion. The above result is concisely expressed by saying that $\mathscr{E}$ is closed under limited recursion.

4.5. *Corollary*

The state function σ_n, hence the functions c_n and j_n, defined in the proof of theorem 5-1.2 *(computability of the universal functions) are elementary. Hence also the predicate T_n of Kleene's normal form (theorem* 5-1.4*) is elementary.*

Proof. We refer to the formal proof of theorem 5-1.2 as given in chapter 5 and completed in the appendix to that chapter. It is mostly routine to establish, by using the above results, that the functions used to build σ_n are all elementary. For the actual definition of σ_n by primitive recursion, note that we can obtain an *elementary* bound on σ_n as follows.

It is easy to see that for any t

$$c_n(e, \boldsymbol{x}, t) \leq \prod_{1 \leq i \leq \rho(P_e)} \mathrm{p}_i^{\max(\boldsymbol{x})+t}$$

and

$$j_n(e, \boldsymbol{x}, t) \leq \ln(e).$$

These two bounds are elementary functions of $e, \boldsymbol{x}, t$ once we have shown that $\rho(P_e)$ and $\ln(e)$ are elementary functions. Putting these bounds together we then have an elementary bound for σ_n, and theorem 4.4 may be applied. The remainder of the proof that σ_n is elementary consists of showing that $\rho(P_e)$, $\ln(e)$ and all the other functions defined in the appendix to chapter 5 are elementary. This is left as an exercise for the reader. (The only general principle needed but not explicitly mentioned already is that elementary functions are closed under definition by cases; see exercise 4.12(4a) below).

The elementary nature of c_n, j_n and T_n follows immediately since these are all defined explicitly by substitution from σ_n and other elementary functions. □

The following corollary is often expressed by saying that functions computable in elementary time are elementary.

4.6. *Corollary*

(a) *Suppose that* $b(\boldsymbol{x})$ *is elementary and* $\phi_e^{(n)}$ *is a total function such that* $t_e^{(n)}(\boldsymbol{x}) \leq b(\boldsymbol{x})$ *a.e.*[4] *Then* $\phi_e^{(n)}$ *is elementary.*

(b) *If* $b(x)$ *is elementary, then* $\mathfrak{C}_b \subseteq \mathscr{E}$.

Proof. (b) is obviously a restatement of (a) for unary functions. To prove (a), suppose that $t_e^{(n)}(\boldsymbol{x}) \leq b(\boldsymbol{x})$ a.e. Then the function

$$k(\boldsymbol{x}) = \mu t \leq b(\boldsymbol{x})(j_n(e, \boldsymbol{x}, t) = 0)$$

is elementary, and we have

$$\phi_e^{(n)}(\boldsymbol{x}) = (c_n(e, \boldsymbol{x}, k(\boldsymbol{x})))_1 \text{ a.e.}$$

[4] Here we are extending the use of a.e. to n-ary predicates $M(\boldsymbol{x})$ in the obvious way: $M(\boldsymbol{x})$ holds a.e. if it holds for all but finitely many n-tuples $\boldsymbol{x}$.

By the results we have proved, the right hand side is an elementary function. To conclude that $\phi_e^{(n)}$ is elementary, we observe that a function that is almost everywhere the same as an elementary function is elementary (see exercise 4.12(4*b*) below). □

At this stage the reader might well be wondering whether the elementary functions coincide with the primitive recursive functions. All particular examples of primitive recursive functions from earlier chapters have been shown to be elementary. The only detectable difference between these classes is that for $\mathscr{E}$ we have only been able to prove closure under *limited* recursion. Could it be that this is only an apparent distinction? The answer, as we shall see below, is *no*. Limited recursion is a definition principle that is really weaker than primitive recursion. We will find a function that is primitive recursive but not elementary as a consequence of the next theorem to be proved below.

Nevertheless, $\mathscr{E}$ is an extremely large class of functions, and contains most of the functions used in practical mathematics. The class $\mathscr{E}$ is a natural first suggestion for the class of total effectively computable functions, based as it is on the ordinary operations of arithmetic. Indeed, it has been argued (for example, by Brainerd & Landweber [1974]) that $\mathscr{E}$ contains all *practically* computable functions. They argue that if $f(\boldsymbol{x})$ is practically computable, then there must be some number k such that $f(\boldsymbol{x})$ can be computed in at most

$$\left.2^{2^{\cdot^{\cdot^{\cdot^{2^{\max(\boldsymbol{x})}}}}}}\right\}k$$

steps for almost all $\boldsymbol{x}$. After all, for practical purposes, this number of steps quickly becomes very large in comparison with $\boldsymbol{x}$, even for small values of k. Now, since the function

$$\left.2^{2^{\cdot^{\cdot^{\cdot^{2^{\max(\boldsymbol{x})}}}}}}\right\}k$$

is elementary (for fixed k), this means that f is elementary, by corollary 4.6.

Our goal in the remainder of this section is to show that the elementary functions can be characterised as *precisely* those functions that are computable in time

$$\left.2^{2^{\cdot^{\cdot^{\cdot^{2^{\max(\boldsymbol{x})}}}}}}\right\}k$$

for some k. As a first step towards that goal, we have the following, which incidentally will give a non-elementary primitive recursive function.

4.7. *Theorem*

If $f(\boldsymbol{x})$ is elementary, there is a number k such that for all $\boldsymbol{x}$,

$$f(\boldsymbol{x}) \leq \underbrace{2^{2^{\cdot^{\cdot^{2^{\max(\boldsymbol{x})}}}}}}_{k}.$$

Proof. Let us write $b_k(z)$ for

$$\underbrace{2^{2^{\cdot^{\cdot^{2^{z}}}}}}_{k};$$

then, explicitly, we have $b_0(z)=z$, $b_1(z)=2^z$, and $b_{k+1}(z)=2^{b_k(z)}$ in general. (Thus, by 2^{2^z} is meant $2^{(2^z)}$, not $(2^2)^z$, etc.). Note that $b_{k+l}(z)=b_k(b_l(z))$. We shall use implicitly below the fact that b_k is increasing and that $z^2 \leq 2^{2^z}$ for all z.

To establish the theorem, we consider each of the clauses whereby a function f can get into $\mathscr{E}$. Referring to definition 4.1:

(i) $x+1 \leq 2^x$;

$U_i^n(\boldsymbol{x}) \leq \max(\boldsymbol{x})$;

$x \dot{-} y \leq \max(x, y)$;

$x+y \leq 2\max(x, y) \leq 2^{\max(x,y)}$;

$xy \leq (\max(x, y))^2 \leq 2^{2^{\max(x,y)}}$.

(ii) Suppose that $h(\boldsymbol{x})=f(g_1(\boldsymbol{x}), \ldots, g_m(\boldsymbol{x}))$, and $k_1, \ldots, k_m, l$ are such that $g_i(\boldsymbol{x}) \leq b_{k_i}(\max(\boldsymbol{x}))$ $(1 \leq i \leq m)$, and $f(\boldsymbol{y}) \leq b_l(\max(\boldsymbol{y}))$. Let $k=\max(k_1, \ldots, k_m)$. Then we have

$$\begin{aligned} h(\boldsymbol{x}) &\leq b_l(\max(g_1(\boldsymbol{x}), \ldots, g_m(\boldsymbol{x}))) \\ &\leq b_l(\max(b_{k_1}(\max(\boldsymbol{x})), \ldots, b_{k_m}(\max(\boldsymbol{x})))) \\ &\leq b_l(b_k(\max(\boldsymbol{x}))) = b_{l+k}(\max(\boldsymbol{x})). \end{aligned}$$

(iii) Suppose that $g(\boldsymbol{x}, y)=\sum_{z<y} f(\boldsymbol{x}, z)$, and that $f(\boldsymbol{x}, z) \leq b_k(\max(\boldsymbol{x}, z))$. Then we have

$$\begin{aligned} g(\boldsymbol{x}, y) &\leq \sum_{z<y} b_k(\max(\boldsymbol{x}, z)) \\ &\leq y b_k(\max(\boldsymbol{x}, y)) \\ &\leq b_k(\max(\boldsymbol{x}, y))^2 \\ &\leq 2^{2^{b_k(\max(\boldsymbol{x}, y))}} = b_{k+2}(\max(\boldsymbol{x}, y)). \end{aligned}$$

The case when g is a bounded product is similar, and is left as an exercise (4.12(6) below). □

4.8. *Corollary*
The function

$$f(x)=2^{2^{\cdot^{\cdot^{\cdot^{2^x}}}}}\Big\}x$$

is primitive recursive but not elementary.

Proof. To see that f is primitive recursive, notice that $f(x)=g(x, x)$, where g is defined by

$$g(x, 0)=x,$$
$$g(x, y+1)=2^{g(x,y)},$$

(so g is primitive recursive).

To see that f is not elementary, notice that for every k

$$f(k+1)=b_{k+1}(k+1)>b_k(k+1),$$

so there is no k such that $f(x)\leq b_k(x)$ for all x. (Note that f is obtained by 'diagonalising out of $\mathscr{E}$'.) □

The penultimate step towards our goal is to show that elementary functions can be computed in elementary time.

4.9. *Theorem*
If $f(\mathbf{x})$ is elementary, there is a program P for f such that $t_P^{(n)}(\mathbf{x})$ is elementary.

Proof. We must examine the ways in which a function gets into $\mathscr{E}$. It is helpful to prove first the following general lemma.

4.10. *Lemma*
Let $\mathbf{x}=(x_1, \ldots, x_n)$. Suppose that $h(\mathbf{x}, y)$ is elementary, and has a definition by recursion from functions $f(\mathbf{x})$ and $g(\mathbf{x}, y, z)$ which can be computed in elementary time. Then h can be computed in elementary time.

Proof. Take programs F, G for f, g, in standard form, such that t_F and t_G are elementary. (For notational convenience we omit here and elsewhere the superscripts from $t_P^{(n)}$ for any program P whenever the meaning is clear.) We shall take the program H for h as given in the proof of theorem 2-4.4, and show that t_H is elementary. We simply calculate $t_H(\mathbf{x}, y)$ by reference to the flow diagram in fig. 2c and the explicit program H that is its translation. We reproduce this flow diagram in fig. 12c, indicating alongside each component the number of steps it contributes when executed by the program H. It is now a simple matter to calculate that

$$t_H(\mathbf{x}, y) = n + 1 + (\rho(F) + t_F(\mathbf{x}) + 1) + (y + 1)$$
$$+ \sum_{k<y} (\rho(G) + t_G(\mathbf{x}, k, h(\mathbf{x}, k)) + 3) + 1,$$

which is clearly an elementary function, since t_F, t_G and h are all elementary. □

Proof of theorem 4.9

Let us consider each of the clauses in the definition of $\mathscr{E}$:

(i) The functions $x+1$ and $U_i^n(\mathbf{x})$ can each be computed by single step programs. For $x \dot{-} y$, $x+y$, xy we use lemma 4.10. Consider $x+y$, for example: this is defined by recursion from the functions $f(x) = x$ and $g(x, y, z) = z+1$, both of which are computable in

Fig. 12*c*. The number of steps in a computation by recursion.

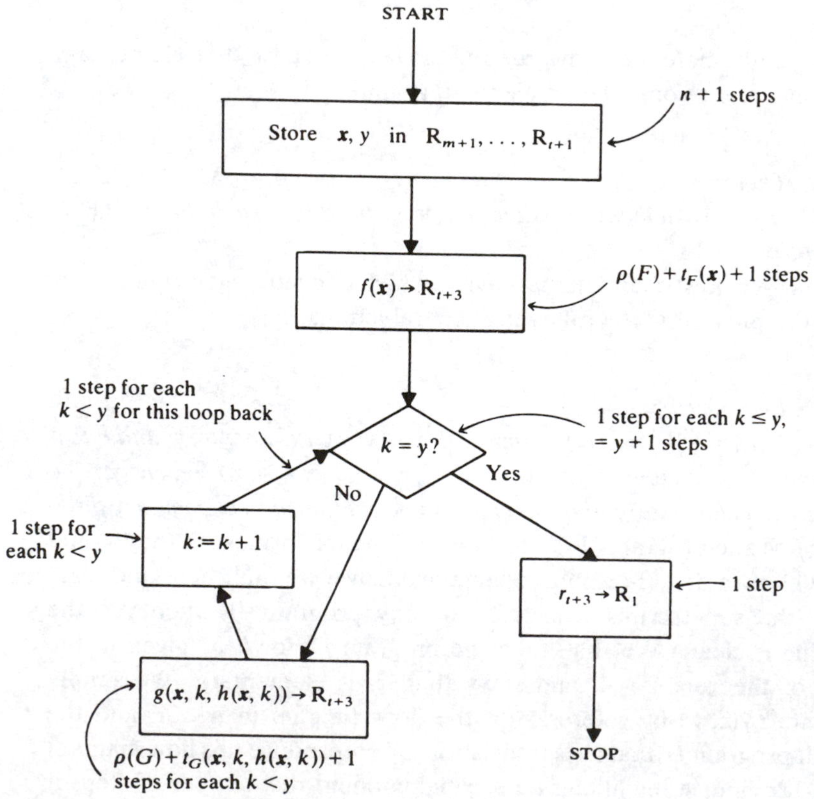

elementary time. Now apply lemma 4.10. Similarly for $x \dot{-} y$ and xy (for $x \dot{-} y$ we must first prove the result for $x \dot{-} 1$, again by using lemma 4.10).

(ii) *Substitution.* Suppose that $h(\boldsymbol{x}) = f(g_1(\boldsymbol{x}), \ldots, g_m(\boldsymbol{x}))$, and each of $f, g_1, \ldots, g_m$ is computable in elementary time by programs $F, G_1, \ldots, G_m$ in standard form. Let H be the program for h given in the proof of theorem 2-3.1. Calculating directly from that program we have

$$t_H(\boldsymbol{x}) = n + \sum_{i=1}^{m} (\rho(G_i) + t_{G_i}(\boldsymbol{x}) + 1) + \rho(F) + t_F(g_1(\boldsymbol{x}), \ldots, g_m(\boldsymbol{x})) + 1,$$

which is an elementary function, by substitution.

(iii) *Bounded sums and products.* The result is established by using lemma 4.10. Suppose that $g(\boldsymbol{x}, y) = \sum_{z<y} f(\boldsymbol{x}, z)$, and f is computable in elementary time. Then g is obtained by recursion from the functions $\mathbf{0}$ and $z + f(\boldsymbol{x}, y)$ both of which are computable in elementary time (from (i) and (ii) above). Hence, by lemma 4.10, g is computable in elementary time.

The proof for bounded products is similar, and is left as an exercise (4.12(8) below). □

We have now done all of the hard work! To express the characterisation of $\mathscr{E}$ towards which we have been working, it is helpful to extend complexity classes to include n-ary functions for all n. Suppose, then, that $b(x)$ is a total function; let us write

$$\mathfrak{C}_b^* = \{f : f \text{ is total and } f = \phi_e^{(n)} \text{ for some } e \text{ with } t_e^{(n)}(\boldsymbol{x}) \le b(\max(\boldsymbol{x})) \text{ a.e.}\}.$$

Clearly $\mathfrak{C}_b = \mathfrak{C}_b^* \cap$ Unary functions.

Now our final theorem is

4.11. *Theorem*

A total function $f(\boldsymbol{x})$ is elementary iff it is computable in time $\le b_k(\max(\boldsymbol{x}))$, for some k. I.e.

$$\mathscr{E} = \bigcup_{k \ge 0} \mathfrak{C}_{b_k}^*.$$

Proof. Since for each k, $b_k(\max(\boldsymbol{x}))$ is an elementary function, we have $\mathfrak{C}_{b_k}^* \subseteq \mathscr{E}$ by corollary 4.6; hence

$$\bigcup_{k \ge 0} \mathfrak{C}_{b_k}^* \subseteq \mathscr{E}.$$

For the converse inclusion, let $f(\mathbf{x})$ be an elementary function. By theorem 4.9 there is a program F for f such that t_F is elementary; now by theorem 4.7 find a number k such that $t_F(\mathbf{x}) \leq b_k(\max(\mathbf{x}))$. Then $f \in \mathfrak{C}^*_{b_k}$, so our proof is complete. □

4.12. *Exercises*

1. Show that it was not strictly necessary to include the functions $x+y$ and xy in the definition of $\mathscr{E}$. (*Hint.* First obtain xy as a bounded sum; *then* obtain $x+y$ from suitable products, using $\dot{-}$).
2. Prove lemma 4.2(*b*).
3. Complete the proof of theorem 4.3.
4. (*a*) Show that $\mathscr{E}$ is closed under definition by cases, when the functions and predicates in the definition are all elementary.
   (*b*) Show that if $f(\mathbf{x})$ is elementary and $g(\mathbf{x}) = f(\mathbf{x})$ a.e., then $g(\mathbf{x})$ is elementary.
5. Check all the details in the proof of corollary 4.5.
6. Complete the proof of theorem 4.7 by showing that if $g(\mathbf{x}, y) = \prod_{z<y} f(\mathbf{x}, z)$ and $f(\mathbf{x}, z) \leq b_k(\max(\mathbf{x}, z))$, then $g(\mathbf{x}, y) \leq b_{k+3}(\max(\mathbf{x}, y))$.
7. Give an example of a unary primitive recursive function that is not elementary, different from that of corollary 4.8.
8. Prove that if f is computable in elementary time and $g(\mathbf{x}, y) = \prod_{z<y} f(\mathbf{x}, z)$, then g is computable in elementary time.
9. Suppose that Φ_e is a complexity measure for unary functions that is related to t_e by an elementary function r. I.e. for any e, and almost all x for which $t_e(x)$ is defined,

   $\Phi_e(x) \leq r(x, t_e(x))$ and $t_e(x) \leq r(x, \Phi_e(x))$.

   For any total function $b(x)$, let $\mathfrak{C}^{\Phi}_b$ be the complexity class of b relative to Φ, i.e.

   $\mathfrak{C}^{\Phi}_b = \{\phi_e : \phi_e \text{ is total and } \Phi_e(x) \leq b(x) \text{ a.e.}\}$.

   Prove that $\bigcup_{k \geq 0} \mathfrak{C}^{\Phi}_{b_k} = \mathscr{E}_1$, the unary elementary functions.

Further reading For a fuller treatment of the machine independent theory of complexity, the reader should consult the basic paper of Blum [1967], or the readable overview of the theory by Hartmanis & Hopcroft [1971]. The paper of Young [1973], which we have already cited in earlier sections, simplifies some of the proofs of basic theorems. The book of Brainerd & Landweber [1974] has a good chapter on complexity, and also gives the characterisation of various subrecursive classes of functions (including $\mathscr{E}$) in terms of time of computation. Similar characterisations are also discussed in the early (in the history of complexity theory) papers of Ritchie [1963] and Cobham [1965], using the Turing machine tape measure of complexity.

13
Further study

Our basic study of computability has been designed so that it could serve as a stepping stone to more advanced or more detailed study in any of several directions. In this brief postlude, we shall mention some of the areas in which further study could be pursued, and we offer some suggestions for further reading. The divisions below are not hard and fast, and there are many interrelations between the various areas we mention.

Computability Further study of the theoretical notion of computability (the starting point of this book) could be pursued in two directions: (*a*) more detailed examination of other equivalent approaches to computability (which we surveyed in chapter 3); (*b*) examination of more restricted notions of effective computability, involving, for instance, *finite automata* and similar devices.

Some references (several historical) for (*a*) were given in chapter 3. For both (*a*) and (*b*) we suggest the books of Minsky [1967] (a very comprehensive treatment), Arbib [1969], or Engeler [1973].

Recursion theory We use this traditional title under which to mention more advanced ideas arising out of the notion of computability on $\mathbb{N}$, such as we began to pursue in chapters 7, and 9 to 11. Specific areas include:

Hierarchies: there are various ways to extend the sequence beginning 'recursive, r.e., . . . ' to obtain a hierarchy of kinds of set, each kind of set having more difficult decision problem than the preceding one. Among the important hierarchies that have been studied are the *arithmetic hierarchy*, the *hyperarithmetic hierarchy*, and the *analytical hierarchy*.

Reducibilities and degrees: between $\leq_m$ and $\leq_T$ there is a spectrum of reducibilities that could be investigated. For the student wishing to delve further into Turing reducibility, the next step would be to master a proof of the Friedberg–Muchnik solution to Post's problem, before proceeding to further results and proofs in this area, some of which we mentioned in chapter 9.

Recursion in higher types: we considered briefly in chapter 10 the question of computable functions of functions. This study can be extended to computability of functions of functions of functions, etc. Hierarchies occur naturally here also.

The book of Rogers [1967] is the best single reference for each of these areas, in that it is a more advanced and comprehensive textbook which continues these topics where we have concluded our introduction. More specific sources of information about degrees are Sacks [1963], Shoenfield [1971] and Simpson [1977].

Under this heading we should also mention

Generalised recursion theory: This is a relatively new field of study, in which ideas arising in computability on $\mathbb{N}$ are transferred to other structures that are not merely coded-up disguises of $\mathbb{N}$. This development has been particularly successful on certain sets called *admissible ordinals*. An introductory article having a large annotated bibliography is provided by Shore [1977] in the *Handbook of Mathematical Logic* (Barwise [1977]).

Decidability and undecidability A good survey of unsolvable problems in general is provided in the article by Davis [1977] in the *Handbook of Mathematical Logic*.

For an introduction to mathematical logic, and decidability and undecidability in this area, there are numerous basic tests, such as Mendelson [1964] or Robbin [1969]. These books also give a complete treatment of Gödel's theorem and related results. For more advanced study in this area there are texts such as Bell & Machover [1977], and Boolos & Jeffrey [1974]. The article by Rabin [1977] surveys methods and results on the decidability of mathematical theories.

Computer science The study of topics included under the heading *Computability* above, especially finite automata, is of course relevant to computer science – which could be called the realm of *practical* computability. Within this realm there are two areas we have touched on, albeit briefly:

Programs and programming: further study here could include topics such as the generation of programming languages and the structure of programs; and the semantics of programming languages (which we touched upon in chapter 10). Texts which cover these matters include Arbib [1969], Bird [1976], Brainerd & Landweber [1974], Engeler [1973] and Manna [1974].

Complexity theory: at the end of chapter 12 we offered some suggestions for further reading in this area. There is considerable interest in identifying functions $f(x)$ that can be computed in an amount of time bounded by some polynomial in x. A major unsolved problem here is the so-called $P = NP$ problem: machines are considered in which there is a certain amount of freedom in choosing the next step in a computation (such machines are called *non-deterministic*). By making good guesses (or choices) one can often obtain a quicker computation than by systematically working through all possible cases in a deterministic way. The $P = NP$ problem asks whether every function computable on a non-deterministic machine in polynomial time is computable in polynomial time on ordinary (deterministic) machines. This problem is mentioned in Rabin [1977] and discussed fully by Karp [1972].

Bibliography

Arbib, M. A. [1969]. *Theories of Abstract Automata.* Prentice–Hall, Englewood Cliffs, N.J.

Barwise, J. (ed.) [1977]. *Handbook of Mathematical Logic.* North-Holland, Amsterdam.

Bell, J. & M. Machover [1977]. *A Course in Mathematical Logic.* North-Holland, Amsterdam.

Bird, R. [1976]. *Programs and Machines.* Wiley, London–New York.

Blum, M. [1967]. A machine-independent theory of the complexity of recursive functions. *J. Assoc. Computing Machinery* **14**, 322–36.

Boolos, G. & R. Jeffrey [1974]. *Computability and Logic,* Cambridge University Press.

Brainerd, W. S & L. H. Landweber [1974]. *Theory of Computation.* Wiley, New York.

Church, A. [1936]. An unsolvable problem of elementary number theory. *Am. J. Math.* **58**, 345–63. (Reprinted in Davis [1965].)

Church, A. [1941]. *The Calculi of Lambda-Conversion.* Annals of Mathematics Studies no. 6, Princeton.

Cobham, A. [1965]. The intrinsic computational difficulty of functions. In *Proceedings of the 1964 International Congress for Logic, Methodology and Philosophy of Science* (ed. Y. Bar-Hillel), pp. 24–30. North-Holland, Amsterdam.

Cohn, P. M. [1977]. *Algebra,* vol. 2. Wiley, London–New York.

Davis, M. [1958]. *Computability and Unsolvability.* McGraw-Hill, New York.

Davis, M. (ed.) [1965]. *The Undecidable.* Raven, New York.

Davis, M. [1973]. Hilbert's tenth problem is unsolvable. *Am. Math. Monthly* **80**, 233–69.

Davis, M. [1977]. Unsolvable problems. In Barwise [1977, pp. 567–94].

Engeler, E. [1973]. *Introduction to the Theory of Computation.* Academic Press, New York.

Friedberg, R. M. [1958]. Three theorems on recursive enumeration: I Decomposition, II Maximal set, III Enumeration without duplication. *J. Symbolic Logic* **23**, 309–16.

Gödel, K. [1931]. Uber formal unentscheidbare Sätze der Principia Mathematica und verwandter System I. *Monatschefte Math. Phys.* **38**, 173–98. (English translation in Davis [1965].)

Hartmanis, J. & J. E. Hopcroft [1971]. An overview of the theory of computational complexity. *J. Assoc. Computing Machinery* **18**, 444–75.

Karp, R. M. [1972]. Reducibility among combinatorial problems. In *Complexity of Computer Computations* (eds. R. Miller & J. Thatcher), pp. 85–104. Plenum Press, New York.

Kleene, S. C. [1952]. *Introduction in Metamathematics.* Van Nostrand, Princeton and North-Holland, Amsterdam.

Kleene, S. C. [1967]. *Mathematical Logic.* Wiley, London–New York.

Manin, Y. I. [1977]. *A Course in Mathematical Logic* (Graduate Texts in Mathematics 53). Springer-Verlag, New York.

Manna, Z. [1974]. *Mathematical Theory of Computation.* McGraw-Hill, New York.

Margaris, A. [1966]. *First Order Mathematical Logic.* Blaisdell, Waltham, Mass.

Markov, A. A. [1954]. *The Theory of Algorithms,* Trudy Math. Inst. Steklov, vol. 42. (English translation, 1961, National Science Foundation, Washington D.C.)

Mendelson, E. [1964]. *Introduction to Mathematical Logic.* Van Nostrand, Princeton.

Minsky, M. L. [1967]. *Computation: Finite and Infinite Machines.* Prentice-Hall, Englewood Cliffs, N.J.

Paterson, M. S. [1970]. Unsolvability in 3×3 matrices. *Stud. Appl. Math.* **49**, 105–7.

Péter, R. [1967]. *Recursive Functions.* Academic Press, New York.

Post, E. [1943]. Formal reductions of the general combinatorial decision problem. *Am. J. Math.* **65**, 197–215.

Rabin, M. O. [1977]. Decidable theories. In Barwise [1977, pp. 595–629].

Ritchie, R. W. [1963]. Classes of predictably computable functions. *Trans. Am. Math. Soc.* **106**, 139–73.

Robbin, J. W. [1969]. *Mathematical Logic – a First Course,* Benjamin, New York.

Rogers, H. [1967]. *Theory of Recursive Functions and Effective Computability.* McGraw-Hill, New York.

Rogers, R. [1971]. *Mathematical Logic and Formalized Theories.* North-Holland, Amsterdam.

Rotman, J. J. [1965]. *The Theory of Groups: An Introduction.* Allyn and Bacon, Boston.

Sacks, G. [1963]. *Degrees of Unsolvability.* Annals of Mathematics Studies, no. 55, Princeton.

Shepherdson, J. C. & H. E. Sturgis [1963]. Computability of recursive functions. *J. Assoc. Computing Machinery* **10**, 217–55.

Shoenfield, J. R. [1971]. *Degrees of Unsolvability.* North-Holland, Amsterdam.

Shore, R. A. [1977] α-Recursion theory. In Barwise [1977, pp. 653–80].

Simpson, S. G. [1977]. Degrees of unsolvability: a survey of results. In Barwise [1977, pp. 631–52].

Smullyan, R. M. [1961]. *Theory of Formal Systems.* Annals of Mathematics Studies no. 47, Princeton.

Tarski, A. [1951]. *A Decision Method for Elementary Algebra and Geometry.* The Rand Corporation, Santa Monica, Ca.

Tarski, A., A. Mostowski & R. M. Robinson [1953]. *Undecidable Theories.* North-Holland, Amsterdam.

Turing, A. M. [1936]. On computable numbers, with an application to the Entscheidungsproblem. *Proc. Lond. Math. Soc.* **42**, 230–65; **43**, 544–6. (Reprinted in Davis [1965].)

Van der Waerden, B. L. [1949]. *Modern Algebra,* vol. 1. Ungar, New York.

Young, P. [1973]. Easy constructions in complexity theory: gap and speed-up theorems. *Proc. Am. Math. Soc.* **37**, 555–63.

Notation

Chapter 1

Chapter 2

Chapter 3

Chapter 4

Chapter 5

$j_n(e, \boldsymbol{x}, t)$
next instruction 87

$\sigma_n(e, \boldsymbol{x}, t)$
state function 87

$T_n(e, \boldsymbol{x}, t)$
Kleene T-predicate 89

$\mathrm{Rec}(f, g)$
function obtained by recursion from f, g 91

$\mathrm{Sub}(f, g_1, \ldots, g_m)$
function obtained by substitution from $f, g_1, \ldots, g_m$ 91

Chapter 6

$\mathbb{Q}$	rational numbers 108
$\wedge, \rightarrow$	logical symbols for 'and', 'implies' 111
$\mathsf{0}, \mathsf{1}, \ldots$; R; $\mathsf{x}, \mathsf{y}, \ldots$	symbols in a logical language 110

Chapter 7

$A \oplus B$	$\{2x : x \in A\} \cup \{2x+1 : x \in B\}$ 122
$A \otimes B$	$\{\pi(x, y) : x \in A$ and $y \in B\}$ 122
K	$\{x : x \in W_x\}$ 123

Chapter 8

$\neg, \vee$	logical symbols for 'not', 'or' 143
$\mathscr{S}$	statements of language L 144
$\mathscr{T}, \mathscr{F}$	true, false statements of L 144
θ_n	$(n+1)$th statement of $\mathscr{S}$ 144
$\mathsf{n} \in \mathsf{K}$	formal counterpart of $n \in K$ 145
$\mathscr{P}_{\imath}$	provable statements 147
Pr^*	$\{n : \mathsf{n} \in \mathsf{K}$ is provable$\}$ 148
Ref^*	$\{n : \mathsf{n} \notin \mathsf{K}$ is provable$\}$ 148

Chapter 9

$A \leq_{\mathrm{m}} B$	A is many–one reducible to B 158
$\equiv_{\mathrm{m}}$	many–one equivalent 161
$\mathrm{d_m}(A)$	the m-degree of A 161
$\boldsymbol{a} \leq_{\mathrm{m}} \boldsymbol{b}$	partial order on m-degrees 162
$\mathbf{0}_{\mathrm{m}}$	m-degree of recursive sets 163
$\mathbf{o}, \mathbf{n}$	m-degrees of $\varnothing$ and $\mathbb{N}$ 162
$\mathbf{0}'_{\mathrm{m}}$	m-degree of K 163

$\mathscr{E}$	elementary functions	225
$b_k(z)$	$\left.2^{2^{\cdot^{\cdot^{\cdot^{2^z}}}}}\right\}k$	230

Index